Yale Romanic Studies, Second Series, 19

ART AND MEANING IN

BERCEO'S *Vida De Santa Oria*

T. Anthony Perry

New Haven and London, Yale University Press

1968

Library of Congress catalog card number: 68-24781

To my parents and to Gustavo Correa

Ca essi ovo siempre cumplida caridat,
qui en poder ageno puso su voluntat.

VIDA DE SANTO DOMINGO

Preface

Toward the end of his life Gonzalo de Berceo (ca. 1180–1250) decided to set his weary hand once more to parchment. In some missal he had discovered a forgotten *Vita,* written about two centuries previous, of a local and obscure mystic. His translation of it into Romance verse must have astonished an audience accustomed to his liturgical poems and pious exploits of saints as famous as Saint Dominic or even the Holy Virgin herself. The new subject matter was also different in another way: Saint Oria had been a visionary, and the setting of the story would hence not be this world of sinners but heaven itself. The ceaseless activity of his poetic world becomes contemplation; instead of praising and condemning, the poet will describe and admire.

The story is simple and beautifully told. A child of devout parents, Oria decides at a young age that this mortal life is of little value and takes refuge in an ascetic's cell. Through prayer and penance she is granted a series of visions that reveal the nature of heaven and predict her future sanctification. She dies and tells her mother in a dream that she has won her reward.

Although Berceo is the first poet of the Spanish language known by name and the author of an impressive list of poems, there exist virtually no literary studies of his works and no monograph on *Santa Oria.* We have endeavored to make a beginning.

In its original form this study was presented to Yale University as a doctoral thesis. It has since undergone considerable alteration. My special thanks go to Professor Gustavo Correa, who initially suggested the topic to me and helped me greatly at every stage of the way. I also wish to thank Professors Howard Garey, Ciriaco M. Arroyo, and Brian Dutton for their many valuable suggestions, and Professor Anthony Zahareas for his encouragement.

T.A.P.

Northampton, Massachusetts
January 2, 1968

Contents

Abbreviations

Berceo's works

Duelo	*Duelo de la Virgen*
Loores	*Loores de Nuestra Señora*
Milagros	*Milagros de Nuestra Señora*
Sacr	*El sacrificio de la misa*
SDom	*Vida de Santo Domingo*
Signos	*De los signos que aparescerán ante del juicio*
SLor	*Martirio de San Lorenzo*
SMil	*Vida de San Millán*
SOr	*Vida de Santa Oria*

Secondary works

BAE	*Biblioteca de autores españoles*
PL	Migne, *Patrologia latina*

Introduction

Our biographical knowledge of Gonzalo de Berceo is scant indeed. Notarial documents [1] suggest that he lived from about the end of the twelfth century until the middle of the thirteenth, that he was known as Don Gonçalvo de Berceo (Berceo is a small village in northern Spain in the province of Rioja) ,[2] and that he was affiliated with the Benedictine Monastery of San Millán de la Cogolla, but probably as a secular cleric rather than as a monk. This lack of external information is compensated in Berceo's case by the rich supply of personal materials in the works themselves. While these do not increase our objective knowledge of the man, they provide an intimate view of his subjective life that has inspired modern poets [3] and that is the distinctive charm of his poetry.

Berceo has the distinction among modern readers of

1. The first study of the documents in which the name of Don Gonçalvo de Berceo appears as a witness was made by Father Plácido Romero of the Monastery of San Millán and printed in the first edition of Berceo's works by Tomás Antonio Sánchez, *Colección de poesías castellanas anteriores al siglo XV* (4 vols. Madrid, 1779–90), 2, iv; 3, xliv–lvi. See also R. Menéndez Pidal, *Documentos lingüísticos de España, 1: Reino de Castilla* (Madrid, 1919), documents Nos. 87, 91, 94, 95. The whole question is concisely discussed in Antonio G. Solalinde's edition of the *Milagros de Nuestra Señora* (Madrid, 1922), pp. vii–x and notes.

2. The poet himself provides this information on several occasions. He ends his *Vida de San Millán* as follows:

> Gonzalvo fue so nomne qui fizo est tractado
> En Sant Millan de suso fue de ninnez criado,
> Natural de Berçeo, ond Sant Millan fue nado.　　　(489a-c)

He repeats this in the *Vida de Santo Domingo:*

> Yo, Gonçalo por nonbre, clamado de Verçeo,
> de Sant' Mjllan criado, en la su merçed seo.　　　(757ab)

For the meaning of *criado,* "disciple," Solalinde (*Milagros,* p. vii) asks the reader to compare *Milagros* 354.

3. Azorín, *Al margen de los clásicos* (Madrid, 1915), p. 19.

1

being chronologically the first poet in the Spanish language known by name and also the first exponent of a new manner of writing poetry, the *mester de clerecía*.[4] Whereas epic poetry (*mester de juglaría*) allowed wide variation in both length of strophe and syllabic count, the new *mester* or school composed in strict monorhymed quatrains and with verses of approximately the same number of syllables.[5] Along with this heightened concern with the form of the poetry, one can note a parallel tendency toward a more erudite subject matter. Berceo is the best example of this, since all of his nine extant works are written in the standard *clerecía* form and all deal with a learned or religious theme.[6] Although it is not known precisely when or

4. A good study on the *mester de clerecía* remains the one by M. Menéndez y Pelayo, *Antología de poetas líricos castellanos* (Madrid, 1891), pp. xxxi–lxxxiii.

5. The author of the *Libro de Alexandre* (*BAE*, 57 [1898]) opens with a sort of literary manifesto in which he distinguishes between the two kinds of *mester* and gives the basic requirements of the new quatrain, the "fourfold way":

> Mester trago fermoso, non es de ioglaria,
> Mester es sen peccado, ca es de clerezia,
> Fablar curso rimado per la quaderna uia,
> A sillauas cuntadas, ca es grant maestria.   (2)

The limits within which the counting of syllables was understood will be discussed below, Chap. 5, pp. 141–46.

6. Berceo's work may be classified into three categories: (1) poems about the Virgin Mary (*Milagros de Nuestra Señora, Loores de Nuestra Señora, Duelo de la Virgen*); (2) liturgical poems (*El sacrificio de la misa, De los signos que aparescerán ante del juicio*); (3) lives of saints (*San Millán, Santo Domingo, Santa Oria*, and the *Martirio de San Lorenzo*). In addition to these nine works there are also three extant hymns attributed to Berceo (*BAE, 57, 144*): "Veni Creator Spiritus," "Ave Sancta Maria," and "Tu Christe que luz eres." The *Loor de don Gonzalo de Berceo*, published by Sánchez as a tribute by an anonymous ancient author and naïvely reprinted in *BAE, 57, 144–46*, has long been recognized as an innocent deception executed in the style of the *mester de clerecía* by Sánchez himself. The *Libro de Alexandre* has occasionally but probably falsely been attributed to Berceo among others. See Raymond S. Willis in *HR, 19* (1951), 168–72. Finally, there is a hint that Berceo may have been the author of a "historia de la traslación de Santa Sabina,

in what order these poems were composed, it is common
practice to cite the poet's own words in support of the
thesis that *Santa Oria* was Berceo's final work. He opens
the prologue with a personal remark:

> Quiero en mj uegez, maguer so ya cansado,
> De esta sancta uirgen romançar su dictado.   (2ab)

The statement of Berceo just quoted suggests that he
was not the author of the original story of Santa Oria but
rather, as in the case of many of his other works, simply the
translator and versifier of texts previously executed in
Latin. Berceo repeats throughout the poem that he is but
the faithful reproducer of the authoritative Latin *Vita*
written by Oria's confessor, a certain Munno:

> Munno era su nonbre, omne fue bien letrado,
> Sopo bien su fazienda, el fizo el dictado.   (5ab)

However, in contrast to the happy discovery by modern
scholars of the Latin sources of Berceo's *Milagros, Vida
de San Millán,* and *Vida de Santo Domingo,* no manuscript containing Munno's original *Vita* has been un-
earthed. (This is unfortunate, because this work is ap-

Christeta y Vicente," now lost. See Justo Pérez de Urbel, "Manuscritos de
Berceo en el archivo de Silos," *BH, 32* (1930) , 5–15.
    In this study the following editions have been used: *Milagros de
Nuestra Señora,* ed. A. G. Solalinde (Madrid, 1922) ; *El sacrificio de la
misa,* ed. A. G. Solalinde (Madrid, 1913) ; *Vida de Santo Domingo,* ed.
John D. Fitz-Gerald (Paris, 1904) ; *Martirio de San Lorenzo,* ed. C. C.
Marden, *PMLA, 45* (1930) ; for *Loores, Duelo, Signos, SMil* I used the
text of the *BAE, 57.* Inaccessible to me was the critical edition of *SMil* by
S. Kravtchenko-Dobelman (Paris, 1952) : *La langue de G. de B. suivie de
l'éd. critique de S. Millán de la Cogolla.* For the *Vida de Santa Oria* I
have used C. C. Marden's edition of manuscript *A* in *Cuatro poemas de
Berceo* (Madrid, 1928) . This is the earliest extant MS and is perfectly
adequate as a basis for stylistic study. Readers interested in the MS tradition and variants may consult Marden's Introduction and notes. Emendations for the irregular readings of *A* have been proposed by María Rosa
Lida de Malkiel, "Notas para el texto de la *Vida de Santa Oria,*" *RPh,
10* (1956–57) , 19–33. See also below, App. II, p. 197, n. 1.

parently the only record of Oria's life actually written
during her lifetime and by a direct acquaintance, and the
confrontation of the source with Berceo's version could
lead to interesting insights into the poet's art.) Thus Férotin's observations remain as true today as when they were
made in 1902: ". . . Sainte Auria, dont les Actes son con-
sidérés comme perdus." [7] B. de Gaiffier echoes the same
remark and adds an important clue: "Le texte castillan
[published by C. C. Marden, *Cuatro Poemas de Berceo*]
s'inspire d'une Vie latine, aujourd'hui perdue, *et que
Sandoval put encore consulter au début du xviie siècle.*" [8]
Fray Prudencio de Sandoval [9] (d. 1620) began as an
archivist and chronicler of the Benedictine Order, until
political events raised him to the level of Court historiog-
rapher and Bishop of Pamplona. Although he is best
known for his *Historia del Emperador Carlos V*, it is his
Crónica de la orden de San Benito [10] that concerns us here.
This work is an attempt to trace the history of the Benedictine Order in Spain from the very beginnings and is
often the only extant record of many ancient manuscripts,
although Sandoval's lack of critical standards of scholarship
rarely permit satisfactory conclusions unless confirmable

7. D. Marius Férotin, in *Analecta Bollandiana, 21* (1902), 40.
8. Ibid., *48* (1930), 427. My italics.
9. For an accessible and readable account of Sandoval, see Carlos Seco
Serrano, "Vida y obra de fray Prudencio de Sandoval," *BAE, 80* (1955),
vii–xlviii. More important is the series of two studies by Ludwig Pfandl,
"Studien zu Prudencio de Sandoval," *ZRP, 54* (1934), 385–423; continued
in *55* (1935), 88–125.
10. (Madrid, 1601). This is the first and only publication of this work.
Its importance as a historical document has been appraised by Pfandl
(*ZRP, 54*, 412–13) as follows: "[Sandoval] bildet . . . eine Art Acta Sanctorum der aus jenen Klöstern entsprossenen heiligmässigen Ordensmit-
glieder. In der Gruppierung des Stoffes nicht gerade sehr klar, in seiner
Verarbeitung nicht immer kritisch genug . . . aber nach echt sando-
valischer Art mit Auszügen aus Urkunden und Dokumenten, die inzwi-
schen längst verloren sind, bis zum Rande gefüllt, ist dieses Werk eine
Fundgrube antiquarischen Wissens und bleibt vor allem für die Ges-
chichte des Benediktinerordens in Spanien ein Quellenbuch ersten Ranges."

through other means as well. Frequently his source is simply listed as a "very ancient document," and no attempt is made to arrive at a critical text.[11]

These problems may be seen in Sandoval's article on Santa Oria.[12] At the outset the author asserts that the following story is taken from a very ancient book written by Munno. There is no way of knowing if this is the same book ("mjssal," *SOr* 171d) of Munno used by Berceo or rather another Latin version or even a Latin prose rendering of Berceo's own poem. Further on in the same article, after having retold Oria's death, Sandoval states (fol. 40) : "Otras revelaciones hechas a santa Auria, y otras que la santa despues que passó al cielo hizo, consolando a su madre, cuenta esta historia, que las déxo por el mal estilo con que las dize el poeta." Now this poet who wrote in such an abominable style is none other than Berceo, according to Sandoval's marginal indication ("Don Gonçalo monge la puso en verso"). But one wonders how long Sandoval had been following Berceo rather than, supposedly, Munno. For the historian never states explicitly that he has Munno's Latin prose version before him, but mentions merely a "libro antiquissimo" written ("escrita" —i.e. the *Vida* and not necessarily the book from which he is reading) by Munno. Sandoval may easily have found this bit of information in Berceo and used Munno's name rather than the poet's in order to give greater authority to the story. It is indeed likely that Sandoval's account is based entirely on Berceo, judging from the similarities

11. Pfandl writes that this was characteristic of Benedictine historiography of the time: "Ihr Respekt vor der Urkunde an sich ist so gross, dass jede gilt. [Sandoval] hat nicht so sehr die historisch-kristische Synthese, als vielmehr die Sichtung und Darbietung des Quellenmaterials im Sinne" (*ZRP*, 55, 111).

12. Sandoval's article appears in Pt. II, fols. 39–41, with the following heading: "Vida de la bienaventurada virgen santa Auria, monja de San Benito, sacada de un libro antiquissimo, escrita por un monge, que la vió, y trató."

between the two: the order of events coincides perfectly, and Sandoval seems at times to have incorporated whole phrases from the poet. The one major deviation, Sandoval's deletion of most of the first vision, may be easily understood as the historian's greater interest in didactic detail than in poetry. Yet it is impossible to assert that Sandoval followed only Berceo or even that he followed him very much at all, given the faithfulness with which the poet is known to have copied his Latin sources.[13] It may be that Sandoval followed the true Latin source, of which Berceo's poetic version is also an accurate reproduction. At any rate, it is no longer safe to assume, along with Gaiffier and others,[14] that Sandoval's account is definitely based on Munno's text.

Because Sandoval's *Vida* stands to date as the only transmission of Munno's Latin version beside Berceo's,[15] and because it has to my knowledge never been reprinted since its original publication, it may be of service to scholars to reproduce it in an appendix.[16] Yet it must be remembered that Berceo's account of Oria's life remains the fullest as well as the oldest, since it includes all information given by Sandoval and, in addition, the entire description of heaven and the vision of the Garden of Olives, both deleted in Sandoval.[17]

Concerning the dates of Oria's life, the one indication provided by Sandoval, the name of a certain Abbot Peter,

13. For example, after a close comparison of the *Vida de Santo Domingo* with the monk Grimaldus' *Vita Beati Dominici Confessoris Christi & Abbatis*, John D. Fitz-Gerald concludes: "Dans tout le poème . . . le poète suit presque servilement le livre dont il nous parle." *Vida de Santo Domingo* (Paris, 1904), p. lx. Greater stylistic originality has been claimed for the *Milagros* by Carmelo Gariano, *Análisis estilístico de los "Milagros de Nuestra Señora" de Berceo* (Madrid, 1965), pp. 25–51.

14. For example, in the article "De B. Auria in Hispania" in the Bollandists' *Acta Sanctorum* (Paris-Rome 1865), March, 2, 99–100.

15. The Bollandists' article (ibid.) is by their own admission but a translation of Sandoval's text into 19th-century Latin.

16. See below, App. I, pp. 193–96.

17. On the other hand, Sandoval uses 4 metaphors not included by

has seemed inconclusive.[18] Recently, however, Fray Joaquín Peña de San José has identified several of the characters mentioned in Berceo's *Vida* and shown that Oria lived from about 1042 to 1070.[19] Her tomb and cell were seen by Berceo, who composed his poem about two centuries after her death, and are, in fact, still to be visited today.[20]

Berceo. All appear in the first quarter of the text and 2 are concerned with light. It is said of Oria that "sus ojos eran fuentes" and that she "lucía como la hacha encendida en el candelero." Sandoval carries even further the symbolic development based on the verbal pun *oro/Oria* by stating that the Saint was converted into gold by the "Sol de justicia." Finally, although Oria was withdrawn from the world, she appeared to it "como la ciudad en el monte."

18. The difficulty was pointed out in the Bollandists' critical introduction to Sandoval's article (*Acta Sanctorum*, March, 2, 99): "However much he [Sandoval] names the Abbot Peter among those who attended the dying Saint, he remains ambiguous as to which of two he intended: the one who succeeded the Abbot Gometius in 1062 and who ruled the convent until 1070; or the one who in the year 1118 of the Christian era was elected to the position of the deceased Joannes and whose prelature Sandoval extends from public documents beyond the year 1142" (trans. mine).

19. Fray Joaquín Peña de San José, "Glosas a la vida de Santa Oria, de Gonzalo de Berceo," *Berceo* (Logroño), *60* (1961), 371–82.

20. I am grateful to Professor Brian Dutton for both the reference cited in n. 19, above, and also the information concerning the continued existence of Oria's cell and tomb.

1. Structure and Narrative Elements

In a picturesque image Berceo has described himself at work:

> Gonçalo li dixieron al uersifficador
> Que en su portaleio fizo esta lauor. *(SOr* 184ab)

His work is hard, a "lauor," and, as the diminutive suggests, humble. He is but the "obrero" of God *(SDom* 4b), whose task it is to render Latin texts into Romance. It is well known, however, that Berceo's boasted fidelity to the source book concerns only the historical or pseudo-historical facts. Far from being a mere "versifier," the poet has taken upon himself the arduous task of composition, of ordering the various elements and passing from one to the other. He is a workman with specialized training, a craftsman, and his craft involves not only skill in verse-making but also an elaborate series of narrative techniques and conceptions.

Tripartite Structure in Berceo's *Vidas*

Of Berceo's four *Vidas* (*SMil, SDom, SLor, SOr,*), the two longest are expressly divided into three sections: (1) the holy, earthly life; (2) miracles performed while living, followed by an account of the saint's illness and death; and (3) supernatural events connected with the saint after death, usually in the form of miracles performed through the saint's intercession or near the holy relics.[1] This three-

1. This threefold division has been pointed out by A. Valbuena Prat, *Historia de la literatura española, 1* (2 vols. Barcelona, 1937), 73. See also Frida Weber de Kurlat, "Cronología de las 'Vidas' de Berceo," *NRFH, 15* (1961), 113. Such a division corresponds roughly with normal practices in traditional hagiographical writing as summarized by Hippolyte Delehaye, *Les légendes hagiographiques* (Brussels, 1906), pp. 110–11: "Si l'on désire

in-one construction, Berceo observes, has a symbolic justification in its suggestion of the Holy Trinity: three Persons, one God; three "Books," one "composition" (*dictado*)[2] (*SDom* 533–35). *Santo Domingo* and *San Millán* are most explicit in elaborating the structure, each section of which constitutes a separate "libro." Strophes 1–108 of the latter narrate "de la sues andadas secund lo que leemos" (108c) —whereupon Berceo addresses his audience as follows:

> Aun si me quisieredes, sennores, escuchar,
> El secundo libriello todo es de rezar:
> Unos pocos miraclos vos querria contar,
> Que dennó Dios al mundo por elli demostrar. (109)

This second "little Book" has two distinct themes: the miracles and the death. The first and longer section (109–293) relates some of the miracles. There then follows the holy death (294ff.) of the "confessor precioso," the assemblage of friends and disciples at the bedside, the immediate reception of the soul by a procession of angels, and its glorious entrance into heaven. Once the soul has been secured, attention is directed once more to the deceased body (309), the great honor with which it is cared for, and finally the sepulcher and relics—of such importance in Christendom as the goal of pilgrimages and the agent of cures and other miracles. This idea is a natural transition (309–20) to the third Book, in which are related the miracles performed after the saint's death, either through his intercession or through the power of the relics:

---

une biographie bien complète, la vie du saint aura trois parties. Avant sa naissance: sa patrie, ses parents, sa future grandeur miraculeusement annoncée; sa vie: l'enfance, la jeunesse, les actions les plus importantes de l'homme fait, les vertus, les miracles; culte et miracles après la mort."

2. "By the use of numerical composition the medieval author attained a twofold end: a formal scaffolding to build upon, and a symbolic profundity." Ernst Robert Curtius, *European Literature and the Latin Middle Ages*, trans. Willard Trask (New York, 1963), p. 508.

El terçero libriello avemos de deçir
De preçiosos miraclos sabroso de oyr. (321ab)

These same divisions are also carefully preserved and spelled out in *Santo Domingo*. Book One is 288 strophes long and ends as follows:

Sennores, Deo gracias, contado uos auemos
dela su sancta ujda lo que saber podemos:
desaquj ayudando nos el Dios en qui creemos,
esti libro finamos, en otro contendremos. (288)

Book Two begins immediately: [3]

Queremos uos un otro libriello començar
e delos sus mjraglos algunos renunçar,
los que Dios en su ujda qujso por el mostrar:
cuyos ioglares somos, el nos deñe guyar. (289)

In Book Two of this poem a structural problem, already present in *San Millán,* gains such proportions as to cause Berceo and scribes some hesitation. It is already obvious in *San Millán* that the second "libriello" is rather an assemblage of different elements than an organic unity characterized by a single subject matter. Statistically, Book Two contains 185 strophes on miracles and 26 on the death (294–319). In *Santo Domingo* the figures show the same tendency and are even more exaggerated. There are 198 strophes on miracles, roughly the same as in *San Millán.* However, there are now 45 strophes on the death of the Saint. The sheer bulk, 180 verses, is enough to call into question the appropriateness of grouping both sections under the same "libro." In consequence, Berceo ends this miracle section with a typical closing invocation:

3. Andrés' edition carries the following rubric in the central margin: "Delos miraculos que fiço en vida" (Fray Alfonso Andrés, ed., *Vida de Santo Domingo de Silos. Edición crítico-paleográfica del códice del siglo XIII* [Madrid, 1958]). This edition contains notable differences from Fitz-Gerald's critical edition of MSS *E, V,* and *H.*

> Prueuas auemos muchas en esto e en al
> que uaso era lleno de graçia çelestial;
> el ruegue por nos todos al Rey Devinal,
> en ujda, e en muerte, que nos guarde de mal. Amen.[4]
>
> (486)

Thereupon Berceo addresses his audience in the first person, a procedure always used to make perfectly clear the joints in the structure:

> Quiero passar al transido, dexar todo lo al,
> sy non y espendremos todo vn tcmporal;
> aun despues nos finca vna gesta cabdal,
> de que faria el omne vn libro general.   (487)

This strophe is preceded in two manuscripts (MS V again has nothing) by the rubrics: "De la fin de su espicion [sic]" (E) : "De coño fino Santo Domingo" (H) . Andrés' manuscript, instead of taking its cue from Berceo's text (487), waits until strophe 496, where the interior margin carries the following notation: "Commo fino Sancto Domingo." In other words, two of the three scribes (following Berceo?) felt the need to separate the death from the miracles, thus constituting two independent sections within Book Two, and to indicate this separation by the appropriate closing formula ("Amen") and rubrics. Whether these rubrics correspond to Berceo's original text is uncertain; they are, however, clearly warranted both by the threat of structural obscurity and by Berceo's own attempts to obviate this obscurity: the closing invocation and the first person transition.

The narration of the death that follows is remarkably similar to that of San Millán described above. The holy man delivers a sermon to those gathered at his bedside (492–502), dies, and is carried up to heaven by a band of

---

4. The reader will note the closing formula. In Fitz-Gerald's edition both MSS *H* and *E* carry the word "Amen." It is missing in *V*.

angels. Berceo then returns to the mortal remains, comments on the honor done them and their value as relics, and then passes on to the third "libro" (533). Ironically enough, it is precisely at the end of an episode whose unwieldiness threatens the unity of Book Two and hence of the tripartite structure itself that Berceo feels the need to assert the presence of that very structure: so that there will be three books just as there are three Persons in the Holy Trinity (*SDom* 534–35). At any rate, the third books of both *Santo Domingo* and *San Millán* relate various miracles occurring after the saints' deaths (*SDom* 536ff., *SMil* 321ff.).

The structure of *San Lorenzo* is less clear, in part because of the abrupt break in the narration during the Saint's martyrdom. In his edition of the poem Sánchez comments after strophe 105: "Faltan al fin de esta poesía algunas hojas, en los dos códices de las obras de Berceo que existen en el Monasterio de San Millán." [5] Why is the poem interrupted? What were its probable contents? Sánchez speculates: "Esta poesía está defectuosa al fin, o por haber perecido algunas hojas de los códices de San Millán, o porque el poeta no la concluyó" (p. 228). Sánchez then continues, thoroughly familiar with Berceo's usual tripartite structure:

> Como quiera que haya sucedido, puede conjeturarse que le faltara acaso la tercera parte. Porque en la última copla se nos representa vivo todavía a San Lorenzo, bien que puesto ya sobre las parrillas acrisolandose con el fuego. Pero no sabemos quantas coplas compondría para explicar las circunstancias de su preciosa muerte, ni las que emplearía en referir los milagros obrados después de ello, que no serían pocas, segun el estilo que en las demás poesías vemos observado. (p. 228)

5. Sánchez, *Colección de poesías castellanas*, 2, 228.

Sánchez observes that the account of the death is incomplete, that the miracles post mortem are not included, and therefore that Part Three is missing. He does not discuss the question as to whether the death belongs to the second or rather to the third section.

Sánchez' speculations on the incompleted section of *San Lorenzo* confirms our general conclusions as regards the tripartite structure of Berceo's *Vidas*. As the editor admits, he induced the probable structure from Berceo's other works. The problems, however, are whether Berceo ever had any such clear notions of structure in mind while composing *San Lorenzo*, and, if so, whether the poet saw fit to implement them in this particular poem. For, the question of Part Three aside, the division between the first two parts remains wholly undeveloped. The *Vida* proper and the earthly miracles, rather than being separated and consigned to separate sections, are blended together without the usual warning from the manuscripts' rubrics or the author's intervention in the first person.

Aside from the possible exception of *San Lorenzo*, however—aside even from the threat to structural balance posed by the somewhat forced application of the symbolic number three to an unyielding subject matter—the fact remains that in both *San Millán* and *Santo Domingo* Berceo has developed a structural organization that is, at least with respect to his Latin sources, original and impressive.[6]

6. Weber de Kurlat (*NRFH, 15*, 116) has studied this aspect of Berceo and summarizes her findings as follows: "Tal división tripartita no se da en las vidas latinas que con minuciosa sujeción al contenido factual del relato sigue Berceo: la de San Millán, escrita por San Braulio, consta de 21 capítulos, no agrupados entre sí en unidades mayores; la de Santo Domingo, escrita por el abad Grimaldo, tiene divisiones, pero no se corresponden con las adoptadas por Berceo, que subdividió el primer libro de Grimaldo en dos y, en cambio, no parece haber conocido un tercer libro, también con relatos de milagros."

STRUCTURE IN *Santa Oria*

Berceo's insistence on the tripartite structure in *Santo Domingo* and *San Millán* seems to emphasize, by contrast, the structural peculiarities of *Santa Oria*. The poem may be analyzed into the following sections:

(a) *The earthly life proper:* Oria's origins, parents, pious life, entrance into the monastery, and rigid asceticism there (1–24).

(b) *Oria's first vision* (25–108).[7] Transition: Oria's disenchantment upon returning to earth; she redoubles her efforts and does not yield to vanity (109–15).

(c) *The second vision:* conversation with the Virgin Mary and prediction of Oria's death (116–36). Transition: illness, bedside scene (137–39).[8]

(d) *Oria's death* (141–84). The following subdivisions may be made: Oria's third and final vision: she is taken up in spirit to the Mount of Olives (141–44); anticipation of death: Oria's conversation with Munno, in whom she confides her vision (145–59). Transition (160). Amunna's (Oria's mother) first vision: her deceased husband announces Oria's imminent death (161–68). The death proper (169–77). The company of friends; the burial (178–79). The author's aside on the place of burial (180–83). The fake conclusion, a typical closing formula: apparently Berceo had originally intended to close at this point (184). Transition (185–87).

(e). *Amunna's second vision:* Oria appears to her and announces her reception into heaven (188–202). Conclusion (202–05).

---

7. For content analysis, see below, Chap. 2, pp. 72–88.

8. I accept without qualification María Rosa Lida de Malkiel's suggested emendations of the order of strophes in the poem (in *RPh, 10,* 23): strophes 141–44 follow directly upon 139, then 140, then the continuation with 145. Further emendations of Marden's text are the following: strophe 39 must be followed by 42, then 40, 41, and 43. After 118 it seems more natural to insert 126–32, then 119–25, then 133–36.

Following upon our previous discussion, the first striking feature of the structure in *Santa Oria* is the absence of the tripartite division. The only exception to this statement, Oria's *three* visions, do not constitute a serious objection. First of all, even granted that they are the most important elements of the whole narrative, they remain segments of the larger *Vida;* they are not structural units within which all other elements are gathered. Secondly, it is clear from the transitions into Oria's visions that Berceo did not intend—at least not explicitly—that Oria's visions constitute separate "libros."

In the study of Berceo's other hagiographic works above, it was seen that the narration of the life proper is followed by two sections of miracles, which are separated by the death of the saint. Two-thirds of the whole *Vida,* therefore, depend, so far as content is concerned, on miracles. Indeed, it can be said that in *Santo Domingo* and *San Millán* the narration of miracles are the sine qua non of the structure. This may explain why the tripartite structure is inappropriate here. Less famous than Santo Domingo and San Millán, Oria perhaps had no substantial body of miracles attached to her name. Thus not only is there not a single miracle narrated in *Santa Oria,* but the word "miraglo" never even occurs.[9]

The total absence of miracles may be understood in two ways. In the first place, Munno's text probably gave no specific examples, and this is sufficient reason for a popularizer who constantly boasts of scrupulously following the

9. In the one instance where Munno possibly mentioned miracles, Berceo avoids even the word. Sandoval states: "La fama de su vida y milagros, que Dios por sus ruegos obraua, se estendió por la tierra." Berceo's version of these lines occurs in the same place as in Sandoval's account, between Oria's entrance into the monastery and the first vision. Yet Berceo translates as follows: "Los pueblos de la tierra fazian li grant honor, / Salia a luengas tierras la su buena loor" (18cd). The poet merely renders the general "fama" and does not bother to specify that this fame was due to Oria's life and miracles.

original Latin "Book." Secondly, in the genre of the *vida,* miracles and visions had similar didactic functions and could therefore be used interchangeably.[10] Thus in *Santa Oria* the absence of miracles is compensated by the extensive use of their substitute: 138 strophes out of 205, 67 per cent of the poem, is devoted to the narration of visions.

These similarities between *Santa Oria* and Berceo's other *Vidas* leads one to suspect structural similarities as well. And, in fact, it is only the idea of the tripartite construction that can unify the whole poem and satisfactorily explain the final episode: Amunna's vision of Oria. As in Berceo's earlier *Vidas,* the *Vida* proper (1–24) constitutes the first book. The second section (25–184) narrates Oria's visions while living and then her death, the difference being the mere substitution of one didactic method for another, the vision for the miracle. The third and final section (185–205), as might be expected, deals with a vision effected by the Saint after her death. Of course, from the point of view of content, it would have been possible to end the poem at strophe 184.[11] Amunna's vision is after all secondary, and Oria's ascent to heaven could have been supposed from the evidence of her life. The older structures, however, were at least obscurely in Berceo's mind: he had always found it too abrupt to end a *Vida* with the death. Furthermore, the narration of miracles or visions post mortem proved both the Saint's divine election and the validity of our continued devotion to her. The poet thus reopens the narrative out of sound didactic principles but also because of a vague but persistent feeling of structural imbalance.

10. Weber de Kurlat (*NRFH, 15,* 130, n. 42) rigorously separates Berceo's other *Vidas* from *Santa Oria* on the grounds that the latter, "desde el punto de vista del contenido, pertenece a la literatura místico-visionaria." The error here consists in confusing content and use. Clearly visions may differ from miracles, but both were used by medieval didactic authors. See below, pp. 53 ff.

11. That this was at one time Berceo's intent may be seen from strophe 184, a typical closing formula.

Finally, we may note two structural problems that are happily resolved in *Santa Oria*. First of all, Berceo's habitual manner of presenting miracles is uninteresting: they are merely juxtaposed in an endless series until the Latin source runs dry or the author becomes weary. By contrast, Oria has only three visions (not a chance figure, to be sure), and these are finely graded in order of diminishing biographical importance and of ascending spiritual value, as we shall see. Secondly, the death no longer stands in embarrassing relief between two series of miracles. Predicted in the second vision, partly revealed in the vision of the Mount of Olives, Oria's death both fulfills its didactic purposes and completes the structural and thematic movement of the middle section.

Narrative Terms Used in *Santa Oria* and the Other *Vidas*

Berceo's failure to elaborate the structural unity of *Santa Oria* in an explicit manner is the exception rather than the rule. Indeed, there are an impressive number of principles of conceiving and executing literary compositions for which a specific vocabulary exists within the *Vidas* themselves. For clarity these may be divided into terms referring to parts of the poem and terms referring to the whole poem. This latter group may further be considered from the point of view of either the author's task or the original source of the materials (in this case, Munno).

TERMS REFERRING TO PARTS OF THE POEM

Prologo.
> Auemos en el prologo mucho detardado;
> Siguamos la estoria, esto es agujsado.   (*SOr* 10a)

Dámaso Alonso has offered the following commentary to Berceo's prologue: "Casi todos sus poemas tienen un breve preámbulo. El de *Santa Oria* le salió de más extensión: en nueve estrofas ha dado una especie de resumen de toda la

materia que va a escribir y los datos concretos más esen-
ciales (nombre y naturaleza de la santa, nombre de los
padres y del que redactó el 'dictado,' etc.) ." [12] More precisely, the order is as follows: the sign of the Cross, statement of subject matter, and the poet's task (strophe 1) ;
invocations to Santa Oria and to the Virgin Mary (2–3) .
Strophes 4–9 telescope in roughly chronological order important facts concerning Oria's earthly life: place of origin, parents, Munno's veracity as author of the original
Vita, Oria's withdrawal from the world, the wonderment
caused by her meritorious acts, and her visions. Berceo
then reflects that it would be a good idea to give Oria's
baptismal name as well as the reason why it is especially
appropriate. But he realizes that he has already spent too
much time with his introduction, and so, "let's get on
with the story." Of the "estoria" that follows, only strophes
11–24 narrate the earthly life proper: Oria's parents (11–
14) , Oria as a Child (15–16) , as ascetic (17–18) , as child
(19–20), and her departure from the world, fame, asceticism, and devotion (21–24) . From this point on, most of
the poem is concerned with visions. In other words, Oria's
earthly life, viewed as content, is but a variation of the
prologue with no important thematic changes.

With the exception of the famous opening allegory to
the *Milagros,* the prologue to *Santa Oria* is the longest such
introduction in any of Berceo's works. *San Millán* has two
such strophes, but they merely serve to draw the audience's
attention to the subject and contain no summary of the
Vida. San Lorenzo has a single strophe: Berceo invokes
God the Creator, announces his subject matter and his own
task ("fer . . . en romaz"), much like the opening
strophe of *Santa Oria.* The four-strophe introduction to
Santo Domingo is a successful application of the rhetorical
device of *amplificatio.* Again the author opens by stating

12. "Berceo y los *topoi,*" in his *De los siglos oscuros al de oro* (Madrid,
1958) , p. 83.

the three themes of God, subject matter, and poet's task, and then simply elaborates or "amplifies" them in the three following strophes. In other words, this rather lengthy introduction must be viewed, from the point of view of content, as but one strophe, corresponding to the opening strophe of the three other *Vidas*. Thus only the preamble to *Santa Oria,* properly speaking, can be called a prologue, if we are led either by the importance of its development or by the fact that the term actually occurs only in this poem. It seems best, therefore, to refer to the opening strophes of the other *Vidas* as simply "introductory." [13]

Comjenço, Primeria, Entrada. Berceo develops a series of expressions—really all variations on a basic pattern—both to indicate the place of honor ("Enel nonbre de Dios, que nonbramos primero," *SDom* 4a) and to serve a narrative function by delimiting, however vaguely, a section of the poem: the opening. Thus in Berceo such phrases occur in the introduction or prologue. "Luego en el comjenço e en la primeria" (*SOr* 3a) : "Right off at the outset and before anything else," says Berceo to introduce an invocation. "Bien es que vos digamos luego en la entrada" (*SOr* 9a) : "It is a good idea to tell you right off at the start" the story about Oria's name. Similarly, in the introduction to *Santo Domingo* (3ab) : "Quiero quelo sepades luego dela primera / cuya es la ystoria." The basic pattern, then, is *luego* followed by any one of a number of synonyms for "beginning." [14] It might be noted in passing that, as is semantically appropriate, the phrase always occurs in Berceo in the first line of a strophe.

13. Following Dámaso Alonso, who also avoids the label "prologue" (ibid., p. 83, n. 12) , except for *SOr* and the *Milagros*. The term also occurs in *Alexandre* 4a.

14. This was a stock construction of the period: "Desend en el setiembre luego en la entrada" (*SMil* 380a) . See also the *Libro de Apolonio* 485c. The formula allowed wide variation: "luego enla mañana" (*SDom* 22a) , "luego de las primeras" (*Duelo* 12a) .

Estoria.[15] In Berceo the term carries two basic meanings which are not distinguished: (1) *history,* the veracious account of an earthly event or existence; (2) the narration of that history, *story:* "Siguamos la estoria, esto es agujsado" (*SOr* 10b) . The story and its telling are one and the same: the history-story exists to be told (and, from a didactic point of view, it is told so it can be relived) .

So much for the narrator's use of the term. When spoken by one of the characters and thus freed from narrative utility, "estoria" is accordingly understood only in sense (1) :

> Respondió la reclusa, que auja nonbre Oria:
> "Yo non seria digna de veer tan grant gloria;
> Mas sy me reçibiessedes vos en uuestra memoria,
> Alla seria conplida todo la mj estoria."   (*SOr* 35)

"If you take me into heaven now, my story [history, earthly life] will be fulfilled." Here the first sense of the word predominates, but the semantic suggestions of (2) seem inescapable: life is to be told as well as lived. Similarly, at Oria's bedside Amunna urges her to disclose the content of her visions before she dies:

> Conjuró la Amunna a su fijuela Oria:
> "Fija, sy Dios uos lieue a la su sancta gloria,
> Sy ujsion uidiestes o alguna istoria
> Dezit melo de mjentre auedes la memoria." (*SOr* 172)

"If you saw a vision or any [true] event worth relating. . . ."

In the above examples Berceo suggests important levels of value through the different derivatives of the Latin *historiam.* In reference to sacred personages Berceo is care-

15. Strictly speaking, the *vision* should be included here for completeness, since in addition to its concrete meaning it also denotes both a section of a narrative and a genre with fairly precise rules of composition. However, we have preferred to deal with visions separately and in conjunction with other matters, owing to their central importance in *SOr.*

ful to use the more learned form: San Millán's *Vida* is an
"ystoria" (1b), and Santo Domingo's likewise (*SDom* 3b).
Berceo's other use of this spelling has been noted above
(*SOr* 172c), where the reference was to a heavenly event.
If this be the case, what about *Santa Oria* 10b or 35d, where
the references are clearly to Oria? The explanations seem
to us obvious. In the first instance the term is primarily a
rhetorical one, as can be seen by contrast with the preceding verse: Berceo has spent too much time on the prologue
and wants to get on with the story. It might be noted
parenthetically that along with *Loores* 99a, this is the only
purely rhetorical use of the term in Berceo; here it
designates all the story that follows and distinguishes it
from the prologue. On the other hand, the explanation of
Santa Oria 35d is stylistic. It must be remembered that it
is no longer the narrator speaking and dignifying the
Saint with the more honorific "ystoria": the speaker is
Oria, humble to the point of self-abasement. From her
point of view her life could only be designated by the more
popular "estoria." [16]

TERMS OF REFERENCE TO THE LATIN SOURCE

Berceo uses the following expressions in *Santa Oria* to
refer to Munno's *Vita: dictado* (2b, 5b, 84b), *letra:* "en
letra lo avemos" (4d), *leyenda* (15a), *lo que leemos* (89d),

16. The final level of semantic shading, the highest, is reserved for *the
Book*: "commo diz la historia" (*Sac* 64c and also 127a). Here the Latin
form is retained (minus, of course, the case inflection), and the form of
the phrase in which it occurs does not vary. Thus the difference between
the learned *historia* and *istoria* or *ystoria,* although purely orthographical,
is nonetheless meaningful, at least as a scribal convention. In the worldly
Juan Ruiz the popular form *estoria* predominates and can mean either
true story or fable indiscriminately, as suggested by the juxtaposition in
297c: "Desto ay muchas fablas e estoria." It obviously means "true story"
in reference to the "trist estoria" of Christ's passion (1048c). However,
the usual tone can be got from the frequent phrase "grant estoria": "es
de grant estoria" (353c), "contar una grand estoria" (166c), "dezir una
grand estoria" (1222b). It has much the same connotation as the English
"tall tale."

ujda (6d), *libro caudal* (171c), and *materia* (19c, 89b, 90a). Of these final three, only the last need refer specifically to Munno's Book: "la materia lo daua." The other two simply indicate the biographical material: "grant materia tenemos"; "La materia es alta." Aside from these nouns there is one adjective, *escripto:* "vision . . . escripta" (115ab); "Ca nos quanto dezimos escripto lo fallamos" (203d). Excepting the possibly more general reference of "materia," all denote, as might be expected, the written source. Thus Munno is referred to as "El quj lo escriujó" (204a).[17]

"Materia" was a formal term of rhetoric in use at the time [18] and meant "simply what has to be said":[19] "Sunt enim artificia duo, quorum alterum est dilatandi et reliquum abbreviandi materiam."[20] There is only one purely rhetorical use of the term in Berceo: "Cambiemos la materia, en otro son cantemos" (*Loores* 103a). Elsewhere the reference is rather to the materials handed to the poet.[21]

TERMS IN WHICH BERCEO CONCEIVES HIS POEM AND HIS TASK

Contrary to his exclusive use of substantives to designate the source Book, Berceo refers to his own work with verbal

17. Whence *escriptura* (*SDom* 5a, 73b, 573a) or *leccion* (*Milagros* 41c). In his studies of the *Perceval Continuations,* Pierre Gallais ("Formules de conteur et interventions d'auteur dans les manuscrits de la *Continuation-Gauvain,*" *Romania, 85* [1964], 203–04) lists more than 60 references to source material. The most frequent are the following: *conte* (36 times), *matière* (10 times), *estoire* (6 times), *escrit, escriture* (4 times), *aventure* (3 times), *livre* (2 times), *romant* (2 times). This is about what one would expect in the more worldly and imaginative atmosphere of the romances. However, the use of *matière* should be noted, along with designations of *written* sources: *escrit* and *livre.*

18. See Edmond Faral, *Les arts poétiques du XIIe et du XIIIe siècle* (Paris, 1962), pp. 203, 271, 273.

19. Curtius, *European Literature,* p. 491.

20. Faral, p. 271.

21. Cf. *Loores* 3d, 13d, 225a; also *Alexandre* 2334, 276: "La materia lo manda."

forms; or rather, he prefers to talk about the actual writing more than about the finished product. There are only three instances where his work itself is designated. The first does not occur until the poem is nearly done: "La *obra* començada bien la quiero conplir" (185c). The second reference is to works that are purely conjectural:

> Vido syn estas otras muy grandes ujsiones
> De que formaria omne assaz buenas *razones*. (202ab)

"If I had the time, I could write a good story about these visions." The third instance refers to the things Oria saw in her first vision:

> Onze meses senneros podria auer passados
> Desque ujdo los *pleytos* que auemos contados.
> (*SOr* 114ab) [22]

The three substantives, then, are *obra, razones,* and *pleyto.* By contrast, verbs referring to his present task are plentiful: *cantar* (19c), *contar* (114b, 203b), *dezir* (185b, 203d), *escriujr* (10d, 89d), *romançar su dictado* (2b), *uersificar* (1d, 203a).[23] Finally, there is one noun denoting the poet's task: *uersifficador* (184a).[24]

The effect of this shifting use of verbal and substantive forms can, I think, be readily seen. Munno's text has the static (not a pejorative idea in the Middle Ages, on the contrary) dignity of an established thing or of a historical fact. Berceo's immediate work, however, is still in the process of becoming; it is not yet anything until the final breath of relief: *"Hic liber est scriptus."* Munno has written a Book: Berceo would (or is condemned to) versify rather than write verse.

Sermon. Going beyond references to the actual composi-

---

22. Compare *Duelo* 22c and *Milagros* 703a.

23. Compare *meter en ditado* (*SDom* 537d), *renunçar,* "to relate" (*SDom* 536c), and the noun *regunçerio* (*SLor* 17b); *desta razon tractar* (*SMil* 320a).

24. Compare *joglar* (*SDom* 289, 775) and *trobador* (*Loores* 232).

tion of the text, we now turn to rhetorical terms used in the poem to denote some type of verbal communication:

> Sopo Dios entender bien el su coraçon,
> Demostró li Amunna vna grant ujsion,
> Que sopo de la fija que era o que non;
> Avn esso nos finca de todo el *sermon*.   (187a-d)

Here the meaning seems to be no more precise than "spoken discourse," having perhaps some degree of edifying content. This can be confirmed by *San Millán* 65ab:

> Creatura fue sancta de Dios mucho amado,
> Que sin sermon ninguno de Dios fue aspirado.

This holy creature was inspired by God without the usual method of the spoken word used for Oria.

Recontar. Although Munno is the written source, he is often but the faithful scribe of Amunna:

> Non echó esti suenno la duenna [Amunna] en olbido,
> Recontógelo todo a Munno su querido.   (170ac)

Here "recontar" simply means "to tell" as opposed to "to tell a story." Amunna does the former when passing on the events to Munno; Berceo does the "contar" by putting the story into literary form.

Razonar, Razones, Passiones.

> Munno era su nonbre, omne fue bien letrado,
> Sopo bien su fazienda, él fizo el dictado;
> Auia gelo la madre todo bien razonado,
> Q [u] e non querria mentir por vn rico condado.   (5)

The reference is once more to Amunna passing on information to Munno. Here "razonar" is synonymous with "recontar" (170c).

The substantive form occurs twice. One of the virgins, perhaps Agatha, is extolling Oria's virtues:

"Tu mucho te deleytas en las nuestras passiones,
de amor e de grado leyes nuestras razones." (34ab)

As Oria continues through paradise, she recognizes two "barones" who are praised for composing such works:

Bartolomeo, ducho de escriujr passiones;
Don Gomez de Massiella que daua bien raçiones.

(55cd)

Now "passion" has a precise literary meaning in Berceo as well as during his period in general: the written *vida* of a martyr. Thus Berceo can only write a "passion" of San Lorenzo (*SLor* 1c), since only he of Berceo's four saints suffered a martyr's death. Similarly, it is appropriate to speak of the "passiones" (*SOr* 34a) of the three virgins of the first vision, since "todas tres fueron martires en poquiella edat" (*SOr* 27b). It is clear, therefore, that "razones" in *Santa Oria* 34b is synonymous with "passiones": it is a written *vida* of a martyr which Oria reads ("[tu] leyes").[25]

INTERVENTIONS OF THE AUTHOR AND NARRATIVE FORMULAS IN *Santa Oria*

One of Berceo's most delightful and puzzling habits is his tendency to intrude his own self into the story. At regular intervals the author comments on the progression of the narrative, provides doctrinal clarification, pleads, chides, and prays.[26] While bringing order and welcome change, such occurrences are also apt to disturb by not providing either "subjective" information or the independent per-

25. It is probable that "raçiones" (*SOr* 55d) is an alternative spelling for "razones."

26. Stylistically, Berceo's personal interventions can usually be identified by the use of either the first person or the second person plural "vos" in direct address. However, this is not always the case. For example: "Sy lis dió otros fijos non lo dize la leyenda" (*SOr* 15a); "Non las podrian contar palabras njn sermones" (*SOr* 24d).

spective on the story that such subjectivity might seem to imply. A systematic attempt to solve this paradox must begin by observing that in Berceo there are two first persons: singular "I" or "me" and plural "we" or "us." The distinction is important because each category has its own functions.

It may be said that *Santa Oria* is informed by two main kinds of consciousness: Berceo as narrator, or *conteur,* and Berceo as Christian. Although the two usually coincide (since his art is didactic, at the service of Christian ideals), their differences may nevertheless best be seen in the distinct uses of personal interventions throughout the poem. Now when the Christian consciousness is dominant, the "I" sponsors a reflection on the author's personal spiritual destiny, while the "we" integrates him into the larger community of Christians and emphasizes their common destiny (as, for example, in the frequent invocations). By contrast, Berceo's personal interventions, even when clearly religious in intent, may also have artistic functions. In such cases even the highly personal "I" tends to reveal not so much a personality as a series of distinct and often stylized narrative techniques. In the actual solution of compositional problems, however, Berceo resorts preferably to the "we" form, as we shall now see.[27]

TRANSITIONS

The copulative kind of transition already seen in the ordering of the larger structural units is also used to link

27. The importance of artistic self-consciousness and the tendency to express it through personal intervention has been noted by Curtius in the case of the *Vie de St. Alexis:* "Suchen wir nach der stilistischen Eigenart des Gedichtes, so treffen wir zunächst auf einen Zug, der durch das ganze Denkmal gleichmässig hindurchgeht und sich als die allgemeinste, damit aber als die am wenigsten individuelle, Voraussetzung für das Verfahren des Dichters erweist. Der Dichter besitzt ein starkes Bewusstsein von seiner selbständigen Gestaltungstätigkeit. Dies wird ersichtlich aus zahlreichen persönlichen Interventionen." Ernst Robert Curtius, "Zur Interpretation des Alexiusliedes," *ZRP, 56* (1936), 115–16.

other elements of the poem, such as a series of miracles [28] or the prologue and story proper:

> Auemos en el prologo mucho detardado;
> Siguamos la estoria, esto es agujsado. (*SOr* 10ab) [29]

Such transitions arrange sequences in a linear and often chronological order, thus enforcing an orderly development of the narrative. Feeling he has allowed the story to get sidetracked, the poet harks our attention back to the point at hand: "Dexemos de la madre, en la fija tornemos" (*SOr* 19a). In the same manner, when he wishes to return to a former topic for amplification: "Dexemos lo al todo, a la siella tornemos" (*SOr* 89a).[30] The guardian of the throne is a certain Voxmea (79ab). Fearing her name might not be remembered (its last mention is separated by 11 strophes), Berceo recapitulates:

> De suso lo dixiemos, la materia lo daua,
> Voxmea auja nonbre la que la siella guardaua.
>
> (*SOr* 90ab)

The same formula is used in 6a, where the function is not so much to recall the name as to bring the story back to Oria: "De suso la nonbramos, acordar uos podedes." [31]

28. For example, *SMil* 132ab: "Entre los sos miraglos en el terçer logar / De una paralítica vos queremos fablar"; cf. also *SDom* 315.

29. Cf. also *SDom* 8d: "Nos sigamos el curso, tengamos nuestra uia."

30. The strongly formulaic character of these transitions should be noted. Compare *Fernán Gonzalez* 15ab (*BAE*, 57): "Tornemos nos al curso, nuestra rrason syguamos, / Tornemos nos en Espanna a do lo començamos." Cf. also *SMil* 482ab: "En Sant Millan vos quiero la materia tornar, / Siguir nuestra istoria, nuestro corso guardar."

31. Since Oria's name does not occur in the five preceding strophes, Frida Weber de Kurlat (*NRFH, 15*, 114), in order to confirm her incidental thesis that *SOr* is posterior to *SDom*, refers to that section in *SDom* (316–33) concerning the exorcism of the demons that were attacking Oria. Her claim is that *SOr* 6a ("de suso la nombramos") is an allusion to this passage. However, I know of no other instance in Berceo of direct cross-reference to another of his works. Rather, the formula "que de suso contamos" (*Milagros* 331a), a rather frequent stylistic trait in Berceo,

Instead of reverting to a former topic, the poet may wish
to introduce fresh elements, to "change the subject":

> Vna cosa me pesa mucho de coraçon,
> que auemos vn poco acanbiar la razon.
>
> (*SDom* 126ab) [32]

Such procedure, especially if it involves an *amplificatio*,
seems to require some kind of explanation, and the following passage may be taken as Berceo's best statement on the
matter:

---

always refers to what immediately precedes in the same poem (cf. also
Sacr 85a; *SDom* 489d, 522d). In the same way, it is more likely that (*SOr*
6a) is simply an allusion to previous mention of Oria (1d, 2b, 4a) or,
more probably, to the title "La Vida de Santa Oria." This explanation
may be expanded by trying to reconstruct the circumstances under which
the poem was presented and for which it was written. Georges Cirot liked
to imagine the recitation of Berceo's *Vidas* as follows: "Je penserais plutôt
à ces 'veladas' tenues dans un Athénée de village, avec le concours des
autorités, 'merinos,' 'alcaldes,' 'andadores,' les dignitaires de l'abbaye, et
la fine fleur du monde campagnard" (*RFE, 9* [1922], 169). One might further speculate on the particular occasion of such a meeting, such as, perhaps, the saint's feastday. It is well known that such events were prime
motivation for composing poems, plays, and the like. Jean Bodel's great
"Jeu de Saint Nicolas" was first presented on the Saint's feastday and
probably before just such a crowd as Cirot imagines. Similarly, Berceo's
audience had perhaps just heard a Mass or pious tale in honor of Oria:
"Essa Uirgen preciosa de quien fablar solemos" (4a). On the tradition of
oral presentation, see Ruth Crosby, "Oral Delivery in the Middle Ages,"
Speculum, 11 (1936), 91–93. One may also consult Erich Auerbach, *Literary Language and Its Public in Late Latin Antiquity and in the Middle
Ages*, trans. Ralph Manheim (New York, 1965), pp. 284–86. The view
that the poems of the *mester de clerecía* were written for oral delivery has
been questioned by G. B. Gybbon-Monypenny, "The Spanish *Mester de
Clerecía* and its Intended Public," *Medieval Miscellany Presented to
Eugène Vinaver* (New York, 1965), pp. 230–44. However, it seems rather
difficult to doubt the literal truth of such passages as *SDom* 259d: "Oyr
tales promessas quales uos e leydas."

32. "Cambiemos la materia, en otro son tornemos," *Signos* 48a. Cf. also
SDom 113ac: "Dexemos al buen omne folgar ensu posada, / . . . demos al
Monasterio de Sant Mjllan tornada." Formulaic transitions of this kind
were popular in both Spain and France of the period. Cf. Weber de
Kurlat, *NRFH, 15*, 121, n. 20, for examples.

> Dexemos al buen omne con el Rey afolgar,
> conujene nos vn poco la materia cambiar,
> *non podriamos sin esso la razon acordar,*
> por que nos alonguemos bien sabremos tornar.
>
> (*SDom* 186)

It is against this background that one must read *Santa Oria* 185:

> Aun non me querria, sennores, espedir;
> Avn fincan cosiellas que uos e de dezir.
> La obra començada bien la quiero conplir,
> Que non aya njnguno por que me escarnjr.

As in *Santo Domingo* 185a, Berceo announces an amplification—or better yet, a continuation—by a double negative, by asserting that he will not yet sign off. The interesting novelty here is in the double justification: the first artistic, the second personal. Lines 185bc may be considered analogous to Berceo's artistic aims in *Santo Domingo* 186c: "non podriamos sin esso la razon acordar." Once an author has begun a work, he feels compelled to finish it, especially when there remain "little things" to write down. But to this, Berceo adds a personal, intimate note: "so that no one may scoff at me." Both his professional and personal honor are at stake.

Finally, the poet may decide to skip ahead or accelerate the narrative:

> Non uos querria mucho enesto detener,
> querria adelante aguyjar e mouer   (*SDom* 222ab)

> Deçir non vos podriemos todas sues trasnochadas.
> Destaiarvos queremos de las fuertes andadas,
> Sacarlo de los yermos a las tierras pobladas.
>
> (*SMil* 68a, cd)

In summary, all personal transitions studied so far occur in the form of the first person plural, "we" or "us." The following might seem an exception:

> En esta pleytesia no qujero detardar,
> Sy por bien lo tobierdes quiero uos destaiar.
> A la fin de la duenna me quiero acostar,
> Leuarla a la siella, despues yr a folgar.   (SOr 160)

Here, however, the transitional function of the formula is doubled with the autobiographical motif "despues yr a folgar," and it will be seen that the latter is always the more dominant.[33] As in *Santa Oria* 185a, the author's motives are personal as well as artistic.

There seem to be other and less self-conscious kinds of transition in *Santa Oria*. For example, between the Virgin Mary's announcement in heaven of Oria's death and its actual earthly fulfillment (136–37), one might expect an interpolation such as "let's return to the bedside." Instead, the narrator passes directly to the concrete event and achieves greater dramatic intensity in so doing. But this is the exception.[34] The rule in *Santa Oria* is that transitions are performed by personal interventions: [35] purely functional devices, efficacious and unsophisticated, and with little lyrical or autobiographical range.

33. See below, Chap. 6, p. 187. The fact that "yr a folgar" is a frequent formula in Berceo does not, ipso facto, preclude any autobiographical content.

34. The abruptness of the transition has caused María Rosa Lida de Malkiel to suppose, perhaps correctly, that the text is incomplete at this juncture, since one might expect Berceo to narrate "el cumplimiento del anuncio y la dolencia de la reclusa" before passing on to her final moments. See *RPH, 10, 23.*

35. Transitions from the narrative to visions are exceptional in that visions have their own formulaic openings.

REFERENCES TO THE SOURCE AND CLAIMS
OF AUTHENTICITY

Berceo modestly conceives his task as that of a versifier who translates Latin texts into Romance. He invents nothing, makes no additions to the text; on the contrary:

> Quj en esto dubdare que nos uersificamos,
> Que non es esta cosa tal como nos contamos,
> Peccara dura mente en Dios que adoramos;
> *Ca nos quanto deximos escripto lo fallamos.* (*SOr* 203)

References to the written source, fidelity to the story, sincerity: these are rhetorical commonplaces in the narrative art of the period.[36] The practice may be seen in any of those phrases that captures the banality of the repeated allegation: "non uos mjento njn grano" (*SDom* 262d), "deuedes lo creer" (*SDom* 613b), "por uerdat uos dezir" (*SOr* 41d), "esta es la uerdat" (*SOr* 180c). Occasionally the formula can be expanded to a whole verse: "Sy entender queredes toda çertanjdat" (*SOr* 180a). Authenticity must be established at every possible source of error. Thus Amunna "bien gelo contó ella" (*SOr* 171b), and Munno's veracity especially must be placed beyond doubt. The way of doing this is, again, through repetition of formula: "non querria mentir por vn rico condado" (*SOr* 5d), "non diria falsedat" (*SOr* 204a), "dixo toda uerdat" (*SOr* 204d). In one of his variations of the formula, however, Berceo's insistence suggests a *rhétoriqueur* playfulness:

> Essa Uirgen preciosa de quien fablar solemos,
> Fue de Ujlla Uellayo *segunt lo que leemos;*
> Amunna fue su madre, *escripto lo tenemos;*
> Garcia fue el padre, *en letra lo auemos.*   (*SOr* 4)

Although protestations of sincerity were common practice at the time, they often have a ring of truth and urgency

36. See Gallais, *Romania, 85,* 181–230.

in *Santa Oria* because of the tone of serious religiosity that pervades the poem. This impression is compounded by Berceo's humility before his subject—first of all as a Christian: "La materia es alta, temo que peccaremos" (*SOr* 89b) ; then as an author:

> Sy nos cantar sopieremos grant materia tenemos,
> Menester nos sera todo el seso que auemos. (*SOr* 19cd)

Here also, when asserting the veracity of his own work, Berceo uses the "we" form of the personal intervention.

THE ABBREVIATIO

One of the most familiar commonplaces of medieval rhetoric is the announcement of the author's intention to delate a section, to pass over certain details, to avoid delay. The usual explanation of this practice may be gleaned from a passage in *San Millán:*

> Sennores la façienda del confessor onrado
> Non la podrie contar nin romaz nin dictado,
> Mas destaiarvos la quiero, hir a lo mas granado,
> Quando ganó los votos, commo ovo lidiado. (362)

Gallais' remarks, based on similar literary practices found in the *Perceval Continuations,* apply here:

> La préoccupation des auteurs est toujours la même: éluder telle description trop difficile à faire, ou jugée par eux superflue, l'objet dépassant infiniment tout ce qu'ils pourraient en dire. Une hyperbole bien amenée [e.g. "Non la podrie contar nin romaz ni dictado"] vaut bien une description et évite bien du travail à l'écrivain.[37]

The usual reasons, then, were ineptitude or laziness; the alleged excuse: to avoid irrelevant and boring detail and to observe an appropriate silence or to express lyrical stupe-

37. Ibid., p. 217.

faction before an awesome subject matter. This is the general background against which all such formulas must be considered.

To refer to this narrative phenomenon, we have settled on the term "abbreviatio," taken from medieval and antique rhetorical terminology, although its precise meaning remains vague.[38] However, it may be said that the Middle Ages had lost the ancient notion of brevity as a "virtus narrationis." The term simply means, generally speaking, the (often artificial) deletion of elements from the narrative, itself conceived as pure linear extension or development. The abbreviatio is not a problem of compressing a given passage into a more succinct statement; rather, it is a matter of deleting or omitting one or more elements which either the author or the audience or both could normally expect to be given.

In Berceo the abbreviatio, like the transition, is effected through formulaic personal interventions. Moreover, while retaining the central intention to delete the text, the abbreviatio can be distinguished by three distinct narrative attitudes. First of all, Berceo may allege personal ignorance or inadequacy of the Latin text. Or he may declare himself unable to describe such a complex or wonderful subject. Finally, he may both have the source material at hand and feel himself equal to the task but nevertheless refuse to describe for artistic or personal reasons. We shall discuss each of these in turn.

Edmond Faral has pointed out the central importance of the technique of amplificatio in medieval literature. F. W. de Kurlat summarizes, with Berceo in mind, that "ya sabemos que el arte medieval es el arte de la *amplificatio,* no de la *abbreviatio.*"[39] Since the main source of inspiration was usually a Latin text, the author's own

38. As may be seen from Curtius' discussion in *European Literature,* pp. 487–94.
39. *NRFH, 16,* 117. See also Faral, *Les arts poétiques,* pp. 61–85.

personality could shine through only at those junctures
where he amplified and went beyond the given. The
amplificatio is thus an artistic device and can be identified
by a simple comparison between the vulgar text and the
Latin original. The *Vie de Saint Alexis* is a good example.
In general the author follows the source faithfully. However, the 22 strophes between 78–99—about one-fifth of
the whole poem—is an invention of the author of the
Romance version. To this may be added the independent
exordium and *conclusio*.[40]

Personal invention may be encouraged in works of the
imagination, but its uncontrolled practice presented a real
and widespread danger in didactic works having historical
pretensions. A modern expert observes, concerning the
author of the passion of Saint Vincent:

> This dearth of material, which does not appear to
> have checked in any degree the fertility of his pen, is
> the common lot of a large number of hagiographers,
> who, for that matter, have been equally little incon-
> venienced by it. As they were compelled to write, and
> frequently, so they themselves say, by order of their
> superiors, they boldly took the only course open to
> them, and either made a generous use of the method
> of development as practised in the schools, or else had
> recourse to borrowing.[41]

Such a state of affairs may help one to understand not only
the insistent assertions of veracity of the fabricators but
reactionary attempts at historical truth. Against such ten-

40. About one-fifth of the poem is "ganz selbständig, ohne Anlehnung
an seine Quelle," according to Wendlin Foerster (*Sankt Alexius* [Halle,
1915], p. 3), quoted by Curtius, who himself adds the observation concerning the originality of the exordium and the *conclusio. See ZRP, 56*,
117.

41. Hippolyte Delehaye, *The Legends of the Saints*, trans. V. M. Crawford (New York, 1907), pp. 91–92. The method of development referred
to is none other than the amplificatio.

dencies, an author who sincerely desires to follow the Book as closely as possible will react against both personal fabrication of fact and the consecrated literary means for carrying it out: the amplificatio. From this perspective the abbreviatio may be considered not so much a stylistic device as an antistylistic one—that is, an attempt to counteract personal amplification of unauthentic material and to remain within the narrow limits imposed by the Latin source.

Such formulas are frequent in Berceo: [42]

El nonbre dela madre dezir non lo sabria,
como non fue escripto non lo devinaria.

(SDom 8ab)

Sy lis dió otros fijos non lo dize la leyenda. *(SOr* 15a)

Sy era de linage, o era labrador,
non lo diz la leyenda, non so yo sabidor;
ma dexemos lo esso, digamos lo meior,
lo que caye en preçio del sancto conffessor.[43]

(SDom 338)

Berceo shows greater personal concern when the missing information has didactic relevance. For example, places where a saint resided were important for worship and the working of miracles. Yet an important year and a half of St. Dominic's life was not associated in the source book with any specific locale:

42. Formulas of this kind are already present in the *Vie de Saint Alexis:* "Mais ço ne sai com longes i converset" (84) ; "Dis e set anz, n'en fu neent a dire, penat son cors" (161–62) .

43. Similarly: "Caetió y vn çiego, de qual parte que ujno, / non departe la ujlla muy bien el pargamjno, / ca era mala letra, ençerrado latino, / entender no lo pudi, par Señor Sant Martino" *(SDom* 609) . And, more humorously: "non quisiemos la ujlla en escripto meter / ca non es nomneçiello de muy buen paresçer" *(SDom* 613cd) .

> Cuntió grant negligençia alos qui lo supieron,
> el logar do estido que non lo escriujeron.
>
> (*SDom* 71ab)

The necessity of staying within the factual limits of the
Latin source is especially urgent:

> Anno e medio estouo enla hermjtanja,
> dizelo la escriptura, ca yo non lo sabia,
> *quando non lo leyesse, dezir non lo querria,*
> *ca en firmar la dubda grant peccado abria.*
>
> (*SDom* 73) [44]

From what we have already said, it is clear that abbreviatio does not necessarily imply an actual deletion of
the source. It refers to the author's announced decision to
omit from his narrative certain data which either he or his
audience might expect to be given. It may in fact faithfully reflect the source (only a comparative study can show
this) or, on the contrary, depend on the personal reasons—
often laziness—of the author.

A variation on this kind of formula—particularly abundant in medieval literature and usually also in the form
of a personal intervention—is the author's enraptured in-
capacity to express the miraculous. Already in "St. Alexis"
the poet states his failure of speech: "Ne vos sai dire com
il s'en firet liez" (125) ; "Ne vos sai dire com lor ledece est
grande" (610). Gallais lists other samples from the narrative literature of the *Continuations: ne voil, ne sai, ne puis,
nus ne poroit, anuis seroit, ne me loist, que vos diroie,* and
the like.[45]

Berceo is fond of such devices:

---

44. By contrast, despite the heated debate in Berceo's time over the
place of St. Millán's origin, the poet does not hesitate to assert: "El barrio
de Berçeo, Madriz la iaz present: / Y nasçió Sant Millan, *esto sin falli-
ment*" (*SMil* 3cd). It is precisely the formula of authenticity that causes
one to suspect.

45. Gallais, *Romania, 85,* 216.

> ca de las sus bondades, maguer mucho andemos,
> la mjlesima parte dezir non la podremos.   (*SDom* 33cd)

Later, probably referring to this passage:

> Ante vos lo dixiemos (sibien uos remenbrades) ,
> que seria luenga soga dezir las sus bondades.
>
> (*SDom* 93ab)

Although the idea is always the same (the greatness or richness of the material in contrast to the impotence of the author and his narrative) , Berceo avoids the short, dull formulas in vogue at the time and manages to achieve variety of expression, usually by expanding the formula to at least a full verse: "Todos los sus mjraglos, ¿quj los podria contar?" (*SDom* 384a) ; "fazia Dios por el tanto que non seria asmado" (*SDom* 537b) ; "non podriamos los medios nos meter en ditado" (*SDom* 537d) ; "Sennores la façienda del confessor onrado / Non la podrie contar nin romaz nin dictado" (*SMil* 362b) . It must be emphasized that these are simple formulas common to narrative techniques of the times and may be no more than exclamations intended to give the saint or subject matter more relief. This is clear from the three examples of this device in *Santa Oria:* "de duro serian contadas" (46d) ; "La su claridat omne non la podria contar" (86d) ; and:

> Tanto fue Dios pagado de las sus oraçiones
> Que li mostró en çielo tan grandes ujsiones
> Que deujan a los omnes canbiar los coraçones;
> Non las podrian contar palabras njn sermones.
>
> (*SOr* 24)

Here a traditional formula is inserted to emphasize the magnitude of the visions. Indeed, the context shows that the formula has lost its literal meaning. The next strophe begins the narration of precisely one of those very visions that were just declared beyond the range of "palabras njn sermones." [46]

The preceding analysis has shown, by contrast with the other *Vidas,* the minimal role of abbreviatio formulas in *Santa Oria.* We were able to find only one example of the *topos* of "insufficiency of the source," and likewise, only three examples of "inability to describe." Moreover, all were rather nonfunctional uses, mere formulas having no organic relation to the context and, indeed, not even carrying the meaning that their words imply. But there is a third series of abbreviatio formulas, and these have little to do with the source or with either the magnitude of the subject or the particular indispositions of the author. This third category has a more strictly literary function: to quicken the narrative, to avoid tedium, to construct a better story. Since this always involves a deliberate choice on the part of the author, abbreviatio in such cases hinges neither on textual inadequacy nor on ability but rather on a refusal to describe.

To avoid tedium: this was a prime reason for abbreviatio in medieval literature.[47] Berceo also uses it, and very skillfully indeed:

> Cantaruos mj fazienda seria luenga tardança,
> ca las razones luengas siempre traen noiança,
> abreuiar uos lo quiero, non quiero fer longança.
>
> (*SDom* 133a-c)

46. "Such empty clichés" are "typical of this literary genre [hagiography]. The authors who practiced it are fond of assuring us that the saint worked more miracles than he can enumerate. Here the *brevitas*-formula enters the service of panegyric" (Curtius, *European Literature,* p. 488, where examples are cited). Occasionally, when Berceo ventures an answer to his rhetorical question "¿Qui los podria contar?" the effect is one of simple profundity: "De la sue sancta vida qui vos podrie deçir? / . . . Fuera qui la podiesse en si mismo sofrir" (*SMil* 55ad; cf. also *SDom* 74).

47. See Curtius, *European Literature,* pp. 487–94, "Brevity as an Ideal of Style."

This is the usual abbreviatio, one would think; and, to be sure, this narrative function is carried out. But the speaker is not Berceo, it is King Don García demanding that Domingo hand him over the treasures of the monastery. He is impatient and wants to get right to the point: "quiero delos thesoros que me dedes pitança" (*SDom* 133d). By putting the well-known topos into the mouth of the King, Berceo gains both stylistic and realistic advantage. He quickens the narrative and faithfully renders the King's lust for money.[48]

This technique occurs in *Santa Oria* in two significant passages. The first introduces Oria's death scene. The Virgin Mary, in vision, has predicted Oria's imminent death (135–36). She then falls ill and is carried up to the Mount of Olives in a dream, a foreshadowing of her reception into paradise (139–47). Her mother, fearing that the end is near, calls Munno (149). Oria describes the vision and, carried away with enthusiasm ("con sabor de la cosa," 159a), tries to lift herself up. Munno calms her with the observation that her time is not yet come:

> Dixoli Munno: "Oria, fuelga en tu logar,
> Non es agora tiempo por en naues entrar." (159cd)

It is at this point that Berceo breaks into the narrative— after an unprecedented string of 70 strophes without interruption:

> En esta pleytesia non qujero detardar,
> Sy por bien lo tobierdes quiero uos destaiar.
> A la fin de la duenna me quiero acostar,
> Leuarla a la siella, despues yr a folgar. (160)

Apparently Berceo feels that the essential has been said in preparation for the death scene; and, indeed, one is in-

---

48. Berceo also uses the tedium-formula, preceding not a deletion but rather the opposite amplificatio, to brace the audience against inattention: "maguer uos enoyedes, deuedes nos soffrir" (*SDom* 335c).

clined to agree that the interest declines as the dialogue
between Oria and Munno nears its end. The poet began
the death scene 23 strophes ago and now, "if you don't
mind," wants to take her to her throne (i.e. he wants to
describe the death and the entrance into heaven) and then
take a rest. Of course, there may be an element of laziness
or weariness (*folgar*) here; if so, Berceo's blunt admission
that he wants to take a rest is charming in its frankness.
Also, he may simply be repeating a formula such as the
one used in the penultimate strophe of the *Sacrificio:*

> El romançe es cumplido, puesto en buen logar,
> Dias ha que lazdramos, queremos ir folgar.   (296cd)

Nevertheless, one is inclined to judge that the abbreviatio
is justified by the necessity of the narrative.

The second passage occurs near the end of the poem.
Oria is in heaven and has just announced this to her
mother in a vision. She returns to heaven, and her mother
wakes up. At this point Berceo intervenes:

> Vido syn estas otras muy grandes ujsiones
> De que formaria omne assaz buenas razones.
> Mas tengo otras priesas de fer mjs cabazones;
> Qujero alçar me desto fasta otras sazones.   (202)

The mystery of this passage is compounded by comparison
with parallel texts. At the end of *Santo Domingo,* as here,
Berceo asserts that there is much more to tell about his
Saint; nevertheless, he is happy because he has finished—
i.e. he has exhausted his written source (755, 754). In like
fashion, *San Millán* concludes with the praise: "El libro
es complido, graçias al Criador" (488d). As noted above,
the *Sacrificio* frankly confesses that "queremos ir folgar";
but this is because "El romance es cumplido" (296dc).
Similarly, the poems in honor of the Virgin are not deleted
at the end and hence require no formula of explanation or
apology.

In contrast, there is a triple mystery about the *Santa*

Oria passage. First of all, does Berceo delete his source at the end? Secondly, if he does, why? Thirdly, what is the reference of the cryptic (202cd), or does the very vagueness have its own meaning? [49]

APOSTROPHE

Although most examples cited above may be termed apostrophe, since they directly address the audience or make at least tacit reference to the audience's presence and complicity by the plural "we," nevertheless we shall reserve this rubric for those uses of direct address which do not have a clearly definable narrative function. There are two such passages in *Santa Oria*. In the first:

> Auja ujda lazrada qual entender podedes,
> Sy su ujda leyerdes assy lo prouaredes.   (6cd)

"Qual entender podedes" is comparable to *Santo Domingo* 337b or its variant, "Entender lo podedes . . . / que auja muchos males de diuersas colores" (*SDom* 349ab). These are padding formulas that Berceo uses in connection with the mention of hardship: "You can well understand or imagine the hard life." The remaining verse (6d) is but another formula of sincerity.

The second apostrophe occurs after the narration of the honors done to the mortal remains of the Saint:

> Sy entender queredes toda çertanjdat
> Do yaze esta duenna de tan grant sanctidat,
> En Sant Mjllan de suso esta es la uerdat.
>
> *SOr* (180a-c)

This intervention may be classified simply as information useful to an audience that revered relics and made pilgrimages to the places where they were to be found.[50]

---

49. These problems are discussed below, Chap. 6, pp. 188–89 and n. 27.

50. Another use of personal intervention might be termed exegetical and arises because of Berceo's need to explain the figures of his allegories: "Sennores e amigos, lo que dicho avemos, / Palabra es oscura, esponerla

PRAYERS, INVOCATIONS, AND DOCTRINAL
CLARIFICATION

In summary, when Berceo's consciousness as an author predominates or when problems of a technical nature occur, the function of the first person may be described as structural or narrative. However, already with the second use of the apostrophe described above, as well as with the exegetical use of the device, Berceo moves from the purely technical problems toward his mission as a Christian author. He undertakes allegorical exegesis because of his doctrinal beliefs; he announces the locus of Oria's relics because he is a preacher. Such personal intrusions may retain both their formulaic character and structural relevance (insofar as they introduce new elements). But the important distinction must be stressed: the personal intervention no longer organizes or discusses content; it *is* content.

Santa Oria begins with the sign of the Cross and closes with the prayer-formula "Amen." Since the whole poem is thus written and spoken under the sign of prayer, it is no surprise to find Berceo interlarding the narrative with brief orations. And since the prayer is a highly personal form of discourse, these interventions into the text occur in the first person.[51] In *Santa Oria* Berceo addresses his prayers, for the most part, to Oria, asking her intercession (2cd, 3bd, 180d, 183cd). In the latter passage he invokes both Oria and her mother, Amunna. Secondly, Berceo may invoke the Virgin Mary (3c) and God directly (1a-c, 43a, 184cd).

The following are examples of the invocations, which may vary in length from one to four lines, although in this

---

queremos" (*Milagros* 16ab). The reasons for the absence of such an exegesis of Oria's visions will be developed in the next chapter.

51. Compare the *Vie de Saint Alexis:* "E reis celeste, tu nos i fai venir" (335).

poem Berceo preferred the form with two verses. One
line:

> Faga nos Dios por ella merçed e caridat. (180d)

Two lines:

> Que Dios por el su ruego sea de mj pagado,
> E non quiera uengança tomar del mj peccado. (2cd)

> Ellas fagan a Dios ruegos multiplicados
> Que nos salue las almas, perdone los peccados.
> (183cd)

> Ponga en el su graçia Dios el nuestro sennor,
> Que uea la su gloria en el regno mayor. (184cd)

> Dios nos dé la su graçia el buen Rey spiritual
> Que alla njn aquj nunca ueamos mal. (205cd)

Four lines:

> Luego en el comjenço e en la primeria
> A ella merçet pido, ella sea mj guja.
> Ruegue a la Gloriosa Madre Sancta Maria
> Que sea nuestra guarda de noche e de dia. (3)

With the exception of the opening invocation to the Trinity, all of these brief orations in *Santa Oria* occur at the end
of the strophe. They are spoken on the last breath of the
quatrain and add to the feeling of conclusiveness that the
ponderous *cuaderna via* normally produces anyway.[52] Furthermore, they are all spoken in the "we" form of communal prayer. The single exceptions to this rule (2cd and
3bc) form part of the opening invocation. In strophe 2

52. Of course, it may also be a convenient device simply to round off
a strophe before proceeding to the next, as is obvious from the following:
"Sennor Sancto Domjngo de primas fue pastor, / despues fue delas almas
padre e guiador; / bueno fue encomjenço, apostremas meior, / el buen
Rey delos çielos nos dé el su amor (*SDom* 31). The metrical convenience
of such prayer-formulas may be further seen in the terminal "Dios sea
end laudado' (*Milagros* 175d).

Berceo has been speaking in the first person singular ("Quiero en mj uegez") and carries the form over into a plea for personal guidance; then, within the same strophe, he expands with the usual "we" into a general request for protection.

Opening invocations are good examples of the way Berceo uses formulaic devices and yet adapts them to the needs of the specific narrative. All of his works begin either with direct address to the audience (*SMil, Signos, Milagros*) or, as in *Santa Oria,* with an invocation. The latter may be directed (1) to God: "rey . . . fin e comienzo de toda creatura" (*Sacrificio*); "Rey omnipotent / que faze sol e luna nazer en Orient" (*SLor*); (2) to the Virgin Mary (*Loores, Duelo*); or, finally, (3) to the Trinity. *Santo Domingo* opens as follows: [53]

> En el nonbre del Padre, que fizo toda cosa,
> E de don Jhesu Christo, Fijo dela Gloriosa,[54]
> E del Spiritu Sancto, que egual dellos posa,
> de un confessor sancto quiero fer vna prosa.[55]

53. The idea of opening a narrative poem with an invocation to the Trinity was in use before Berceo. The *Chanson de la croisade albigeoise* (ed. Eugène Martin-Chabot [3 vols. Paris, 1960]) begins as follows: "El nom del Payre e del Filh e del San Esperit / Comensa la cansos que maestre Guilhems fit." One may further compare the opening of *Fernán Gonzalez* (quoted below, n. 55) or the *Libro de buen amor* (ed. J. Ducamin [Toulouse, 1901]): "Dios Padre, Dios Fijo, Dios Spiritu Santo" (11a).

54. *Don Jhesu Christo.* Perhaps a reference to the Incarnation, as can be seen from the rest of the verse: "qui nos ujno salvar." Christ is the only Person of the Three who became man. See *Milagros* 169a; *SLor* 44a, 55c; *SDom* 252c: "don Christo." Or, following its etymology, the title may be equivalent to "Señor": "Tornó en la Gloriosa Madre del nuestro don" (*Milagros* 168a). A comic effect is achieved in the *Libro de buen amor* (200a, etc.) in speaking of "don Jupiter."

55. Imitations of Berceo's formulas are not wanting. The opening strophe of *Fernán Gonzalez* is almost word for word a repetition of *SDom,* except for the mention of the subject matter ("Del conde de Castilla") and a slight variant on the reference to Christ: "Del que quiso nasçer de la Virgen preçiosa." The same formula, in prose this time, may be found in the codex of the *Sumario de crónicas hasta el año 1368,* described by

Berceo has retained the traditional order of the sign of the Cross and reserved one line for each Person of the Trinity, the author and his subject being naturally mentioned last. The opening invocation in *Santa Oria* follows this same pattern:

> En el nonbre del Padre que nos quiso criar,
> E de don Iesu Christo qui nos ujno saluar,
> E del Spiritu Sancto, lumbre de confortar,
> De vna sancta uirgen quiero uersificar.

This invocation retains virtually intact the first hemistich of each line of the *Santo Domingo* invocation. The improvement occurs in the rhyming words, in which Berceo has succeeded in compressing the essential action appropriate [56] to each Person: the Father's appropriate activity is *criar*, the Son's is *salvar*, the Spirit's is *confortar*, and the poet's is merely *versificar*. But this is not all. In *Santa Oria* the formulaic opening is not a mere mechanical device but rather bears an organic relationship to the narrative that follows. In naming the three Persons of the Trinity, Berceo introduces them as dramatic personages. And, indeed, all three play important and independent roles in the poem (insofar as the Persons may be said to act independently) : the dove, symbol of the Spirit (37–40) ; the voice of the Father (105–07) ; and Christ, implied in the scene of the Garden of Olives.

Menéndez Pidal in his *Catálogo de crónicas generales,* p. 125 (quoted in *Fernán Gonzalez,* ed. C. C. Marden [Baltimore, 1904], p. 163, n. 1). The codex begins with the following paragraph: "Enel nonbre del padre que fiso toda cosa del que quiso nasçer de la virgen gloriosa e del spiritu santo que es iglesia dellos prosa [*sic*] dala crónica delos Reyes e enperadores quiero fablar una breve cosa." Menéndez Pidal seems to prefer to compare this passage to *SDom,* although it is clear from a comparison with the second verse of *Fernán Gonzalez* that the latter is the more probable source.

56. The term "appropriate" is taken here in the sense of "being a property of," as in St. Thomas Aquinas: "Utrum esse bonum per essentiam sit proprium Dei." *Summa Theologica* 1–4.3.

PERSONAL INTERVENTION OF THE
NARRATOR MUNNO

It has been implicit in all the examples studied thus far
that "personal intervention of the narrator" refers to Berceo, since he is the author of the poems. In *Santa Oria*,
however, there is a development unique in Berceo: the
poet steps aside and lets the original narrator of the Latin
version speak in his own words. At a certain point in the
Vida the narrative "I" is no longer Berceo but Oria's confessor Munno.

The section in question is dramatically crucial. Oria is
in a delirium, and the "good ladies" attending her wonder
whether this is all for the good or bad. Oria's confessor is
summoned:

> "La madre de la duenna fizo a mj clamar,
> Fizo me en la casa de la fija entrar."   (149ab)

The girl speaks of her visions, in comparison to which "the
world is nothing." Munno is pleased: "Ouo destas palabras
don Munno mucho plazer" (153a). The reader is perhaps
still unaware of the fact that within 6 strophes the narrator
has changed from Berceo to Munno and back again to
Berceo.

In the second such passage (163–68) Berceo has just
announced that he wishes to pass directly to Oria's death
("non qujero detardar," 160a) and immediately uses a
rhetorical formula indicating that he is about to narrate a
vision (164ab). The drama becomes intense and soaked
with realism. It is the hour of the midday siesta; the ascetic, "who always dressed in wool," is in pain; the mother
is tired but can neither sleep nor eat. Suddenly, with no
warning:

> "Yo Munno e don Gomez çellerer del logar
> Oujemos a Amunna de firmes a rogar

> Que fuese a su lecho vn poquiello a folgar,
> Ca nos guardariamos si quisiesse passar."   (163)

How long Munno has been narrating it is impossible to say. The switch of narrators is nowhere indicated and is yet easily accepted or perhaps again not even noticed by the reader absorbed in the drama. Somewhere after Berceo's own personal intervention (160), he imperceptibly yields to Munno and equally imperceptibly resumes his own task by strophe 170, where he mentions how Munno learned the whole story by heart.

Such examples demonstrate better than all formulas Berceo's conception of his relation to the Latin source and its author: as far as the essential fact goes—the life of the Saint—they are one voice.

In summary, the use of personal interventions of the author speaking for himself as individual or Christian must be carefully distinguished from the structural and narrative devices of the *conteur*. The large majority of such instances belong precisely to the literary (and not the personal) category. Berceo has a well-developed system of narrative techniques and uses them consistently. Prominent among these are the preference of "we" over "I" and formulaic patterns of expression involving repetitions of hemistichs and even whole lines. With this perspective in mind, we shall better be able, at the proper time,[57] to appraise those unique interventions where Berceo views himself no longer as a *conteur* but rather as a man with a personal destiny.

57. See below, Chap. 6.

2. Genre and Themes of *Santa Oria*

DIDACTICISM: THE EXEMPLUM

THE EXEMPLUM IN MEDIEVAL LITERATURE: THEORY AND PRACTICE

Berceo's *Vida de Santa Oria* belongs to that prolific branch of didactic narrative known as the exemplum. In its traditionally Christian context the exemplum may be said to teach in at least two senses. Strictly speaking, it exposes and elaborates doctrine; in a more affective sense it attempts to convert souls to God. It may thus be directed to both the mind and the heart, although in practice it tends to stress the latter. It seems needless to add that these goals are not opposites but complementary. Further, although the exemplum is not necessarily hagiographic,[1] this is often the case, since the saints are considered ideal exemplars of the Way and the Truth.

Historically, the Christian could trace the origins of such practices to the Bible itself.[2] Christ used three different types of exemplum: parables, comparisons with nature, and prosopopoeia or visions (see Luke 16:19-31). In addition to biblical sources there were available the prodigious *Acta Sanctorum,* the *Acta Martyrum,* and countless hagiographical records, pious tales, and apparitions, as well as personal religious experiences. Berceo was surely familiar with such materials. Referring to the life of St. Dominic:

---

1. St. Augustine interrupts a scriptural exegesis with an illustration that has "occurred to him": "Tamen scripturis diligentius perscrutatis, occurit mihi unum exemplum." Quoted in J. T. Welter, *L'exemplum dans la littérature religieuse et didactique du moyen âge* (Paris, 1927), p. 13. This excellent study contains an important collection of original materials on the subject.

2. Ibid., pp. 10, 11, 16.

Muchos son los padres que fizieron tal ujda,
yaze en *Vitas Patrum* dellos vna partida.

(SDom 61ab)

St. Gregory the Great (590–604) was extremely fond of
such methods of instruction.[3] He seems to have been one
of the main channels of diffusion of the *Vitae Patrum*,[4]
and his famous dialogues were influential throughout the
Middle Ages.[5] Dominic's words are compared to his:

Los dichos que dizia melados semeiauan,
como los que de uoca de Gregorio manauan.

(SDom 121cd)

The general practice and popularity of such stories is succinctly summarized by Welter: "Les *Acta Sanctorum* ont
donné naissance au type hagiographique, de beaucoup le
plus répandu de tous les types dans la littérature médiévale
religieuse. Ils embrassent, en effet, une infinité de vies de
saints, existant isolément ou réunies en de vastes légen-
diers, soit locaux, soit universels."[6]

This statement suggests an especially important concern
among didactic authors, that of bringing the story closer to
the audience so as to make it more credible. This was done

3. "Plus enim plerumque exempla quam ratiocinationis verba com-
pungunt." *PL, 76,* col. 1300.

4. For the text of the *Vitae Patrum* see *PL, 21,* cols. 387–462. See
Welter, p. 14, n. 8: "Il semble bien que Saint Grégoire ait cherché à
imiter les *Vitae Patrum* en entreprenant d'écrire une pareille collection
pour les Pères de l'Occident." For further bibliography see Welter, p. 25,
n. 41.

5. "Les grands maîtres de la mystique bénédictine et cistercienne . . .
l'accueillent [the exemplum] avec une grande faveur et en font pour ainsi
dire la base de leurs traités destinés à alimenter, sous forme de lectures
spirituelles, la piété des religieux de leurs très nombreux monastères. Les
types d'*exempla* qui ont leur préférence sont ceux qui s'adaptent le mieux
aux conceptions religieuses de leurs confrères. Ce sont les mêmes qu'on
voit déjà mis en œuvre dans les *Vitae Patrum,* les vies des saints et, plus
spécialement, dans les célèbres dialogues de Grégoire le Grand, qu'ils
prennent du reste comme modèles à imiter." Welter, p. 42.

6. Welter, p. 105.

in several ways. First of all, along with the remote *Vitae
Patrum* and the like, examples were taken from more
recent history and even from contemporary events. Caesarius von Heisterbach (d. 1240) states in one of his sermons: "Nonnulla etiam quae nostris temporibus sunt gesta
et a viris religiosis mihi recitata." [7] Or, as the passage from
St. Augustine shows, the *exemplum* may be taken from
personal experience. Bourgain notes a similar concern in
the preaching of the day: "Le prédicateur a toujours été
témoin de ce qu'il rapporte." [8] Or, again to make the story
closer and livelier to the audience, the author would locate
it with great precision in time and place.[9] This was common practice in medieval allegory and tended to give an
otherworldly or otherwise fantastic narrative greater authenticity.[10] It is highly relevant that in *Santa Oria* four
visions are directly preceded by an indication of the exact
date. Take, for example, the first vision:

> Terçera noche era despues de Naujdat
> De Sancta Eugenia era festividat.   (25ab) [11]

Finally, the use of the vulgar tongue became increasingly
the proper medium for approaching the common people
through exempla:

> La littérature en langues vulgaires recourra elle-même
> de bonne heure au même procédé [i.e. visions]. Ce ne

7. Caesarius von Heisterbach (1180?–1240), *Homilis de Infantia,* in
Fascibus moralitatis Caesarii Heisterbacensis monachi (Coloniae, 1615),
Prol., p. 2; quoted in Welter, p. 115.

8. L. Bourgain, *La chaire française au XIIIe siècle* (Paris, 1879), pp.
258–61.

9. Welter (pp. 116–17, n. 7) notes this practice in Caesarius von
Heisterbach and contrasts the exemplum having no time and place data
with the more lively anecdote that has such indications.

10. Chandler Post, in his *Medieval Spanish Allegory* (Cambridge, Mass.,
1915), p. 122, notes this desire for greater realism and credulity and goes
on to observe, in his discussion of *Santa Oria*, that the "scrupulous ob-
servance of the date" is a "commonplace of medieval allegory."

11. See also strophes 116, 161, 88.

sont d'abord, il est vrai, que des traductions, des
visions précédentes. Mais dès le debut du xive siècle,
les visions, les songes ou les pèlerinages dans l'autre
monde . . . entreront sous une forme originale dans
le domaine du genre didactique.[12]

Berceo never tires of mentioning that he invents nothing;
he is only a "versifficador." What is perhaps unique—or at
least charming—is his unpretentious excuse for writing in
"roman paladino" as opposed to Latin: ". . . non so tan
letrado por fer otro latino" (SDom 2c). While acknowl-
edging the grain of humor, one must not miss the main
reason for composing in the vulgar tongue: its greater
effectiveness in sermonizing the people.

The purpose of such practices, then, was simply to increase piety. One may, however, distinguish several
preferred areas of concentration that are relevant to our
subject. The Cistercian Alanus ab Insulis (d. 1202) gives
the following advice to preachers: "Praedicator concludat
admonitionem suam in exemplari doctrina, ostendens quo-
modo antiqui contempserint mundum." [13] Another basic
concern, complementary to this contemptus mundi, was
propaganda in favor of the religious life. Welter observes
that the principle actors in the exemplum were God, Mary,
the saints, the Devil, and man: "Et parmi ceux-ci, c'est
l'homme qui est le plus représenté par les différents types
sociaux et notamment par ceux que fournit le monde
ecclésiastique: prêtres, moines, clercs, ermites." [14] The
dominant concern is of course the conversion of souls. God
showed Oria such great visions, "Que deujan a los omnes
canbiar los coraçones" (SOr 24c).

If the exemplum was intended to convert souls to God,
it was nevertheless carefully distinguished from other more

---

12. Welter, p. 94.
13. Summa de arte praedicatoria, in PL, 210, cols. 111–98.
14. Welter, pp. 79–80.

elevated didactic modes. Although they all teach doctrine, the exemplum was frequently contrasted with *praecepta*—with *verba*,[15] *ratio, auctoritas,* and *interpretatio*.[16] And beyond the demands of the type of audience to which the exemplum was addressed, it had positive advantages. It was shorter and easier: "In duobus igitur haec doctrina constitit praeceptis scilicet et exemplis. 'Longum enim iter est, ut ait Yeronimus, per praecepta, commodum autem et compendiosum per exempla'." [17] These different approaches to doctrine may complement one another: "4ᵉ Circa annexa vel concomitancia. Laborandum est enim quod semper aliqua auctoritas vel ratio efficax vel utrumque adjungatur exemplo ad confirmacionem majorem." [18] This occasionally accounts for Berceo's interventions into the narrative. Following the long and uninterrupted description of heaven, the author reaches the level of the apostles and evangelists and then pauses to explain:

> Estos son los nuestros padres, cabdiellos generales,
> Principes de los pueblos son omnes principales;
> Jesu Christo fue papa, estos son cardenales
> Que sacaron del mundo las serpientes mortales.
>
> (SOr 87)

This is an instance of Berceo the preacher adding that something else ("utrumque") in an effort to further the doctrinal import of the description.

As may be supposed from these careful distinctions, the

15. St. Ambrose states: "Exempla subjicit, ut facilius suadeat, quia cui verba satis non faciunt, solent exempla suadere . . . quoniam exempla facilius suadent quam verba." Quoted in Welter, p. 13.

16. "Sunt enim multi quibus data est major gracia loquendi per auctoritates, raciones vel interpretationes vel aliis modis quam per exampla." Humbert de Romans (d. 1277), *De habundancia exemplorum;* quoted in Welter, p. 72.

17. Giraldus Cambrensis, *Gemma ecclesiastica,* ed. J. B. Brewer (London, 1862); quoted in Welter, pp. 53–54.

18. Humbert de Romans, *De habundancia exemplorum;* quoted in Welter, p. 72.

exemplum as a manner of teaching or as literary genre was addressed to a certain kind of audience, and its peculiar nature had to conform to their ability to grasp doctrine. This problem was frequently stated during Berceo's time. Jacques de Vitry warns: "Ad aedificacionem rudium et agrestium erudicionem, quibus quasi corporalia et palpabilia et talia que per experienciam norunt frecuencius sunt proponenda, magis enim moventur exterioribus exemplis quam auctoritatibus vel profundis sentenciis." [19] And Saint Bonaventura likewise states: "Tertius modus est ratiocinare per exempla sive per exemplum, quod multum valet laicis, qui similitudinibus gaudent externis . . . Conveniens est dialogum Gregorii, vitas patrum et vitas sanctorum, quorum festa celebrat ecclesia, cognoscere." [20] These factors serve to explain a certain "realistic" tendency of the exemplum. Being often based on supposedly personal experiences and set in the everyday world (Bonaventure's "similitudinibus externis"), they tended toward familiar and concrete portrayals which the simpler minds of the lay people could grasp. And since the appeal was moreover to the heart, it was frequently lively.

THE VISION AS EXEMPLUM

Despite a modern critic's attempt to distinguish "misticovisionary" literature of the period from other forms of didacticism,[21] the vision was traditionally considered as a type of exemplum. It shared the same goals and usually addressed the same kind of audience. Such stories seem always to have been current, but toward the middle of the twelfth century they enjoyed a special increase in popularity. Welter summarizes as follows: "Il n'existe pas moins d'une trentaine de récits curieux à ce sujet dans les traités,

19. *Sermones vulgares;* quoted in Welter, p. 68, n. 5.
20. Quoted in Welter, p. 79.
21. Weber de Kurlat, *NRFH, 15,* 130, n. 42. See above, Chap. 1, p. 16 and n. 10.

les chroniques et les vies de saints jusqu'au milieu de xiie siècle. . . . A partir de la seconde moitié du xiie siècle, ce dernier occupera une place préponderante dans les grandes traités d'édification et de mystique." [22] These tales were widespread in all religious circles and were especially favored among the reform group of the Benedictines—the Cistercians. Peter the Venerable, Abbot of Cluny (d. 1156), composed a treatise on miracles containing over sixty narrative illustrations, over half of which belong to the visionary type of exemplum,[23] as did Hélinand de Froidmont (d. 1220), also a Cistercian: "Ses préférences semblent aller à l'*exemplum* prosopopée." [24] And by virtue of its subject matter the vision had a preferred area of emphasis: life after death and the eternal joy or misery of the soul. Its specialty was to show "dans un but moralisateur que tous les méfaits commis ici-bas seront châtiés dans l'au-delà et qu'au contraire toutes les bonnes actions y recevront la juste récompense." [25]

Now *Santa Oria* is turned steadily toward heaven, and there is but a passing and discreet reference to purgatory or hell (strophe 62). And one has only to select any random passage to note the preponderant importance accorded to eternal reward. It almost seems that heaven is conceived solely in these terms. Oria may not yet remain in heaven, for

> . . . aun essi tiempo non era allegado
> Para recevir soldada del lazerio passado.   (66cd)

The martyrs

> Dexaron se matar a colpes de azconas,
> Jesu Christo por ende diólis ricas coronas.   (81cd)

22. Welter, pp. 92–93.
23. *De miraculis libri duo,* in *PL, 189,* cols. 851–954.
24. Welter, p. 111.
25. Ibid., p. 93.

These observations furnish an important perspective on our poem. *Santa Oria* was written to promote popular piety, to teach common men the way to heaven, and to urge them to attain it through contempt of this world. It teaches invisible truths by visible similitudes and familiar examples; and, although based firmly in doctrine, the appeal is directed mainly to the heart.

THE DOCTRINE OF SALVATION IN SANTA ORIA

THE FLIGHT FROM EVIL

The traditional doctrine of salvation after death that is preached in *Santa Oria* is based on an equally traditional theology of good and evil. The latter has three forms: the world, the flesh, and the Devil.[26] In extreme contrast to this lower world of sin and hardship is heaven, the realm of the afterlife. Since Berceo's whole view of reality is grounded on the static opposition of these two "kingdoms," and since in *Santa Oria* the two domains are always in dramatic contrast, this section will deal with the "lower" world, and the following one will provide the contrast by analyzing the world of Oria's visions—heaven.

"*De Contemptu Mundi.*" The dominant tonality of Berceo's didactic *Vida* is one of praise: the saint's life is worthy to be imitated. Now Santa Oria was a nun ("freyra"), a "reclusa." It is interesting that the greatest number of epithets referring to Oria describe precisely her withdrawal from the world. They are two in number and each is frequently repeated throughout the narrative. The first is *reclusa* (*SOr* 61a, 164d), *la reclusa leal* (177c), *la reclusa don Oria* (111a), *Don Oria la reclusa* (49a), "Respondió la reclusa que auja nonbre Oria" (35a). Although the obvious explanation for this rather awkward line is the neces-

26. This notion is traditional and was familiar to Berceo's contemporaries. The Arcipreste de Hita (*Libro de buen amor,* ed. Ducamin) warns: "Lydian ostrosi con estos otros tres principales: / La carne, el diablo, el mundo; destos nasçen los mortales [peccados]" (1584ab).

sity of rhyme, still the effect is to give importance to the
moral type or category "reclusa," of which the specific instance (Oria) is but a single example and is added almost
as an afterthought.

One of the reasons for seclusion is made clear: it is a
better way to mortify the flesh. But there is a more general
reason as well. Oria describes her final vision in these
terms:

> "Ca entre tales omnes era yo arribada
> Que contra los sus bienes *el mundo non es nada.*"
>
> (152cd)

The world is nothing! Oria has just returned from
heaven and is summarizing the divine perspective. The
world and all its values are annihilated before the divine
transcendance.

The second epithet that reinforces by repetition the idea
of withdrawal from the world is "emparedada": *yazer
enparedada* (98c, 6b), *la njnna que yazia en paredes* (31a),
la fija sancta enparedada (186a), *eres enparedada* (134b),
entró enparedada (17b, 21b), *enparedada* visco (70c), and
finally, the noun *enparedaçion* (23a). The narration of
Oria's rejection of the world is always accompanied with
the solution of solitary withdrawal:

> Pagauase muy poco de los seglares pannos;
> Vistió otros uestidos de los monges calannos.
>
> (20bc)

> Desemparó el mundo Oria toca negrada.   (21a)

The stages of Oria's seclusion are explained in *Santo Domingo* (325). She first takes the Benedictine veil ("soror
toca negrada") and then "fue end apocos dias fecha enparedada." Oria actually becomes "walled up" in San
Millán de Suso.[27]

27. "Se daba el nombre de reclusos o emparedados especialmente a
aquellos soliterios de ambos sexos que se encerraban en una estrecha celda

Asceticism. A modern Benedictine scholar has summarized the traditional Christian understanding and practice of asceticism under three main branches:

(1) There is purely internal self-discipline and spiritual exercising, carried out in mind and heart and soul, without becoming in any way external;

(2) There are the great renunciations, especially those of the three "Evangelical Councils,"—Poverty, Obedience, Chastity,—which have at all times been recognized as the principal external asceticisms;

(3) There are the various forms of corporal austerities or bodily mortifications.[28]

Dom Butler observes that it is therefore wrong to exclude the first two aspects, especially since these are the essence of St. Benedict's own teachings: "there is a common tendency to identify asceticism, wrongly, with this one form (the third), and to understand by the term self-inflicted, or at least deliberately chosen and sought, bodily austerities and discomforts." Such austere practices, he continues, are more characteristic of Egyptian and especially Syrian asceticism; they have no basis either in St. Benedict's *Rule* or in his life as told by St. Gregory.[29]

The first general category of asceticisms presents the greatest problems to the narrator because it consists of "internal" deeds. There are, to be sure, many references to prayer and the performance of the Holy Offices, but the emphasis is, as it were, on their more tangible aspect, on the heavy labors and the ensuing fatigue: *"Siempre rezaua psalmos . . ."* (23c). The Virgin Mary identifies herself

con una sola ventana para recibir por ella el indispensable alimento, pasando su vida en la contemplación de los divinos atributos y en la mortificación de sus carnes." D. Rufino Lanchetas, *Gramática y vocabulario de las obras de Gonzalo de Berceo* (Madrid, 1900), p. 313, art. *Emparedado.*

28. Rev. Cuthbert Butler, *Benedictine Monachism* (London, 1919), p. 39.

29. Ibid., pp. 39–40.

to Oria as ". . . la que tu ruegas *de noche e de dia*"
(124d). At the wake of Oria's body "Fue *muchas de
uegadas* el psalterio rezado" (179c). The labors of the Offices cause great weariness:

> Despues de las matinas, leyda la lection,
> Escuchola bien Oria con grant deuoçion;
> Qujso dormir vn poco, tomar consolaçion.   (26a-c)

Much the same may be said of Amunna:

> Cantadas las matinas, la liçençia soltada
> Que fuesse quis quisiesse folgar a su posada,
> Acostosse vn poco Amunna bien lazrada.   (189a-c)

As for the second category—the great renunciations—
all references to the three Evangelical Councils are in-
direct. For example, it is understood that when Oria leaves
the world and enters the monastery of San Millán as a nun,
she takes such vows.[30] Renunciation is understood in terms
of one entity—the world. There is no allusion to that form
of renunciation of the self known as obedience, although
mention is made of the abbot (178b), the one person to
whom complete submission was due. Although the allusion is incidental, it perhaps suggests the presence of his
counsel throughout Oria's spiritual ascent.

Whether Berceo's emphasis on bodily austerities is due
to an incorrect understanding of the *Rule* or rather that
the other aspects of asceticism were too obvious to Berceo's
audience to require their being pointed out is a question
that others may decide. The intention here is merely to
demonstrate the idea of asceticism in *Santa Oria* as being
explicitly propounded almost exclusively in the third sense
of the term. There is an impressive listing of mortifica-

30. After her death Oria reveals to her mother that she is in heaven
among the "innocentes" (200a). This is meant to suggest innocence to
the ways of the world and hence also includes chastity. This virtue is
also indicated by the symbolic color white (see below, Chap. 3, p. 107).

tions: abstinence in general (21c), fastings (112c), vigils (112c, 117b), and direct bodily punishment with either the "cilicio" (17b), a "saya de lana" (33d), or simply "lana" (161d). She sleeps on the bare ground "que es fria e dura" (128a), and as a place to rest: "Lecho qujero yo aspero, de sedas aguijosas" (130a). Oria, weary from long spiritual exercises, lies down to sleep: "Non era la camenna de molsa ablentada" (117d). Beyond these specific examples Berceo confines his expression of this idea to two basic terms, abundantly repeated and varied: *carne,* "flesh," and *lazrar.* The former is used no less than nine times. Oria's parents

> Nunca querian sus carnes mantener a gran ujçio,
> Ponjan toda femençia en fer a Dios seruiçio.   (13ab)

Here asceticism, by juxatposition, is equated vaguely with "the service of God." The daughter is worthy of such parents; God

> . . . diólis vna fija de spiritual fazienda
> Que ouo con su carne baraia e contienda,
> Por consentir al cuerpo nunca soltó la rienda.
> (15b-d)

Berceo likes to juxtapose this idea with the notion of reward, reinforcing the direct link between the two. St. Eulalie advises Oria:

> "Assy mandas tus carnes e assy las agujsas,
> Que por sobir a los çielos tu digna te predigas."
> (36cd)

During her first vision of heaven Oria meets a company of "colonges" more beautiful than the flowers of May. It is explained that these canons

> Toujeron en el mundo la carne apremjda,
> Agora son en gloria en letiçia conplida.   (54cd)

Stylistically, this same procedure is used repeatedly, often in the final line of the strophe. The hermits

> suffrieron por Christo mucho amargo ujento
> Por ganar a las almas ujda e guarimjento.   (83cd)

The flesh is viewed as the exclusive opposite of the soul:

> Por amor de la alma non perder tal ujctoria
> Non fazia a sus carnes nulla mjsericordia. (111cd)

Such practices are based on the Gospel:

> Martiriaua las carnes, dandolis grant lazerio;
> Cumplia dias e noches todo su mjnjsterio,
> Jeiunjos e ujgilias e rezar el salterio;
> Queria a todas gujsas segujr el Euangelio.   (112)

Berceo's fondness for the word *lazrar* has been well observed and commented by Lanchetas: ". . . los prodiga Berceo hasta el aburrimiento": [31] *lazrar* (72b, 105c), *lazrar el cuerpo* (102c), *vida lazrada* (6c, 21c), *lazrada* as both an adjective (189c) and as a noun (134a). Originality of vocabulary was not Berceo's prime concern, especially when didactic ideas of such importance were involved. "Carne" is evil, "lazrar" its cure.

The Devil. Readers familiar with the worldly setting of the *Milagros* will remember the major and dramatic role played by the Prince of Evil. In the rarefied atmosphere of the *Santa Oria*, by contrast, he never appears as a personage.[32] References to him are incidental, almost rhetorical, and of the three evils he is clearly the least important. In strophe 105, almost the exact midway point of the poem, God the Father promises Oria that she need no longer

---

31. Lanchetas, *Gramática,* p. 421, art. *Lazerio.*

32. Jorge Guillén's observation that "the works of Berceo naturally shelter more sinners than saints" is thus more valid for the *Milagros* than for *SOr* or Berceo's liturgical poems. Cf. "Prosaic Language in Berceo," in his *Language and Poetry: Some Poets of Spain* (Cambridge, Mass., 1961), p. 7.

fear the wiles of the Devil; his existence is thereby rendered ineffectual and he is never again mentioned.

Yet he is a force to be reckoned with in the first half of
the poem—that is to say, until Oria has freed herself completely from his power. Although the Devil is never the
dominant subject of discourse, he has a way of sneaking
into strophes unannounced and quite gratuitously, so that
he is a leitmotiv running through the entire first half. He
is the clever enemy of man: *escantador* (105d), *serpientes
mortales* (87d), *el diablo,* "El que todas sazones a los
buenos asecha" (12cd). In two instances his epithet is
longer and more specific: ". . . al mortal enemigo / Que
engannó a Eva con un astroso figo" (60cd); ". . . conseio
del peccado / El que fizo a Eua comer el mal bocado"
(96cd). The specific relevance to Oria is clear. Each woman
is a direct descendant of the prototype Eve, and over her
the Devil has shown a special power. The admonitory intent of these epithets is further suggested by their context.
They are not used as mere padding devices by the narrator
speaking didactically in his own name. They are both
uttered by heavenly beings directly to Oria, reminding her
indirectly of the special weakness of her womanly nature.

The relationships among the three evils are not elaborated, although it is clear that solitary withdrawal from the
world is conceived primarily as the best way to mortify
one's flesh. Berceo summarizes all three evils in one strophe
and suggests their ultimate connection:

> Qujso seer la madre de mas aspera ujda,
> Entró enparedada, de celicio uestida;
> Martiriaua sus carnes a la mayor medida
> Que non fuesse la alma del diablo uençida.   (17)

The war terminology ("vencida") is traditional, as is the
ultimate issue: the universal battle between the forces of
good and the Devil.

THE ASCENT TOWARD GOD

The negative spirituality of the poem consists of a ceaseless and rear-guard fight against world, flesh, and Devil—the escape from hell (attrition). There now remain the positive virtues and practices, the upward ascent toward heaven (contrition). This implies a set of personal motives as well as precise ways of attaining the desired goal. The exact nature of the goal itself will be discussed in the final section, in the description of paradise.

The Motives for Salvation. Concerning the motives of the religious life, there is little ambiguity in either our poem or in the Christian tradition generally. St. Benedict expressly states in the prologue to his *Rule:* to avoid the pains of hell and win *the reward of heaven.*[33] It is in keeping with the advanced level of spirituality of Oria's life that fear of hell never appears as a powerful deterrent. The choice is represented not as between two opposite kingdoms in eternity: the opposite pole of heaven is this world. Hence there is not the slightest mention of hell, and the Devil appears only as the clever tempter, never as the agent of eternal retribution. Rather than the fear of eternal damnation, Berceo prefers to emphasize the possible loss of salvation:

> "Por seer bien çertera algun signo querria
> Por que segura fuesse que saluar me podria."
> *(SOr* 133cd)

We have already alluded to the didactic device of juxtaposing suffering and reward so as to show their direct causal connection. For her "vida lazrada" Oria won a "rica soldada" (21d; see also 33c, 34). The "omnes de sancta vida" that Oria meets in heaven

---

33. "Et si fugientes gehennae poenas ad vitam volumus pervenire perpetuam." *Benedicti Regula,* Prol., No. 42.

> Toujeron en el mundo la carne apremjda,
> Agora son en gloria en letiçia conplida.   (54cd)

Oria wants to remain in heaven but learns that it is not
yet time, "Para recevir soldada del lazerio passado" (66d).
But the Virgin Mary promises her that

> "Dios es contigo sy tu firme estoujeres,
> Yras a grant riqueza, fija, quando murieres."
>
> (125cd)

In contrast to these, the following passage suggests quite
a different motivation: love of God. The chorus of virgins
tells Oria that of themselves they are not worthy to receive
such glory:

> "Mas el nuestro Esposo a quien voto fiziemos
> Fizonos esta gracia *porque bien lo quisiemos.*" (68cd)

Of course "love" in this context also implies mortification
and suffering, but the important fact is that the motive is
no longer the self. Similarly, the Virgin Mary addresses
Oria as follows: "Yo so Sancta Maria, la que tu mucho
quieres" (125a). Oria's relation to God is expressed in the
same manner:

> "Sennor, dixo, e Padre, pero que non te ueo,
> De ganar la tu graçia siempre ouj deseo"   (103ab)

In addition to "deseo" and "querer," Berceo uses a third
term. Mary predicts Oria's death, following which, she tells
her, "Yras do tu codiçias a la silla honrrada" (136c). On
her death bed Oria expresses her desire with powerful
compactness:

> Dixol Munno a Oria: "¿Cobdicias alla yr [to heaven]?"
> Dixol a Munno Oria: "Yo si, mas que ujujr." (158ab)

But whether or not Oria's motives arise from love of God
or of self, one is finally impressed with their force. Saint

Bonaventura expressed this emotional prerequisite for the mystical life: "Unless he be like Daniel a man of desire." [34]

An important way of expressing the love for God is by the traditional metaphor of Christ the Bridegroom (*SOr* 68c). In addition to the chorus of virgins, one other "bride" of Christ is mentioned: St. Cecilia, "Que de don Iesu Christo qujso seer esposa" (28b). By contrast, Oria has not yet achieved mystical union, since she is still living, still in the waiting stage, a *novia* (64c):

> "Sy como tu me dizes, dixoli Sancta Oria,
> A mj es prometida esta tamanna gloria,
> Luego en esti talamo querria seer nouja."   (97a-c)

This language was part of the nun's initiation ceremony and is still in use in the present day.[35]

The Means of Salvation. The means or program for reaching heaven are characterized by St. Benedict in the prologue to his *Rule:* "Constituenda est ergo nobis dominici scola servitii." [36] The Order will be devoted to the *service of God,* and each member must pledge this service. This general notion is stated no less than eleven times in the first half of the poem; it does not occur in the second half.[37] One of the blessed is called *sierua del Criador* (73d); on earth the Bishops were *sierbos de los Gloriosa* (59d); and God helps his *sieruos* (78c). The verb form also appears. Don García is a "leal conpannon, / Que sirvió

---

34. *Itinerarium mentis in Deum,* Prol.: "nisi cum Daniele sit vir desideriorum."

35. According to F. Callcott, *The Supernatural in Early Spanish Literature* (New York, 1923), p. 77. The author also cites the *Cantigas* of Alfonso X, No. 42.

36. *Regula,* Prol., No. 45.

37. The term is general and designates any act of devotion directed to God or the Virgin Mary. One may do service "de piedes e de manos" (*Milagros* 331d), "en dichos e en fechos" (*Milagros* 219b). A bishop did the Virgin "servicios muchos e muy granados": "Fizo della un libro de dichos colorados"; "Fizoli una fiesta" (*Milagros* 51–52), Cf. also *SDom* 53a, 100c, 129d, etc.

a don Christo de firme coraçon" (61cd). Oria addresses
the Virgins in the following manner: " 'Dezitme, mis sen-
noras, por Dios, a qui servides . . .' " (71b). On Voxmea's
robe there is written "nonbres de omnes de grant ujda /
Que serujeron a Christo con uoluntat conplida" (92ab).

It will be noticed that these two grammatical forms of
service, the epithet and the verb, occur only in reference
to beings who are already in heaven. Other forms exist for
earthly inhabitants. Oria's parents "Ponjan toda femençia
en fer a Dios seruiçio" (13b). Following this idiosyncracy
of restricting a certain grammatical expression of an idea
to separate groups or individuals, Berceo refers to Oria's
service uniquely as *servicio*: "Plazia el su seruiçio a Dios
nuestro sennor" (18b; see also 14c, 33d, 95d). These distinctions are pure idiosyncracies of style and do not alter
the basic concept in any way.

An important aspect of this service of God is prayer, especially for the Benedictine. "Nihil operi Dei praepona-
tur," says St. Benedict,[38] and Dom Butler explains: "by
'Work of God' . . . St. Benedict means precisely the public recital of the office." [39] Summarizing the sense of St.
Benedict's teachings, Dom Butler continues: "the essence
of a Benedictine vocation is the celebration of the Liturgy." *Santa Oria* is fully within this tradition. Aside from
the frequent invocations of the narrator, the content of the
poem is saturated with prayer. Now the central body of
the divine office is made up of psalms: "Siempre *rezaua
psalmos* e fazia oraçion" (23c); "Cumplia dias e noches
todo su mjnjsterio, / Jeiunjos e ujgilias e *rezar el salterio*"
(112bc); "Fue muchas de uegadas *el psalterio rezado*"
(179c, also 137c).[40] It will be noted also that the emphasis,
as in the case of ascetic practices, is on frequency (*dias e*

38. *Regula,* Chap. 43.
39. Butler, *Benedictine Monachism*, p. 30.
40. The psalter is always "recited." *SDom* 67bc: "faciendo muchas
preçes, rezando su psalterio, / diziendo bien sus horas, todo su mjnjsterio."

noches, muchas de vegadas, siempre). One stage of the
daily office is matins: *matinadas* (107d) or *matinas* (26a),
and these are sung (189a). During matins there is also the
reading of the lesson: "Despues de las matinas, leyda la
lection . . ." (26a). In addition to these services there are
frequent instances of prayer, *rogar: de firme coraçon* (14a),
quanto mejor sopieron (101a), *de toda uoluntat* (100a),
de noche e de dia (124d), *muchas de uegadas* (188d). Here
again there is an emphasis on repetitiveness or continuity.

Oria has other virtues, many of which Berceo points
out. She is a "uaso de *caridat*" (22a), a "templo de
paçiençia e de *humjldat*" (22b); [41] her patience is *firme*
(125c), and she has the virtue of *taciturnitas:*

> Con ambos sus labriellos apretaua sus dientes
> Que non salliessen dende palabras desconuenjentes.
>
> (16cd)

She expects the same from others: "Non amaua oyr palabras de uanjdat" (22c). Other than these specific indications, Berceo is content with general terms of praise:
"Omnes eran catholicos, ujujan ujda derecha" (12a).
Berceo's favorite choice is "holy." Oria is a *sancta uirgen*
(1d, 2b); her parents are *sanctos* (7a, 11b); even God is
Dios el buen padre sancto (173b); the bishops are a *sancta
mesnada* (63a); Oria's visions reveal that she was *plena
de sanctidat* (25d); Urraca is *de muy sancta vida* (70a),
and so is Oria's father (164c) and Amunna (182a). It can
be seen from this list that such virtues are traditional terms
of praise and, in keeping with the generalizing nature of

---

41. This kind of metaphoric formula of praise is a favorite of Berceo.
Christ is a "tiemplo de caridat, / Archa de sapiençia, fuente de piedat"
(*Duelo* 76ab); Mary is a "templo de castidat" (*Milagros* 526a). St. Dominic
"uaso era lleno de graçia çelestial" (*SDom* 486b). St. Millán is a "vaso ont
tal vertut manaba" (*SMil* 152d). The epithet "uaso de oraçion" (*SOr* 8b)
is undoubtedly a scribal error for "vaso de election," as in Acts 9:15.

didactic art, could have been applied to almost any good person.

There is, however, one virtue by which Berceo tries to individualize Oria; or perhaps it would be safer to say that Oria is depicted especially by one outstanding virtue— *humility*. Indeed, it would not be at all exaggerated to call *Santa Oria* a eulogy to humility. Oria is a "templo . . . de humjldat" (22c) ; she addresses God "con grant humjldat" (121a). Her expressions of embarrassment ("enbergonzada," 69a) upon being provisionally admitted into heaven are to be understood in this sense:

> Encargada fue Oria con el reçebimiento,
> Ca tenia que non era de tal merecimiento,
> Estava atordida en grant desarramiento.   (65a-c)

She calls herself a "peccadriz mezquina" (104a) ; she is not worthy ("digna," 35b) to go to heaven. Berceo's favorite term in this instance is "merit," and in conformity to his usual practices he repeats the same word frequently, with variations only in the grammatical form. Oria's parents are *merescientes* (7b). Oria persistently disclaims any personal *merito* (199d, 105b), and the holy virgins likewise (68a). Oria "tenia que non era de tal merecimiento" (65b, 88d). The verbal form occurs with reference to the virgins (68b) and to Oria: " 'Non meresçen mjs carnes yazer tan ujçiosas' " (130b). After death she appears to Amunna and describes her reward:

> "Yo non lo merezria de seer tan honrrada,
> Mas plogo a don Christo la su uirtut sagrada."
>
> (200cd)

This latter passage reveals another important preoccupation of the poem. Since man cannot attain heaven unaided, the necessary counterpart to his humility is God's grace. From the start it is stated that "puso Dios en ella conplida bendiçion" (8c). Oria is "la reclusa de Dios mucho amada"

(49a) and is rapt up to heaven because "A Dios auja pagado por manera alguna" (50c). God performs favors ("gracia") for the virgins (68d) and for Oria (116c), and the Virgin Mary also has this power: " 'De la su sancta graçia en mj mucha metió' " (198d). God's grace reveals itself with special force in Oria. Not only is she granted visions of heaven; she, like San Millán, is permitted to know beforehand the hour of her death (135–36).

This conjunction of humility and divine grace, perfectly balanced in emphasis throughout the poem, accounts for the dynamic ascending motion of the whole work. Oria's parents pray for a child:

Que para el su serujcio fuesse [de Dios], que para al non,
E siempre *meiorasse* esta deuoçion.   (14cd)

Their prayer is heard. Oria, "Sy ante fuera buena fue despues muy meior" (18a).[42] Improvement along the path of humility is the spiritual basis for both the structure of Oria's visions and the symbolic development of the poem.

Visions in Santa Oria

Although man has experienced his visions in an incredible variety of situations, in medieval Spain they are described as occurring especially during sleep and as being somehow identified with dreams.[43] The absence of any distinction between the two is characteristic of *Santa Oria*. All visions in the poem take place during sleep, and the coincidence or rapid succession of the two is emphasized at every point:

42. Cf. *Milagros* 493a: "Si ante fora bono, fo desende meior." Continuous spiritual improvement is a topos in Berceo's *Vidas*: "bueno fue encomjenço, apostremas meior" (*SDom* 31c); "Meioró todavia, siempre fue mas osado" (*SMil* 51c).

43. In his study of the *Cantigas de Alfonso X* (cf. esp. Nos. 53, 68, 336), Callcott observes that "the two terms *dream* and *vision* seem to have been only vaguely differentiated in the period we are studying" (*The Supernatural*, p. 107). A good general study of the subject may be found in Howard Patch, *The Other World According to Descriptions in Medieval Literature* (Cambridge, Mass., 1950).

> Qujso dormir vn poco, tomar consolaçion,
> Vido en poca hora vna grant vision.   (26cd)

Similarly, before her death:

> Traspuso se vn poco ca era quebrantada,
> Fue a Monte Oliueti en ujsion leuada.   (139ab)

Amunna's vision is prefaced in the same way:

> Quanto fue acostada fue luego adormjda,
> vna ujsion ujdo . . . .   (164ab)

The end of the vision is described as "espertar" (108) or
"despertar" (139, 145, 169, 201) , a waking up. The identification of dreams and visions is shown especially in reference to Amunna: "Despierta fue Amunna, la ujsion
pasada" (169a) ; "Non echó esti suenno la duenna en
olbido" (170a) . Here, as also in the final vision, the terms
are synonymous. In this latter instance there is an interesting extension of the notion. "To have a vision of" someone is "sonnar" (186c) . Or, rather superfluously, "To have
a vision" is "ensonnar . . . un suenno" (188c) , parallel
to the English "to dream a dream." [44]

It will be remembered that Oria has three visions: in
the first (25–108) she speaks with the three virgins (25–
40) and then ascends to heaven (41–108) ; in the second,
the Virgin Mary appears to her in her cell (116–36) ; in
the third she is transported to the Mount of Olives (141–
44 and 154–57, where she tries to describe her experience
to Munno) . Although Oria is said to have had an infinity
of such visions (25c) , Berceo's decision to narrate only
three of them makes good didactic and artistic sense. Instead of the usual lengthy series of miracles loosely juxtaposed with no apparent order, Oria's visions are limited to

---

44. For the concurrence of visions with sleep cf. also *SDom* 226bc:
"durmjase ensu lecho, ca era muy cansado, / una vision ujdo"; and
"Como qui amodorrida [adormecida] vió grant vision" (*Milagros* 528c) .

the mystical number three and are moreover intimately fused together by content.

The first is the longest and the most important. All of Oria's destiny is foreshadowed, she is advised to "follow the Dove [the Holy Spirit] and forget all else" (37b). The vision, a historical event, thus becomes a program of action and a promise. The other two visions bring solace and encouragement to the ascetic—the second during the tribulations of life, the third at the hour of death. Oria's second vision also announces her imminent death (the central biographical fact of the Saint's destiny), to which Amunna's first vision may be considered an echo since it fulfills a parallel function. Oria's final earthly vision dramatizes even further her passion and death. The final vision of all, Oria's appearance to Amunna, announces the outcome: the story has a happy ending.

These, then, are the central biographical stages: spiritual ascent, foreknowledge of death, and death and salvation, all placed in continuous counterpoint to divine solace. A separate vision is reserved for each, and their unity is secured by Mary's prediction, which links the promise made in the first vision to its suggested fulfillment in the third. It will be further noted that the narrative length of the successive visions diminishes sharply as the poem progresses, while the quality of the visions is progressively heightened: in the first, Oria can hear God but not see Him; in the second she sees the Virgin and speaks with her; in the final vision she is taken to the Mount of Olives with Christ. In this way the content of the individual visions reflects the ascending motion of Oria's spiritual progress, which can also be seen in the *internal* structure or development of Oria's most detailed visionary experience: the first.

Corresponding to the doctrine latent in *Santa Oria* that the universe is geographically (and spiritually) divided into two realms, heaven and earth, there are two possible

levels on which visions may occur. Either a heavenly creature may descend to earth or the earthly creature be transported up to heaven. Now although all the visions introduce heavenly visitors, only the first actually takes place in
heaven. The other two—in contrast to Amunna's two
dreams, the locus of Oria's visions is always specified—
occur in Oria's cell and, finally, on the Mount of Olives.
The first vision thus differs from the others in an important
way: its locus is superterrestrial. And whatever the non-
physical nature of such places, whatever also the symbolic
levels of meaning implied,[45] Berceo constantly emphasizes
the necessity of taking the vision literally, at a historical
and realistic level, as true biography and accurate description of the realities involved. The first vision depicts Oria's
real journey through a real heaven, and it is thus possible,
by describing its topology, inhabitants, and other characteristics, to define the poem's conception of heaven.

In Oria's vision of the Mount of Olives, Berceo carefully gives general categories for describing superterrestrial
places, and it is both wise and convenient to follow his
simple terminology. Oria sees a mountain covered with
olive trees and a company of "preciosos barones" emerging from the background and walking toward her. She is
much disturbed upon being awakened:

Con esto la enferma ouo muy grant pesar,
En aquella sazon non querria espertar,
Ca estaua en grant gloria *en sabroso logar,*
E cuydaua que nunca alla podria tornar.

Aujalis poco grado a los despertadores,
Siquiera a la madre, siquier a las sorores,
Ca estaua en grant gloria *entre buenos sennores,*
Que non sintia vn punto de todos los dolores. (145–46)

45. See below, Chap. 3.

The parallelism of these two strophes is obvious. The first two lines of 146 repeat the idea expressed in the corresponding lines of the previous strophe by merely specifying who the "despertadores" are. The first part of the third line is a word for word repetition, thus putting in bold relief the parallel designations that follow: the "logar" and the "buenos sennores." As if this were not clear enough, Berceo returns to the same categories when he has Oria describe her vision to Munno. Strophe 155 (parallel to 145) begins:

> Vidi y *logar bueno,* sobra buen arbolado.

And, to maintain the balance, strophe 156 (parallel to 146) opens:

> Vidi y *grandes yentes* de personas honrradas.

Finally, as if to make the structure of his exposition (as well as the main aspects of heaven) perfectly transparent, Berceo summarizes in the following strophe:

> Tal era *la conpanna,* tal era *el logar.*   (157)

It is clear, then, that Berceo uses the two notions of place and people as organizational concepts in his narration of the Mount of Olives episode. These two terms are perfectly transferable to the first vision of heaven. Although Berceo is neither so explicit nor structurally neat in this longer vision, it will become obvious that the whole episode is seen in terms of these two categories. For Berceo heaven is especially describable as a "good place" with "good people." Further, in Berceo's hierarchic depiction of heaven these two notions interpenetrate, since in heaven persons may be identified by their places in relation to God.

Seen from a human perspective, heaven is a long "distance" from earth. The three virgins tell Oria that it is for her alone that they have traveled such a long journey,

"esta tan grant carrera" (32c). In addition to being far
away, heaven is also high: ". . . los çielos son altos, enfiesta la subida" (106b). Oria complains in the same terms:
" 'Los cielos son mucho altos, yo peccadriz mezquina' "
(104a). Moreover, the metaphor of the ladder or column
emphasizes both distance and height:

> Alço Oria los oios ariba onde estaua,
> Vido vna colunna, a los çielos pujaua,
> Tanto era de enfiesta que aues la cataua. (38b-d)

The continual upward motion of Oria's journey is
stressed at every stage of the way. Now in the celestial geo-
graphy there seem to be two distinct areas of space. The
first is the one already noted, the great distance from earth.
The second is that hierarchical ordering within heaven
itself which distinguishes the blessed by their closeness to
God. The first area of space, though enormous, is uninteresting and is quickly bridged by supernatural means as
soon as Oria has taken the first few steps:

> Enpeçaron las uirgines lazradas a sobir,
> Enpeçolas la duenna reclusa a segujr;
> Quando don Oria cató lo quiso conplir,
> Fue puyada en somo por uerdat uos dezir.   (41)

Berceo pauses a strophe in order to make a doctrinal comparison and then resumes:

> Ya eran, Deo graçias, las uirgines ribadas.
> Eran de la columpna en somo aplanadas.   (43ab)

Upon arriving at the summit of the ladder ("en somo"),
they see a "good tree" in flower, surrounded by a marvelous
meadow. They gladly climb into the tree and receive great
delight (45cd). The description is purely physical and
sensual, with no attempt to specify the symbolic referents.
It seems that the meadow is distinct from the hierarchical
arrangement of heaven; it is rather the antechamber

through which one gains access to paradise, since, while
the four virgins are joyfully sitting in the tree, "Vieron
enel çielo finjestras foradadas" (46c). The image gives a
perspective of the "palace" from the outside. Three angels
emerge from these windows and lift the virgins into other
regions (48c) where they witness "many honored proces-
sions." Strophe 49 is merely a repetition of this development rather than a description of yet another stage in
the journey. Oria,

> Catando la palonba como bien acordada,
> Subió en pos las otras a essa grant posada. (49cd)

Strophe 50 returns to the idea expressed in strophe 41,
showing that the intervening episode is merely preparatory
to the actual entrance into heaven:

> Puyaua a los çielos syn ayuda njnguna,
> Non li fazia enbargo njn el sol njn la luna. (50ab)

Finally, after the tree and meadow interlude, specific mention is made of the entry into heaven:

> Entraron por el çielo que aujerto estaua,
> Alegrosse con ellas la corte que y moraua. (51ab)

The levels of the heavenly hierarchy may be inferred
from the number of times Oria progresses in her journey
to a higher region. The task is made easy by the care with
which Berceo records each step upward. The entrance into
heaven proper is anticipated in strophe 48: the virgins are
placed

> . . . mas altas en otras regiones,
> Alla ujdieron muchas honrradas proçessiones.
>
> (48cd)

The first group encountered are "colonges" (probably lay
priests) dressed in white, all distinguished by their asceticism: "Toujeron en el mundo la carne apremjda"
(54c). Oria then follows her guides to the second level:

> Fueron mas adelante en essa romeria.   (57a)

Whereas the group of canons was "muy grant" (52a), this company is only rather large ("asaz grant," 57c). They are the bishops, dressed in chasubles of precious colors, and they are greatly superior to the calonges: "De la [compannia] de los calonges avia grant meioria" (57d). Oria moves on:

> Fue a otra comarca esta freyra levada.   (63b)

Here a chorus of virgins, singing responses, comes out to receive her. Oria is pronounced worthy to remain in their company, she sees the throne reserved for her, and her symbolic journey ends at this level of heaven. From this point on she no longer ascends physically but only raises her eyes:

> Alço Oria los oios escontra aqujlon
> Vido grandes compannas . . .   (80ab)

On the fourth level of heaven (Berceo does not enumerate them explicitly) are the martyrs. They are dressed in symbolic red and include both many lay people as well as many "ordenados." Oria raises her eyes even higher ("vido mas adelante," 83a) and sees a convent of hermits "Que suffrieron por Christo mucho amargo ujento" (83c). Apparently this group also includes both lay and ordained people, since the author specifies that a certain Monjo was an "ordenado." However, one is surprised to find Oria's father García among the hermits, although he is known as a holy man who, along with his wife, "never gave their flesh up to any delights" (13a). Oria looks even higher:

> Vido a los apostolos mas en alto logar.   (86a)

This is the sixth level of the hierarchy, reserved for the Apostles and Evangelists. It is among this company that Oria hears Christ: "Mas non podio ueerlo a todo su taliento" (88c). She could not see Him as much as she wanted—perhaps a little, though.[46]

At this point the author intrudes himself into the narrative in an attempt to return to his heroine and the throne that is promised her. This is dramatically simple, since Oria has physically never left that level of heaven. Having followed the dove and seen all the celestial inhabitants from the lowest to the highest, Oria has heard and perhaps even seen Christ. There remains but one personage to appear, the crown of the hierarchy who inhabits the seventh sphere, the "Rey de maiestat" (100b).[47] It is only after the three virgins have petitioned—unsucessfully—the Father that Oria dares to address Him herself. Oria's prayer and the ensuing dialogue with the Father create a good artistic variation and are, indeed, the most effective way of presenting the Father, since He can only be heard:

> Fablolis Dios del çielo, la uoz bien la oyeron,
> La su maiestat grande, pero non la ujeron. (101cd)

46. In the heaven where St. Millán is received after his death (*SMil* 302–08), again 6 categories of the blessed are mentioned, although the listing differs somewhat from *SOr: confessores, patriarcas, prophetas, apostolos, martyres, virgines.*

47. Giovanna Maritano counts 7 levels before the final vision of God by attributing separate stages to the apostles and evangelists, although Berceo is quite clear in combining the two (86c) ("*La Vida de Santa Oria*," *introduzione e note* [Varese-Milano, 1964], p. 42, n. 70). Patch (*The Other World*, pp. 34, 83, 107) traces early Celtic and Gnostic parallels to the notion of 7 heavens and suggests these as possible sources of the 7 heavens in the Irish *Vision of Adamnán* (9th century) and the *Vision of Alberic* (12th century). Berceo's more likely source, however, is the Book of Revelation or even Hebraic apocrypha: "The idea of the seven heavens through which the soul ascends to its original home, either after death or in a state of ecstasy while the body is still alive, is certainly very old. In an obscure and somewhat distorted form it is already to be found in the old apocrypha such as the Fourth Book of Ezra or the Ascension of Esaiah, which is based on a Jewish text. In the same way, the ancient Talmudic accounts of the seven heavens, their names and their contents, although apparently purely cosmological, surely presuppose an ascent of the soul to the throne in the seventh heaven" (Gershom Scholem, *Major Trends in Jewish Mysticism* [New York, 1954], p. 54).

The text emphasizes the hidden nature of the Father: neither the virgins ("non la ujeron") nor Orio herself (103a) can see Him.[48]

In addition to the hierarchical levels of nearness to God, the idea of order is reinforced also by the numbering and configuration of *groups* of the blessed.[49] Celestial beings always appear in, or are preceded by, groups of three. Larger gatherings are usually arranged in an ordered processional, and everyone is understood to occupy a specified place within the organization.[50] Thus the first three levels of heaven are composed of "processiones" (48d, 59b, 61a, 63c). As a variation in vocabulary but not in concept, the virgins appear as a chorus and in single file: "El coro de las virgines, procession tan honrrada" (63c). Oria wants to see her former superior, Urraca, but is prevented because "La az era muy luenga" (76a), and because Urraca is at the head of the line. Of course this "az" is here meant to be read as the symbolic denotation of relative merit.

Thus, in addition to the level distinctions based on the category of one's sainthood (virgin, bishop, hermit, and so forth), there is a more graded ordering within the levels themselves. This double ordering may be seen in Oria's reception into the company of the virgins:

48. The contrast between hearing God and not seeing Him symbolically restates the Christian idea of the necessity of faith, of "hearing" the word without requiring visible proof (cf. Luke 20:24–28) —whence St. Paul's phrase "fidex ex auditu" (cf. esp. Rom. 10). The idea of *deus absconditus* is especially strong in the Hebraic tradition, where it is forbidden to invent graven images of God and where God never appears face to face but only in the form of a burning bush or behind an obscure mist (Ex. 20:21, Deut. 4:11–20).

49. As Oria enters heaven she is said to please "la corte que y moraua" (51b). This metaphor is meant to suggest, among other things, the idea of order. Cf. also *Loores* 132d: "la corte del çielo," and *SLor* 73c.

50. Cf. Dante, *Paradiso*, III 88–89, and C. Singleton's commentary in *Dante Studies*, 2 (Cambridge, Mass., 1958), 21: "Gazing up into the descending light, each attains to such measure of the Beatific Vision as grace and merit may determine, for 'Ogni dove in cielo è paradiso': there are as many mansions here as there are creatures."

> El coro de las virgines, una fermosa az,
> Dieronli a la freyra todas por orden paz.
> Dixieronli: "Contigo mucho nos plaz;
> Para en esta conpanna digna eres assaz."   (67)

On the one hand, they form one "company"; on the other, they give her the kiss of peace in an ordered fashion, one after the other. "Todas por orden" suggests both different levels of merit and good organization.[51]

In contrast to the graded order of the actual inhabitants of heaven, there are the divine messengers who carry out divine commands or accompany important personages. They always appear in groups of three, are always described as equal to one another, and are always clothed in white. They may be either angels or virgins. The three virgins of the first vision

> Todas eran eguales, de un color bestidas;
> Semeiaua que eran en vn dia nasçidas.   (29bc)

As they approach heaven, three angels come out to receive them:

> Salieron tres personas por essas auerturas,
> Cosas eran angelicas con blancas uestiduras.   (47ab)

Oria's second vision also opens with the appearance of three virgins:

> Vido uenjr tres uirgines todas de vna guisa,
> Todas uenjan uestidas de vna blanca frisa.   (118ab)

Like the three virgins of the first vision, they address Oria, although they are never identified with the former.

---

51. The organizer and leader of these heavenly processionals is God Himself: "El Rey de los reyes, alcalde derechero, / Qui ordena las cosas sin ningun consegero, / Con su proçession rica, pero él delantero / Entrará en la gloria del Padre verdadero" (*Signos* 49). "Procession" is Berceo's favorite descriptive term for heavenly groups (*SMil* 302c, 304d, 306c; *Milagros* 169b).

Berceo later develops the theme of equality ("todas de vna guisa") through *amplificatio*. Mary has just spoken, and the author makes the transition back to the virgins by a strophe-long description that belies an attitude of ecstatic admiration:

> Todas eran iguales de vna calidat,
> De vna captenençia e de vna edat;
> Ninguna a las otras non vençia de bondat,
> Trayan en todas cosas todas tres igualdat.   (126)

Just as the virgins of the first vision announced the Holy Spirit and invited ("conbidar" 33a) Oria to heaven, their counterparts in the second vision announce the Virgin Mary and lead Oria to the soothing "lecho," all the while chiding her for her reluctance:

> Tomaron la las uirgines dandol grandes sossannos,
> Echaron la a Oria en essos ricos pannos.   (131ab)

When García appears to his wife to announce Oria's death, he also is accompanied by three mysterious "persons":

> Vido con don Garçia tres personas seer
> Tan blancas que nul omne no lo podria creer;
> Todas de edat vna e de vn paresçer,
> Mas non fablauan nada nj querian sygnas fer.   (168)

Like the previous messengers, they are dressed in white and are equal. They are probably "cosas angelicas" like the "sanctos barones" (48a) of the first vision, although their sex is not given. Like the latter they remain silent.

The identity of the persons in the vision of the Garden of Olives is somewhat less certain. In contrast to the usual three, Oria is greeted by "muchas gentes" (142a), all well-dressed, who have come to carry her up to heaven (142d):

> Eran estas conpannas de preçiosos barones,
> Todos bestidos eran de blancos çiclatones,

> Semeiauan de angeles todas sus guarnjciones;
> Otras tales ujdieran en algunas sazones.   (143)

The color of their garments is white, appropriate to either virgins or angels. Oria later refers to them again:

> Vidi y grandes yentes de personas honrradas
> Que eran bien bestidas todas, e bien calçadas;
> Todas me reçibieron con laudes bien cantadas,
> Todas eran en vna uoluntat acordadas   (156)

The final verse is still another variant on the theme of the spiritual equality that has characterized celestial messengers to this point. It further suggests that they all share the same intention, the carrying up of Oria into heaven: "Querian si fuesse tienpo al çielo la sobir" (142d) .

While the saints in heaven are referred to in general terms of praise: "buenos sennores" (146c) , "tales omnes" (152c), "esta sancta mesnada" (63a, 69c) , and the like, the comparison with earthly people is usually implicit if not stated. When Oria gets to heaven she will become a "conpannera de conpannas meiores" (113d) . And the friendship of the saints may be emphasized when appropriate. Oria is encouraged to follow the virgins to heaven, "Ca as sobre los çielos amigos e amigas" (36b) .[52] Oria is eager to return to "essa confradria" (110b, 119d) . Usually, however, Berceo restricts his epithets designating celestial groups to two or three general terms and their linguistic variants. The most frequent is "companna" and means simply "group, company" (52a, 80b, 113d, 199b) ; a variant is "compannia" (57c, 85a) , which rhymes with "guía." A friend or member of the company of heaven is therefore a "compannera" (73c, 75a, 113d, 196d) . The second term is "convento" and may suggest a grouping of a religious

---

52. Friendship with the divine is a topos in Berceo: Dominic's parents are "del Criador amigos" (*SDom* 6a) , and Oria is "del Criador amjga" (*SDom* 329c) . One can also be an "amigo de la Gloriosa" (*Milagros* 48d).

order (83b), although it is usually used in its general meaning as synonymous with "companna" (63a, 88b, 114c, 137b, 178c). A final designation, "vando" (72c), is synonymous with the ones just noted.

In counterpoint to the generalizing tendency of organizing heaven according to spatial levels and saintly categories, the author illustrates each group with specific examples, taken whenever possible from local history. This tendency toward exemplification and individualization may be noted throughout Berceo's *Vidas,* but the localizing tendency is especially strong in *Santa Oria.* Local examples are given for each of the levels of heaven except, of course, the sixth, the home of the apostles and evangelists.[53]

These individuals do not usually appear in any active sense. They are merely seen by Oria as she passes by. Stylistically, they are simply named along with a single accompanying phrase or epithet indicating either general praise or the typical activity of the saint while on earth. On the first level of heaven Oria distinguishes four from among the canons, and although she has never seen them previously, she recognizes them: [54]

> Bartolomeo, ducho de escriujr passiones;
> Don Gomez de Massiella que daua bien raçiones.
>
> (55cd)

---

53. Weber de Kurlat observes, concerning this aspect of *SOr,* that "el localismo medieval" is "no incompatible con una formación cultural universalizante en sus manifestaciones más elevadas" *NRFH, 15,* 14, n. 4. María Rosa Lida de Malkiel has attempted to identify some of these local personages in *RPh, 10,* 20–22. In this connection see also Maritano, "*Santa Oria,*" pp. 16 ff., and esp. J. Peña de San José, *Berceo* (Logroño), 60, 378–81.

54. It is twice emphasized that Oria is able to identify people during her visions without previous acquaintance: "Conosció la fija buenos quatro barones, / los que nunca ujdiera en njngunas sazones" (55ab, which may be compared in form and sense to 143d: "Otras tales ujdieran en algunas sazones"); "Nunca lo ouo ujsto njl tanso de la mano, / Pero la serranjella conosció al serrano" (144cd).

> Don Xemeno terçero, vn uezino leal
> Del uarrio de Uellayo fue esti natural;
> Galindo, su criado, qual el bien otro tal,
> Que sopo de bien mucho e sabia poco mal. (56) [55]

The second group, the bishops, is illustrated with three persons:

> Conosçio la reclusa en essa proçession
> Al obispo don Sancho, un precioso varon;
> Con el a don Garcia, su leal conpannon,
> Que sirvio a don Christo de firme coraçon. (61)

The third bishop is noted for his absence rather than his presence:

> "El obispo don Gomez non es aqui, hermana.
> Pero que traxo mitra fue cosa mui llana,
> Tal fue como el arbol que florece e non grana."
>
>   (62b-d)

This is not, as one scholar has maintained, casting a character into hell with Dantesque virulence.[56] We have already noted the heavenly orientation of this poem. The Devil plays a diminished role, in contrast to Berceo's other poems, and evil has no active function. This is the sense of the discreet reference to hell: don Gómez is not described as in hell but simply as absent from heaven.

No attempt has been made thus far to characterize the saints in their individuality, other than to mention their place of origin, if local, or their typical activity while on earth. Indeed, some of the epithets seem so vague ("precioso varon," "sopo de bien mucho") as to lack savor and interest altogether. Further, one feels that some of the personages have been assigned disciples or companions

---

55. The place of origin is given whenever the verse permits it and whenever it could have some effect on the local audience.

56. Post, *Medieval Spanish Allegory*, p. 124.

merely to achieve a group number of mystical significance
(there are four examples given on the first and fifth levels
of heaven and three on every other). However, the seem-
ingly uninteresting or irrelevant "criado" Galindo (56c),
as well as the "leal conpannon" García (61c), anticipate
an important principle in Oria's own story: her discipleship with Urraca [57] and her anticipated friendship with
Voxmea, the guardian of the throne. These two, along with
Iusta, another disciple of Urraca (7d), make up the three-
some representing the third level of heaven, the home of
the virgins. Since this place is destined to Oria, it receives
more ample development than the others. Further, this is
the only level of heaven where the inhabitants engage in
actual conversation with Oria; elsewhere they are merely
observed in passing and commented upon by the three
virgins who have accompanied Oria from the outset.

At the level of the martyrs—the fourth—again three
individuals are mentioned:

> Alli es Sant Esteuan el que fue apedreado,
> Sant Lorente el que Çesar ouo despues assado,
> Sant Viçent el caboso de Ualerio criado.   (82a-c)

St. Stephen was known as the first martyr and was considered their archetype. Berceo considered the other two
of local origin, as he states at the beginning of his *Martirio de San Lorenzo:* "Ambos de Uesca fueron" (2b);
"Criados de Valerio" (2d). Again, the discipleship is
stressed, since Valerio was presumably Bishop of Huesca at
that time (*SLor* 3ab).

Finally, the fifth level has four representatives:

> Conosçio entre todos vn monge ordenado,
> Monjo li dixieron, como diz el dictado;
> A otro su discipulo, Munno era llamado,
> Que de Ualuanera fue abbat consagrado.

---

57. And, beyond this, the more general principle of spiritual guidance
and imitation, of such central importance throughout the poem.

Y ujdo a Galindo en essa conpanja,
Ladrones lo mataron en la hermjtanja;
Y ujdo a su padre, que llamauan Garçia,
Aquelli que non qujso segujr nulla follia.

(SOr 84-85)

Stylistically, all of these individuals are neatly handled in
either one or two full verses. The result is a series of vi-
gnettes that one pauses to notice before continuing the
journey. The emotion aroused is a vague admiration,
heightened (in the case of Berceo's audience) by local
pride. There are two exceptions to this procedure, which
require, by contrast, a longer and more deliberative pause.
The reference to the Bishop don Gómez, the one absent
from heaven, is lengthened out to three verses so that the
reader or listener may consider at greater length the general idea that he exemplifies: the tree that bears no fruit
(62). The second deviation from this stylistic practice is of
course the references to Urraca and Voxmea. This is consistent with the much longer development of the third level
of heaven, Oria's future home.

Although Urraca's voice is heard and her presence felt,
she cannot be seen, nor is Oria able to speak with her. She
is at the head of the line of virgins, thus remaining distant
horizontally from Oria, just as God the Father is vertically
removed. Voxmea, the guardian of the throne, is both more
visible and more talkative, but she remains purely functional and is never individualized. Her person and clothing are symbolic, and her conversation either answers
Oria's questions or describes and explains things to Oria
and to the reader. Such, it can be observed, is also the
function of the three virgins accompanying Oria.

The most active and varied roles played by celestial
powers are naturally assigned to God and to Mary. Since
the Holy Spirit appears only in symbolic form and functions in a less explicit manner throughout the poem, he

may best be studied in the following chapter. The Father
and Christ appear more directly. Their name and importance to man are given at the outset:

> En el nonbre del Padre que nos quiso criar,
> E de don Iesu Christo qui nos ujno salvar   (1ab)

Whereas the Holy Spirit appears only in the form of the
dove, the other two are distinguished as separate *persons,*
although their functions overlap considerably since they
are both God. The subtle and not always clear distinctions
between their respective areas of power are suggested by
the places in which they appear in the narrative. The
Father, both "padre" (173b) and "Criador" (73d), resides
in the seventh and highest level of heaven. He can only be
heard and never leaves heaven. Christ the Bridegroom
(28b, 68c) appears on the sixth level of heaven (88),
among the apostles and evangelists. He can be heard and
perhaps partially seen as well. Thus, although the Father
addresses Oria with some tenderness, He remains remote
and His decisions are inscrutable. Oria is permitted to
ascend to heaven because she doubtlessly "had pleased God
in some way" (50c). He does not necessarily answer
prayers, no matter how powerfully they may be addressed.
The saints

> Rogaron a Dios ellas quanto meior sopieron,
> Mas lo que pidia ella ganar non lo podieron.
>   (101ab)

To be sure, God will not abandon a faithful servant:

> Non se partia Dios della en njnguna sazon
> Ca siempre tenja ella en El su coraçon.   (115cd)

Mary reassures her: "Fija, Dios es contigo sy tu firme estou-
jeres" (125c). Nevertheless, He remains highest and un-
assailable:

El Rey de los reyes, Sennor de los sennores,
En cuya mano yazen justos e peccadores.   (113ab)

His will must be accepted without question or hesitation: [58]

"Mas quando no lo quiere el Criador soffrir,
Lo que a el plogujere es todo de soffrir."   (175cd)

Both Father and Christ are objects of frequent "servicio," although different functions are assigned to each. The former dispenses the grace necessary to go to heaven, either during this life (41cd, 100) or after death:

Dios nos dé la su graçia el buen Rey spirital
Que alla njn aquj nunca ueamos mal.   (205cd)

Preceding Oria's first two visions as well as the final vision between her and Amunna, it is made clear that these are the special gift of God:

. . . puso Dios en ella conplida bendiçion,
E ujdo en los çielos mucha grant ujsion.   (8cd) [59]

---

58. The majesty and inscrutability of God the Father, and especially His transcendance or great "distance" from man, have often been symbolized by man throughout his religious history in the image of a king surrounded by his Court. An especially suggestive and relevant parallel to Oria's sublimely transcendent God is the experience of the divine in the Jewish Hekhaloth, in which "God is above all King." The relevant aspects of God are "His majesty and the aura of sublimity and solemnity which surrounds Him. Such a view is characterized by a "complete absence of any sentiment of divine immanence. The mystic or "traveller in search of God, like a visitor at Court, must pass through endless magnificent halls and chambers." The emphasis is on *God's otherness.* Contrary to the *unio mystica,* "the identity and individuality of the mystic does not become blurred even at the height of ecstatic passion. The Creator and His creature remain apart. . . . The mystic who in his ecstasy has passed through all the gates, braved all the dangers, now stands before the throne; he sees and hears, but that is all." Scholem, *Major Trends in Jewish Mysticism,* pp. 54–56.

59. See also 24ab, 113, 187–88.

Oria's reward is always described as coming from "Dios."
Just as the "escalera" is an "obra de Dios" (42c), so her
throne is a "Siella que Dios fiziera a tan grant maestria"
(110d). Just as God is the dispenser of grace and visions,
only He can reward so magnificently: "Dios solo faz tal
cosa que sus sieruos enpara" (78c; cf. also 21d, 66). Since
the Father rules so absolutely over rewards, He is addressed
with humility (2cd) and praise (96b).

Christ also receives service and gives rewards, but the
emphasis is different. When the Father is not mentioned
in connection with Oria, His attributes are generalized.
Christ, by contrast, is usually associated with specific groups
of saints, and usually with those who have lived in the
world. Mentioned in the service of Christ are bishops (61d)
and the "omnes de grant vida," both representatives of the
active life. Or, Christ may give rewards, but He does this
for martyrs like Himself:

> Dexaron se matar a colpes de azconas,
> Jesu Christo por ende diólis ricas coronas.   (81cd) [60]

Whereas the Father is object of "service," Christ also receives suffering: "suffrieron por Christo mucho amargo
ujento" (83c); "suffrieron por Christo lazerios muy granados" (183b). The fact that Oria is placed in heaven among
the Innocents is appropriate, since they also "suffered for
Christ" (200ab). Finally, whereas it is the Father who
permits the visions to occur, it is Christ the Bridegroom
who sends the virgins and invites Oria: " 'Gujate por nos,
fija, ca Christus te conbida' " (37d). This closeness of
Christ to man is symbolized in the Eucharist (191–92).

The Virgin Mary is also central. She announces herself
to Oria as "la que tu ruegas de noche e de dia" (124d).
This is not mere rhetoric, since Mary plays an important
part in all three major events of Oria's life. In the first

60. See also 200.

vision she is the meadow through which the virgins accede to heaven. In the second she is the central personage. She is the mistress of heaven, "Mas fermosa de mucho que non es la aurora" (123b). She embraces Oria (123cd) and states her readiness to help women:

> "Yo so Sancta Maria la que tu mucho quieres,
> Que saque de porfazo a todas las mugieres."   (125ab)

Finally, her presence is comforting both in this life (the symbolic "lecho") and at the hour of death (198).

In conclusion, Berceo limits his narration of the joys of heaven to the two areas of "good people" and "good places." Beyond these, all explicit—i.e. nonfigurative— description merely affirms didactic generalities. All that Berceo can say about the canons, for example, is that "Now they are in glory, in perfect happiness" (54d). It remains to be seen how these literal meanings are expanded by the symbolic aspect of Oria's visions, and, indeed, in what sense figurative expression is operative in *Santa Oria*.

3. Allegory and Symbolism

In its most general sense, allegory means simply saying one thing in terms of another, *alieniloquium*, a definition that has served as a convenient point of departure for scholars of diversified critical tendencies.[1] Nevertheless, it is customary to draw a basic distinction between two kinds of allegory, a distinction that has been said to reflect, in a general way, the world views of the two main sources of Western culture: the Hellenic and the Hebraic.[2] The former tradition is secular and artistic; and, at least among recent critics, its exemplar is the *Psychomachia*. The contrasted tradition is that of biblical exegesis as developed by the Church Fathers for the defense and elaboration of the

1. See Angus Fletcher, *Allegory: The Theory of a Symbolic Mode* (Ithaca, 1964), p. 2. See also D. W. Robertson, Jr., *A Preface to Chaucer: Studies in Medieval Perspectives* (Princeton, 1962), pp. 288, 291. Fletcher's approach is formalistic and seeks to understand the mode *en soi;* Robertson is more historically oriented. This definition is traditional, as may be seen in Isidore of Seville's *Etymologiae* (1.37.22): "Allegoria est alieniloquium. Aliud enim sonat, et aliud intelligitur." For further historical background see Bernard F. Huppé and D. W. Robertson, Jr., *Fruyt and Chaf: Studies in Chaucer's Allegories* (Princeton, 1963), pp. 16–18.

2. See Charles Donahue, "Patristic Exegesis: Summation," in *Critical Approaches to Medieval Literature,* Selected Papers from the English Institute, 1958–59, ed. Dorothy Bethurum (New York, 1960), pp. 62–66. Donahue elaborates a view already suggested by Erich Auerbach (*Mimesis* [Princeton, 1953], pp. 17–18) in his famous contrastive studies between narrative approaches in Homer and in the Old Testament. In an effort to preserve this important historical distinction, a modern historian of the exegetical tradition, Jean Daniélou (*Origène* [Paris, 1948], pp. 137–98), has restricted the term allegory to the Greek sense and has referred to the tradition of biblical exegesis (as, for example, Paul in Gal. 4:24) as typology. Another Origen scholar, Henri de Lubac, has approved the effort to distinguish between Christian and non-Christian kinds of allegory (*Histoire et Esprit* [Paris, 1950]; however, he deplores the terminology as being historically inaccurate (" 'Typologie' et 'allégorisme,' " *Recherches de Science Religieuse, 34* (1947), 180–206.

word of God. Despite inevitable oversimplification, this
historical distinction has provided scholars with the best
preliminary demarcation of the vast terrain of allegory.[3]

In order to approach Berceo's so-called allegorical meadow of the *Milagros* or the mystical visions of his *Santa
Oria,* it will be necessary to reconstruct symbolical modes
of thinking which the medieval Christian took for granted.
In Christian exegetical symbolism, in its most general formulation, the world is "said" and God is meant. God
speaks to man through words and things.[4] God's word par

3. For example, C. S. Lewis: "my subject is secular and creative allegory,
not religious and exegetical allegory" (*The Allegory of Love* [Oxford,
1958], p. 48, n. 2). We need not concern ourselves here with the complex
dispute over the differences between "allegory" and "symbolism" that
originate with Goethe (*Maximen,* 1.211), "since it concerns romantic
conceptions of the mind, and of 'imagination' in particular" (Fletcher, p.
13). Hans Robert Jauss has noted the close connection between such
conceptions and 19th-century "Erlebniskunst" and attempted to restore
the unity of symbolic thinking by reverting to Hegel's formulation of
"die ursprüngliche, religiös-sakramentale Funktion des Symbols" ("Form
und Auffassung der Allegorie in der Tradition der *Psychomachia,*" in
Festschrift für Walther Bulst [Heidelberg, 1960], pp. 179–206). Nevertheless, there remain important pre-19th-century differences between sacramental symbolism and thinking, which, for the sake of convenience, we
shall usually designate as allegorical. Such differences may be glimpsed in
Alanus ab Insulis, who, although his literary reputation was firmly based
on allegorical creations, was perfectly clear as to which tradition he favored: "At in superficiali litterae cortice falsum resonat lyra poetica, sed
interius auditoribus secretum intelligentiae altioris eloquitur, ut, exteriore
falsitatis abjecto putamine, dulciorem nucleum veritatis secrete intus
lector inveniat" (quoted in G. Raynaud de Lage, *Alain de Lille: Poète du
XIIe siècle* [Montréal-Paris, 1951], p. 151).

4. Deus non tantum loquitur per verba, verum etiam per facta" (St.
Bonaventura, *Breviloquium,* Prol. 4.4). According to Huppé and Robertson
(pp. 7, 24), the tendency to extend symbolic values so as to cover the
whole universe of things may be traced back to St. Augustine, who, in
turn, bases his thought on Rom. 1:20: "For the invisible things of Him
from the creation of the world are clearly seen, being understood by the
things that are made" (cf. Augustine, *On Christian Doctrine,* 1.5). The
universal nature of this allegory is constantly stressed: "Omnis mundi
creatura / quasi liber et pictura / nobis est in speculum." Or, with
Richard of St. Victor: "Habent corpora *omnia* ad invisibilia similitudinem." Both references may be found in Edgar de Bruyne, *Historia de la
estética medieval,* 2 (2 vols. Madrid, 1963), p. 580.

excellence is of course Scripture,[5] although other forms
such as specially appointed messengers and visions are also
possible. There are two kinds of things: things as such—
objects (*res*) —and things done (*res facta*) —actions.[6] The
distinction between God's words and his things is a mere
analytical convenience, since "His saying is doing, and His
doing, saying." [7] Both God's Bible and His world constitute symbolical "Books," in which man may read the revealed truths of his salvation.[8] Such revelation through
words, things, and history is a series of signs which, properly understood, lead man from the sign to the signified,
from the world to his Creator. In order to describe this
opposition between the letter and the spirit (2 Cor. 3:6),
between sensual appearance and "the invisible truths of
God" (Rom. 1:20), the tradition had a number of stock
metaphors: fruit and chaff, or, in Berceo's own version,
cortex and marrow.[9]

5. "Auctor sacrae Scripturae est Deus." St. Thomas Aquinas, *Summa
theologica*, I.1.10 ad Resp.

6. This distinction between *res* and *res facta* is no meaningful basis,
however, for a further distinction between "symbolic" things and "allegorical" actions: "Allegory is simply the device of saying one thing to
mean another, and its ulterior meaning may rest on things or an actions,
or on both together." Robertson, *A Preface to Chaucer*, p. 300.

7. " . . . quia ipsius dicere facere est, et ipsius facere dicere" (St.
Bonaventura, *Breviloquium*, Prol. 4.4). This idea is metaphorically
expressed in Hugh of St. Victor's definition of things as the "vox Dei ad
homines" (*Didascalicon*, ed. C. H. Buttimer [Washington, D.C., 1939],
p. 97).

8. Charles Singleton succinctly summarizes as follows: "What the figure
of a book should be found appropriate to express the nature of a world
revealing the creator's intention arises, no doubt, by analogy with that
other book of which God is also the author and which is literally a book:
I mean Holy Scripture. Almost never is the Book of the Universe mentioned without the other, the Bible, coming into the picture. Both 'books,'
we are commonly told, are spread open before the eyes of men that they
may read and that their minds may be turned to the Author of both.
Each book is a revelation of the hidden truths of his Providence. Both
books are given to man for his salvation." *An Essay on the Vita Nuova*
(Cambridge, Mass., 1958), p. 40.

9. "Tolgamos la corteza, al meollo entremos, / Prendamos lo de dentro,
lo de fuera dessemos" (*Milagros* 16cd). Bede had used the same figure:

Although the definition of allegory as alieniloquium seems to have gained general approval, Christian symbolism differs from other kinds of allegory in both the thing signified and the nature of the sign.[10] For the Christian, God's signs signify Him and must be so interpreted.[11] To stop short is to adore the creature for the Creator, to miss the spiritual meaning of things. Now man also can, as it were, create signs. And, as with God's world, so with man's signs: they may be understood simply as signs, in themselves, or as signifying an aspect of creation.[12] In literary allegory, for example, the signified is usually an emotion (anger, love) or a natural entity (nature, the sea). The

God "donet nobis propitius, retecto cortice litterae, altius aliud et sacratius in medulla sensus spiritualis invenire" (PL, 91, 923). For fuller documentation on the enormous popularity of such figures, cf. C. Sqicq, Esquisse d'une histoire de l'exégèse latine au moyen âge (Paris, 1944), pp. 19–20. See also Huppé and Robertson, Fruyt and Chaf, pp. 4–6.

10. Petrarch, speaking from a grammatical point of view, emphasizes the similarity of all uses of allegory and minimizes the differences: "What in truth do the parables of the Savior in the Gospel utter except speech different from the sense meanings, or, as I may express it in one word, alieniloquium, which we are accustomed to term allegory? Moreover, with this kind of speech all poetry is covered. Who denies it? The latter treats of God and of divine things; the former of gods and men" (Familiari, ed. Rossi, Bk. X, letter 4; quoted in Huppé and Robertson, p. 17). Of course, it is precisely on this last point, the signified, that Christians took strong issue.

11. In fact, St. Augustine sees this as the necessary and sufficient test of the exegetical meaning of any given passage of Scripture: "Scripture teaches nothing but charity. . . . I call 'charity' the motion of the soul towards the enjoyment of God for His own sake, and the enjoyment of one's self and one's neighbor for the sake of God." On Christian Doctrine, 3.10, trans. D. W. Robertson, Jr., (New York, 1958), p. 88.

12. This is the well-known distinction between image and idol: "imago ad aliquid, idolum ad seipsum." For example, historical facts or signs (res facta) refer to concrete realities; poetic fables or figures (res ficta) refer to nothing real beyond themselves. It was undoubtedly this kind of awareness of the ambiguous value of verbal signs that caused Hugh of St. Victor to write: "the significance of things is far more excellent than that of words, because the latter was established by usage [exception made, of course, of Scripture], but nature dictated the former. The latter is the voice of men, the former is the voice of God speaking to men." Didascalicon, 5.3, trans. Jerome Taylor (New York, 1961), p. 121.

signs are figures either personified (Ira) or mythological (Neptune). In such cases, however, the sign does not lead to a knowledge of the Creator: its function is literary embellishment or dramatization of natural and psychic forces.

St. Augustine vigorously criticizes both practices: [13] "Of what use is it to me, for example, if Neptune is not taken as a god but as a sign for all the sea . . . ?" Such a figure of speech is a husk that "shakes sounding pebbles inside its sweet shell, but it is not food for men but for swine." For, he continues, "what is it to me that the statue of Neptune is referred to that meaning except to show that I should worship neither? For to me, neither any statue [i.e. any sign] nor the great sea itself is a god." To remain at the literal level is servitude; yet it is more base to serve the invented letter of man (metaphor, statue of Neptune) than those of God (the sea).[14]

St. Augustine's criticism of the carnal interpretation of the *signified* brings us to the second major difference between Christian and other kinds of allegory: the truth-value of the *sign*. Creative allegory attempts to convert the passions into "picturable terms," to represent the immaterial by "material inventions" (C. S. Lewis). The sign may thus signify real entities (passions), but as sign it has no objective existence. It is a "bella menzogna," both because it is invented by man and because it has neither sensual nor historical concreteness. By contrast, for the exegete the sign does not arise in the imagination of man; it is grounded in the created world: "The word *allegory* . . . means . . . 'saying one thing to mean another,' but *the thing said in the first place is also true.*" [15]

13. *On Christian Doctrine*, 3.7.

14. "If it is a carnal slavery to adhere to a usefully instituted sign instead of to the thing it was designed to signify, how much is it a worse slavery to embrace signs instituted for spiritually useless things instead of the things themselves." Ibid., 3.2.

15. Robertson, *A Preface to Chaucer*, p. 291. The now classical study of the sense of the literal level in the exegetical tradition is that of Erich Auerbach, "Figura," in his *Scenes from the Drama of European Literature*

A good access to symbolism in *Santa Oria* is to accept
Berceo's constant assertion that the story is historically
true, that Oria actually had such visions as are described
in the narrative. As such, the poem differs sharply from the
Introduction to the *Milagros,* which is, more properly
speaking, an allegory. The latter is presented in the haze
of a dream not unlike that of *Santa Oria,* but the poet is
careful not to state that what follows is actually a vision.
One notes also the temporal vagueness of the initial con-
trivance: "Iendo en romeria caeçi en un prado," as contrasted with the preciseness with which each of Oria's
visions are presented ("Tercera noche era despues de
Naujdat"). The literal, sensual level is quickly laid aside
("lo de fuera dessemos") so that the marrow can be

(New York, 1955). He observes in speaking of Dante, where the literal is
understood in a historical sense (p. 68): "actually there is no choice between historical and hidden meaning; both are present. The figural
structure preserves the historical event while interpreting it as revelation;
and must preserve it in order to interpret it." Similarly, Charles Donahue
(*Critical Approaches,* pp. 65–66): "Typology finds a hitherto unsuspected
layer of meaning in the original record, but the person, event, or utter-
ance of the record retains all its original existence and value. Melchisedech
is no less Melchisedech when he has been discovered to be a *tupos* of
Christ. In the Greek method, the original meaning is destroyed once the
allegorical meaning has been discovered. The Athene who pulled Achilles
by the hair evaporates into a *bella menzogna* if we say that the passage
really means that Achilles's prudence restrained his wrath. The grain has
been winnowed out, and what is left is only the more or less picturesque
chaff." One's understanding of the literal level of biblical symbolism could
lead to differences between the "allegorical" and sacramental within the
exegetical tradition itself, as may be seen in the dispute between William
of Conches and Hugh of St. Victor over Genesis: "William is willing to
interpret key features of the text allegorically and, from Hugh's point of
view, irresponsibly. Thus, whereas William of Conches denies the existence
of initial chaos and holds that the six days of creation must be taken
figuratively, Hugh insists that the chaos literally existed and that its
ordering in an equally literal six-day period is a mystery, a 'sacrament,'
through which the Creator determined to teach the rational creature that
it must rise from the disorder of its initial and untaught existence to an
intellectual and moral beauty of form conferred by the divine Wisdom."
Taylor, *The Didascalicon of Hugh of St. Victor,* p. 13.

savored. And, in himself explaining the deeper meaning of the fiction, the poet emphasizes his own responsibility in its invention.[16] Berceo's inventiveness, however, concerns only the historical trappings, it constitutes but the framework of the real bearers of symbolic meaning: not personified abstractions but, as in *Santa Oria,* things sensually perceived, *res.* And although this Introduction is one of the two sections of the entire poem for which no source has turned up, abundant literary precedents exist.[17] Moreover, as we shall see, the symbolic things that form the basis of both Oria's visions and the mystical meadow of the *Milagros* are grounded in symbolic patterns of universal provenance.

We may now turn to our narrative. The nun Oria has lived a life of seclusion, proceeding up the path of spiritual perfection through rigid ascetic practices. One night she has a dream or vision, the literal level of which is immediately perceived by her and known to all readers of the poem. She has experienced a series of visible signs. What can they *mean?* When the shell of sensual appearance is penetrated, the allegory may be read in the following manner.

16. This aspect of allegory, the author's attempt to control the hidden meaning of the literal level through explicit indications, has been discussed by Fletcher in *Allegory,* pp. 304–05. See also Northrop Frye, *Anatomy of Criticism: Four Essays* (Princeton, 1957), p. 90; The allegorical poet "explicitly indicates the relationship of his images to examples and precepts." In so doing, he "tries to indicate how a commentary on him should proceed."

17. The scholar who discovered the MS containing the Latin source of the *Milagros,* Richard Becker, writes: "Für diese Einleitung . . . ist es bisher nicht gelungen, eine entsprechende Vorlage zu finden. . . . Der Grundgedanke der Einleitung selbst ist ohne Zweifel nicht Erfindung Berceos, sondern in der Literatur des Mittelalters ziemlich verbreitet" (*Gonzalo de Berceos Milagros und ihre Grundlagen* [Strassburg, 1910], p. 9). Indeed, although the fact is always overlooked, Berceo twice refers to a written source of the *Milagros* allegory within the text of the Introduction itself: "Las flores son los nomnes *que li da el dictado*" (31c); "*como diz la lection*" (41c).

Oria is first met by three virgins dressed in white, all martyrs at an early age. The white means purity, symbolizing their virginity. These virgins are therefore fit to point out the way to heaven to Oria, also a virgin. But what is the significance of their martyrdom. Oria was not a martyr. Yet it is later learned by Oria herself that after her death she has been placed among the Holy Innocents: "Los que puso Erodes por Christo a espada" (200b). The meaning can only be that the three virgin-martyrs signify Oria's figurative martyrdom, her asceticism of the flesh.

The method is already clear. The allegorical persons (considered only on this level, for they are lively enough as characters and real enough historically) prefigure Oria's own fate, they *stand for* important aspects of her spiritual development. Oria is shown a dove and advised to watch it and forget all else. Any Christian understands that by this Oria is summoned to follow the Holy Spirit. However, one may recall that the metaphor applied to the Holy Spirit at the beginning of the poem, "lumbre de confortar," is carefully restated in reference to Oria herself: "Luz era e confuerto de la su uezindat" (22d). Such doubling of the metaphor suggests, insofar as Oria has succeeded in fulfilling her duties, spiritual similarity. It is therefore significant that there be not only one dove but rather one for each personage: each of the three virgins carries an individual dove in her raised hand (30b). Thus the dove symbolizes both the Holy Spirit that descends from heaven and also the individual soul, whiter or purer than snow (30c), which longs to return to its homeland and leads the way there.[18]

Oria "hears" the virgins' advice and looks up to heaven:

18. When the virgins have been lifted up to the mystical meadow, it is said that their doves are now "alegres e pagadas" (46b), their souls are happy and satisfied. M.-M. Davy summarizes this dual reference of the bird symbol in romanesque art as a whole: "L'oiseau est toujours un signe d'ordre spirituel; il désigne l'âme. C'est là un thème très ancien, puisqu'on

Vido vna colunna, a los çielos pujaua,
Tanto era de enfiesta que auez la cataua.   (38cd)

This image states that heaven is both "up" and also a long "distance" from earth. The theological position implied by the latter is that God is transcendent rather than immanent—a notion repeatedly and explicitly emphasized throughout the poem (e.g. "el mundo non es nada"). The metaphoric value of heaven's being *vertically* removed is to suggest perfection of virtue through struggle.[19] Berceo was thoroughly familiar with the traditional expression of this idea: Jacob's ladder. Although he chooses not to use the precise metaphor in *San Millán,* he could not have avoided reading the following in Braulio's *Vita Sancti Emiliani,* the source of his own poem: "Celsiora petit leuesque per ardua gressus agebat spiritus promptus ut non solum corde sed etiam corpore, plorationis ualle gradiens, de uirtute in uirtutem uideretur Iacob quodammodo scalam conscendere." [20] The arduous ascent to virtue is associated with Jacob's ladder in *Santa Oria* as well (42a-d). Moreover, it may be permissible to take the biblical metaphor in a more precise sense. Berceo might easily have recalled a passage from St. Benedict's *Rule:*

---

voit dans l'enfer babylonien des âmes porteuses de vêtements de plumes. L'oiseau figure aussi l'Esprit Saint; il prend alors la forme d'une colombe, les ailes étendues" (*Essai sur la symbolique romane* [Paris, 1955], p. 168). Cf. also J. E. Cirlot, *A Dictionary of Symbols,* trans. Jack Sage (London, 1962), pp. 25, 27. The dove, symbol of the soul, also occurs in Berceo's account of the pilgrims drowned at sea (*Milagros* XXII): "Catando si algunos muertos podrian veer, / . . . Videron palombiellas de so la mar nacer, / *Quantos fueron los muertos tantas podrien seer*" (*Milagros* 599). As in *SOr,* the image emphasizes the soul's liberation from the body.

19. Cf. esp. *SOr* 104–06: "los çielos son altos, enfiesta la subida" (106b). St. Millán's ascent of real mountains is understood symbolically: "Por las montannas yermas las carnes martiriando, / Iba enna Cogolla todavia puiando, / *E quanto mas puiaba mas iba meiorando*" (54a-c).

20. Braulio, Chap. 11; quoted in Weber de Kurlat, *NRFH, 15,* 119, nn. 16, 17.

> Unde, fratres, si summae humilitatis uolumus culmen
> adtingere et ad exaltationem illam caelestem, ad quam
> per praesentis vitae humilitatem ascenditur, uolumus
> uelociter peruenire, actibus nostris ascendentibus scala
> illa erigenda est, quae in sommo Iacob apparuit, per
> quam ei descendentes et ascendentes angeli mostra-
> bantur.[21]

Reading Berceo's "columna" as the ladder of humility coincides with what was found to be Oria's dominant virtue
throughout the rest of the narrative. This passage from
the *Rule* also accounts for Berceo's mention of the ascending angels (42b) as well as Jacob himself.

Oria starts to "follow" the virgins (41b), but God wants
to shorten the way:

> Quando don Oria cató Dios lo qujso conplir,
> Fue puyada en somo por uerdat uos dezir.   (41cd)

This act signifies God's infinite power and beneficent grace
toward those that He loves. The greatness of the miracle
is charmingly punctuated by the poet. After stating the
stark fact, he steps out of the narrative and states, almost
with a gasp: "to tell you the truth" (41d).

On their way up to heaven and before actual entrance
into the divine palace, the four virgins pass through a
mystical meadow similar to the one that introduces the
Milagros: in the center of a "marvelous meadow" there is
a "good tree" in flower, shady and well trimmed, in which
the ladies climb about and take great delight (43–46).
Readers sensitive to rhetorical commonplace will easily
identify this as the *locus amoenus,* a familiar literary ap-
pendage since antiquity and common in Berceo's own
day.[22] In *Santa Oria* the scene is laid out in purely sensual

---

21. *Regula Benedicti,* 7.5, 6. The image is based on Gen. 28:12.

22. Ernst Robert Curtius traces the rich history of the *locus amoenus*
from antiquity to modern times in *European Literature and the Latin
Middle Ages,* pp. 192 ff. According to him (p. 195), "its minimum in-
gredients comprise a tree (or several trees), a meadow, and a spring or

images, with no attempt to explain their symbolic import
(in contrast to the *Milagros*). Readers of the latter are
equipped, however, to supply the withheld information:
meadow—Virgin; green—virginity; shade—prayers of the
Virgin; tree—miracle; flowers—the names of Mary. The
Milagros allegory, being by far the longer, has two details
that do not reappear in *Santa Oria:* the four streams
(Gospels) and the birds (the Prophets and Church Fathers).
In *Santa Oria* the birds do not form part of the landscape
but rather symbolize the souls of the virgins and therefore
arrive with them.

A more basic difference between the two scenes lies in
their symbolic polarization: whereas the meadow was
formerly the central figure, in *Santa Oria* the whole scene
is constructed around a single tree. Thus the attributes of
green and flowers that characterized the meadow of the
earlier version are here arboreal qualities. Since trees were
well-known feminine symbols in medieval times, one wonders whether in *Santa Oria* it is the tree that is meant to
symbolize the Virgin.[23] Such a hypothesis, consistent with
Berceo's strong devotion to Mary and with the central role
she plays in the poem, is also firmly grounded in Christian
symbolic thinking. In an early patristic text Mary is called
the "imperishable wood of mankind," an allusion to the

---

brook. Birdsong and flowers may be added." Viewing Oria's visionary
meadow from the perspective of such rhetorical borrowings, C. R. Post
can only remark disdainfully that "the poet, according to the prevalent
custom, degrades the earthly paradise into the ordinary French bower
with a mystical tree in the centre" (*Medieval Spanish Allegory*, pp. 136–
37). We shall see, however, that such ideal landscapes are in fact de-
generations of primitive religious symbolisms, which have retained in
Berceo, moreover, much of their original significance. A restitution of
such meanings has already been suggested in the excellent article of
Erika Lorenza, to which I am much indebted, "Berceo, der 'Naive,'"
RJ, 14 (1963), 255–68.

23. M.-M. Davy, *Essai*, p. 163, observes that "le bois est un symbole
féminin et que de nombreux textes médiévaux appartenant à la poésie le
présentent sous un aspect maternel." One need only recall Berceo's abundant listings of trees that denote the Virgin: "Oliva, cedro, bálssamo,
palma . . . piértega" (*Milagros* 39cd).

dogma of her freedom from original sin.[24] She was commonly identified as the rod out of the branch of Jesse
(Isa. 11:1), the blossoming staff of Aaron (Numb. 17:5),
or even the burning bush of Moses.[25] Berceo draws on this
long tradition of Old Testament exegesis by refering to
Mary as "de la que fabló tanto el baron Ysaya" (SOr 133b).
She is the "verga" of Jesse, the "baston" of Aaron, and the
"fust de Moyses" with which he opened the Red Sea (Ex.
14:16).[26]

In the Christian tradition, however, the tree is inevitably
associated with the Tree of the Cross, which is believed to
have opened heaven to mankind.[27] As such, it becomes
linked to the column that rises up to heaven (SOr 38c),
since both tree and column form part of that cluster of
images known to the historian of religions as symbols of

24. "Das älteste patristishe Zeugnis von der Erbsündefreiheit Marias
nennt nämlich die Gottesmutter das 'unverwesliche Holz der Menschheit'"
(Erika Lorenz, who refers the reader to Hypolit, gest. 235; cited in
Theodoret, Dial. I, in PL, 10, 863). Berceo's strong interest in Mary's
purity is placed within its historical context by Lorenz (pp. 64–65). The
critic does not sufficiently distinguish, however, between Mary's freedom
from original sin and the doctrine—of much greater emphasis in Berceo—
of Mary's virginity post partum et in partu. Cf. esp. Milagros 20, and
Loores: "conçebiste del Spiritu Sancto . . . Pariste fijo preçioso en tu
entegredat" (1bc); "Et tu pariste Virgo sin toda lesion" (7d).

25. Bishop Proclus (d. 446) calls Mary "der beseelte Dornstrauch der
Natur, welchen das Feuer der göttlichen Geburt nicht verbrannte," because, like the bush that burned without being consumed, she bore Jesus
without losing her virginity. Quoted in F. A. von Lehner, Die Marienverehrung in den ersten Jahrhunderten (Stuttgart, 1886), p. 215. See also
Yrjö Hirn, The Sacred Shrine (London, 1912), pp. 449–50.

26. ". . . de raiz de Iesse una verga saldria. . . . Madre tu fuisti la
verga, el tu fijo la flor" (Loores 8–9). On the rod of Aaron, cf. Milagros
41, Loores 7. The "fust de Moyses. . . . Si non a la Gloriosa, al non
significava" (Milagros 40).

27. J. E. Cirlot, in his Dictionary of Symbols, notes that in religious
symbolism the tree signifies the life of the cosmos, inexhaustible life,
immortality. For Christians it is the "Cross of Redemption, and the Cross
is often depicted in Christian iconography as the Tree of Life" (p. 328).
The traditional connection between the tree of life of Genesis and the
Tree of the Cross is established in Loores 110: "Si por mugier fuemos e
por fuste perdidos, / Por mugier e por fuste somos ia redemidos."

the center, whose function it is to join heaven and earth
and facilitate the passage from one to the other.[28] Further,
since it is the journey *to* heaven that is emphasized, these
images are related in turn with the dove, the flight of the
souls, and the ladder, all of which form yet another group
known as symbols of ascent or transcendence: "the Tatar
or Siberian shaman climbs a tree, and . . . the Vedic
sacrificer mounts a ladder: the two rites are directed to the
same end, the ascension into Heaven." [29] One should recall
that Oria sees "redor el tronco marabilloso prado" (44c);
that is, the tree is in the middle of the meadow and thus
qualifies as a symbol of the center. Another detail of universal provenance: within this brief description Berceo
finds it somehow important to observe that the four virgins
are "ligeras mas que viento" (45a). Eliade summarizes:

Space takes on quite a different aspect in the countless
myths, tales and legends concerning human or super-
human beings who fly away into heaven and travel

28. Cirlot, p. 328, traces the connection between the vertical arm of the
Cross and the tree of life, which function, along with the ladder, as the
world-axis linking hell, earth, and heaven. Mircea Eliade has assembled
an impressive documentation attesting to the universal diffusion of such
symbols, which occur spontaneously in "primitive" religious mentality as
well as in the dream life of more "advanced" peoples. According to Eliade,
symbolisms of the center may usually be reduced to a few archaic images:
the Cosmic Mountain, the central Pillar, and the World Tree, the latter
of which is the most popular, "situated in the middle of the Universe and
upholding the three worlds as upon one axis" (*Images and Symbols,* trans.
Philip Mairet [London, 1961], p. 44). Cf. also, by the same author, *Myths,
Dreams and Mysteries,* trans. Philip Mairet (London, 1960), pp. 99–110.

29. Eliade, *Images and Symbols,* p. 48. In the *Book of the Dead* (cited
ibid., p. 50) it is said that "the gods make him a ladder so that, by making use of it, he may go up to heaven." Eliade explains the rich symbolism of the ladder as follows: "It gives plastic expression to the break
through the planes necessitated by the passage from one mode of being
to another, by placing us at the cosmological point where communication
between Heaven, Earth and Hell becomes possible" (p. 50). Oria's violent
asceticism and desire for death takes on deeper significance when seen
from the perspective of the ladder vision, since stairs in such experiences
symbolize sanctification, love, and the desire for death and deliverance
(cf. ibid., p. 51).

freely between Earth and Heaven, whether they do so
with the aid of birds' feathers or by any other means.
It is not the speed with which they fly, nor the dramatic intensity of the aerial voyage that characterize
this complex of myth and folk-lore; it is the fact that
weight is abolished, that an ontological mutation has
occurred in the human being himself.[30]

Despite superficial similarities between the *Milagros*
Introduction and Oria's vision (such as the *locus amoenus*), the profound differences that separate them may now
be gauged. We have already suggested that the former is
an allegory in the sense that the historical frame is contrived. To this may be added that it contains not a single
symbol of transcendence (there is not *one* tree but trees).
The narrator dismisses his cares ("perdí los sudores," 5c;
"perdí todos cuidados," 7a) or removes his clothes not the
better to take flight but rather to derive greater comfort:
"Descargué mi ropiella *por iazer mas viçioso*" (6c). The
protagonist never leaves the "romería," *this* life. Also, although his images are deeply grounded in Christian symbolism, Berceo seems to know exactly what he means; he
consciously controls the range of his symbols (hence he
is able to explain them). When he says the meadow, for
example, he really means the Virgin Mary. By contrast,
neither Oria's images nor their meaning are limited to
temporary relief from the profane world. Her ascent signifies a conquest of immortality. Further, what is remarkable
in *Santa Oria* is not simply the presence or quality of such
symbols (for they are of universal provenance) but rather
their concentrated profusion and especially the way in
which they are juxtaposed or, rather, superimposed. What
is first a column is converted into a ladder. Doves mys-
teriously appear; the virgins follow them and are quite
abruptly found to be sitting in a tree. The passage from

30. *Myths, Dreams and Mysteries,* pp. 104 ff.

one image to another, the transmutation of levels, the superimposition of symbols—all are connected by the simple "vido." Coherence is internal, as in dream-logic.[31]

The transconscious coherence of Oria's dream—resulting in the poet's failure to give a controlled exegesis of the whole scene—is both deepened and explained by the multiple resonances of the symbols employed. We have already noted the ambiguity of the central tree, which may signify either Christ or the Virgin. Equally suggestive is the traditional association and fusion of Mary and the Dove—no surprise, since the Virgin was said to have conceived through the Holy Spirit.[32] Prototypes of Mary were commonly found in Song of Songs 2:14, where the beloved is called a dove, or again in the dove of Noah, which brings the world the olive branch of peace.[33] Or the poet may have been struck by their common "whiteness." The first thing said about the doves is that they are "whiter than snow" (30c), and Mary's chastity was a doctrine in which Berceo showed special interest.[34] The more profound con-

31. Eliade (*Images and Symbols*, p. 120) posits a "sub- or transconscious 'logic' which is not always heterogeneous to 'normal' logic (. . . that of good sense)." Thus, "at least a certain zone of the subconscious is ruled by the archetypes which also dominate and organize conscious and transconscious experience."

32. Robert Briffault, *The Mothers, 3* (3 vols. New York, 1927), pp. 180–81, writes: "The Son, the Logos, was the offspring of the Father and of Divine Sophia—for the Queen of Heaven had even been the Goddess of Wisdom; the Holy Ghost, which is identical with her, and, in Hebrew, feminine, was regarded by the Nazarenes and early Christians as the mother of Christ." The Holy Ghost "was represented by the dove, the immemorial bird of the Great Goddess, the 'Patroness of Israel.' Philo regarded the sacred bird as identical with Sophia. Jesuit theologians have asserted that the Holy Virgin was omniscient, and described her in that aspect as the 'noetic dove.' . . . 'Mary,' says Alphonso de Liguori [St. Alphonso Maria de Liguori, *The Glories of Mary*, trans. R. A. Coffin (London, 1868), p. 176], 'was prefigured by the Dove of the ark,' and she is addressed as 'the beautiful Dove.' In Eastern Europe the dove is still associated with the Holy Virgin rather than with the Holy Ghost."

33. Cf. Hirn, *The Sacred Shrine*, p. 436 and p. 546, n. 2.

34. Cf. *Milagros* 20: "Ca nunca ovo macula la su virginidat." It is quite

nection, however, is their similar role as intermediaries between heaven and earth, thus relating them both to center symbolism.[35]

Did Berceo consciously associate the Virgin with the Holy Spirit? That he was familar with such a tradition cannot be doubted, since he says of Mary that "Ella es la palomba de fiel bien esmerada" (*Milagros* 36c) .[36] In *Santa Oria,* however, immediately after the first apparition of the doves (30b) , Berceo asserts that Oria is comforted by the "Spiritu Sancto." It may be that Oria's dream simply conforms to traditional patterns of symbolic association and fusion, and such experiences, as Eliade has shown, often occur at levels below or above normal consciousness.

While the virgins are recreating themselves in the tree, they see openings in the sky, and lights and angels issuing forth from them. In fact, it appears that the lights allegorically *are* the angels:

> Lumbres salian por ellas, de duro serian contadas.
>
> (46d)

> Salieron tres personas por essas auerturas,
> Cosas eran angelicas con blancas uestiduras.   (47ab)

(In Berceo the first verse of a strophe is frequently a recapitulation of the previous strophe.) Pictorially, the

---

natural that Mary's purity should be compared with snow (Psa., 51:9) . Hirn (p. 436 and pp. 544–46, n. 1, traces the basis of such a comparison.

35. Hirn states that "the Holy Ghost was regarded as a mediator between heaven and earth" (p. 115). Proclus called Mary "die einzige Brücke Gottes zu den Menschen" (quoted in Lehner, *Die Marienverehrung,* p. 215) . For Berceo, Mary is she who "por los peccadores ruega noch e dia" (*Milagros* 23c) . She "opens the Heavens" for men (*Himnos* 1.5) or is herself the Gate to paradise for sinners: "Puerta de pecadores por al Cielo entrar" (*Himnos* 1.1) ; "puerta de paraisso" (*Milagros* 774a) ; "puerta de salvedat" (*Duelo* 205b) .

36. The modern equivalent is "paloma sin hiel." Hirn points out (p. 546, n. 2) that this popular epithet of Mary was originally applied to the souls of the dead ("pure doves without gall") and was found on tombstones.

scene is impressive. First we see the windows, then the
lights issuing from them, and then, as if riding on those
lights, the "angelic things." It is not until the detail of
their white garments is given that one realizes that the
angels and the lights are somehow the same.[37]

At this point, with the help of divine grace (the three
angels), the virgins enter heaven proper. And in the
heaven of Oria's visions special importance is placed on the
symbolism of *things*. Now such are not the only possible
carriers of symbolic meaning. As seen above, there are also
symbolic actions and words (if uttered by God, as in
Scripture). In fact, Oria engages in conversation with
heavenly beings and is directly addressed by the Father.
Yet the divine words merely restate meanings implicit in
allegorical things already experienced elsewhere. They are
not mysterious "signs" to be interpreted. The same may be
noted of symbolic actions. The refusal of the three angels
who accompany the visionary appearance of Oria's father
is symptomatic:

Vido con don Garçia tres personas seer
Tan blancas que nul omne no lo podria creer;
Todas de edat vna e de vn paresçer,
Mas non fablauan nada *nj querian sygnas fer*. (168)

37. In Oria's second vision Berceo again juxtaposes the arrival of
"lights" (note the plural) with that of heavenly creatures, as if they were
the same thing or at least simultaneous occurrences: "Fue de bien grandes
lumbres la çiella alunbrada. / Fue de uirgines muchas en vn rato pablada"
(132bc). The idea is that, from Oria's viewpoint, the heavenly creatures
function as symbols, as bearers of divine light or grace. The traditional
metaphor of light is a favorite one throughout the poem. The three
virgins "luzian como estrellas, tanto eran de bellidas" (29d). Oria's throne
shines "como rayos del sol" (90c), as does the cloth that covers it: "Non
podria en este mundo cosa seer tan clara" (78b). The symbolic import of
this clarity is emphasized by the fact that the names of the just are in-
scribed with "mayor claridat," while the others are more "tenebrosas" and
even "de grant obscuridat" (93). This is the beautiful light of blessedness,
a direct reflection of that light of comfort or grace that descends from
above (122c; also 1c, 22d, mentioned above, p. 96).

In Berceo's visions actions are limited to the bare minimum necessary to the dramatization of the scene, and these
few actions need not point to any deeper meaning. In fact,
they are usually the simple backdrop against which symbolic things and persons are presented.

A few examples will make this clear. The functions of
the virgins in the first vision are two: to announce Oria's
destiny and to lead her to heaven. Oria's reaction (since
she is an actual participant in the allegorical vision, her
actions may also have symbolic meaning) is to follow
("seguir") or rise to heaven ("subir"). Now the metaphoric value of these acts is quite low, or rather, as in biblical language, they were in such common use that their
metaphorical meanings were never consciously distinguished. These acts, then, are not allegorical in the sense
used above, where they require interpretation or at least
some kind of conscious recognition (e.g. ladder equals
humility).

Other than these frequent verbs of simple movement [38]
upward, one is struck by the almost total absense of action-
verbs in the visions. The celestial beings do not act; they
are. The three virgins

> Todas *eran* eguales, de un color bestidas;
> Semeiaua que eran en vn dia nasçidas,
> Luzian como estrellas, tanto *eran* de bellidas.
>
> (29b-d)

Before entering heaven proper:

> Vieron vn buen arbol, cimas bien conpassadas,
> Que de diuersas flores *estauan* bien pobladas.
>
> (43cd)

> Verde *era* el ramo . . . (44a)

38. To give but a sampling: *subir* (41a, 45c, 49d, 50d), *salir* (47a, 63d,
64a), *seguir* (41b), *puyar* (50a), *entrar* (51a). Only God's grace is active:
"pusieron las mas altas" (48c).

This treatment is consistently followed throughout the visions. Actions are seen only as having been completed ("eran nasçidas"), and the celestial personage is seen through one of his or her qualities, either symbolic ("verde") or simply descriptive ("bellidas"). Moreover, this quality is appended as unobtrusively as possible: either by verbs "to be" (*ser, seer, estar*) or words indicating possession (*aver, tener, vestir*) or expressions describing the appearance or state or present condition of the person (*parescer, semeiar*,[39] and so forth). Equally striking is the high incidence of verbs of simple—usually visual—perception. Heaven not only *is,* it *is seen.* Oria, as just pointed out, does not see actions. She sees people and things, and these are usually symbolic: the things are symbolic in themselves, and the people are symbolic because of the things associated with them (objects, clothes, colors, and the like). A systematic study of these symbols will show how this is so.

   Clothing and colors are the two most dominant symbolic denotations, and stylistically they usually occur together. The range of color is limited to two—white (chastity or charity) and red (martyrdom): "Cosas eran angelicas con blancas uestiduras" (47b). The angels in the third vision "todos bestidos eran de blancos çiclatones" (143b). Similarly, the canons are dressed "en bestiduras albas fermosas por fazanna" (52b), and the martyrs "semeiauan uestidos todos de uermeion" (80c). In an effort to arouse admiration, the poet may replace the precise color by an adjective or formula. The bishops "todos vestian casullas de preciosos colores" (58a); Voxmea has a "preçiosa uestidura"

   39. These two verbs meaning "to seem" can be understood as synonymous with "to be" throughout the poem. They say what *is,* though their implied understatement supplies a feeling of vagueness or awe appropriate to the visions:

   Vido grandes conpannas, fermosa criazon;
   Semeiauan uestidos todos de uermeion.   (80bc)
That is to say, they *were* dressed in vermilion. See also 30d, 93b, 143c.

(91a); and the people of the third vision are "todas bien
agujsadas de calçar e de uestir" (142c, repeated in 156b) .
Again, color and clothing go together, as in the case of the
virgins who are "de un color bestidas" (29b) . Only once
does Berceo mention color without attaching it to some
piece of clothing: the angels in García's appearance are simply "blancas" (168b) . It goes without saying that the symbolism of colors in these examples is of the most elementary
sort. The colors are simple tags emphasizing the kind of
sanctity of the person to which they belong, although their
starkness and brightness do contribute to the pomp and
solemnity of the scenes. The same may be said for clothing.
Only on three occasions is the type of garment bearing the
symbolic color specified: "çiclatones" (143b) and "casullas" (58a) already noted, along with the attire of the virgins in the second vision:

> Todas uenjan uestidas de vna blanca frisa,
> Nunca tan blanca ujdo njn toca nin camjsa.
>
> (118bc)

Actually, these are not symbolic at all; Berceo has merely
selected a garment appropriate to the persons or their pro-
fession, thereby rendering the description that much more
picturesque.

The garment worn by Voxmea, the young girl charged
to guard Oria's throne, seems an interesting exception:

> Vistia esta mançeba preçiosa uestidura,
> Mas preçiosa que oro, mas que la seda pura;
> Era sobre sennada de buena escriptura,
> Non cubrió omne ujuo tan rica cobertura.   (91)

Berceo uses the whole quatrain to say that garment is
"preciosa." Neither the type of garment nor any symbolic
color is specified, and the only definite fact asserted about
the "vestidura" is that:

Auja en ella nonbres de omnes de grant ujda
Que serujeron a Christo con uoluntat conplida;
Pero de los reclusos fue la mayor partida
Que domaron sus carnes a la mayor medida.   (92)

This seems to establish two classes of holy people, with a
slight preference for the ascetics, undoubtedly because the
throne belongs to Oria.

Symbolic things may be carried as well as worn. Indeed,
Berceo is especially fond of ceremonious gestures and up-
lifted hands that place such objects in prominence. In the
case of the bishops the effect is one of symmetry:

Todos vestian casullas de preciosos colores,
Blagos en las siniestras como predicadores,
Caliçes en diestras de oro mui meiores.   (58a-c)

These are obviously symbolic, and upon Oria's request the
proper meaning is given:

Porque daban al pueblo bever de buen castigo,
Por ende tienen los calices cada uno consigo,
Reffirian con los cuentos al mortal enemigo
Que engannó a Eva con un astroso figo.   (60)

The two objects recall two different aspects of the bishops'
earthly careers: preaching and administering Communion.
Two kinds of symbolism may be distinguished here. The
"blago" is a symbol in the sense that it is merely a sign indicating the occupation of preaching. A figurative meaning is of course latent in the word (staff equals support or
protection), but it is not exploited. Rather, the author
prefers to develop the preaching theme independently and
to remain on the literal level: in their sermons the bishops
assailed the Devil. In contrast, they carry chalices because
these have symbolic import: they contain the "bever de
buen castigo," Christ, who nourishes and refreshes with
His sound warnings.

It appears that the divine purpose of the first vision is
to reveal to Oria the promise of glory, if she but hold fast.
In this vision the notion of reward—of such pervasive importance throughout the whole poem—is represented by
the traditional symbol of the throne. Actually, Berceo does
not speak of a throne but rather of a seat, a "siella." He
uses the former elsewhere (86a), but as the throne from
which the Apostles judge the world and without the impli-
cation of reward. Another traditional metaphor for reward
is the crown. It also is used once only.[40] The martyrs

> Dexaron se matar a colpes de azconas,
> Jesu Christo por ende diolis ricas coronas. (81cd)

However, Oria's reward is always termed a "siella," [41] and,
despite its central importance in the vision, it is not presented with any great detail. Specifically, six things are
made known about it:

> *En cabo de las uirgines,* toda la az passada,
> Falló muy rica siella *de oro* bien labrada,
> De *piedras muy preçiosas* toda engastonada
> Mas estaua *uazia* e muy bien *seellada.*   (77)

> Como rayos de sol asy *relampagaua.* (90c)

No one will have great difficulty in understanding the
meaning here. The place of the throne signifies that Oria's
merit is higher than that of all the other virgins. The gold
means simply that the reward is worth much, and also
probably that the "oro" is especially suited for "Oria," a
pun not unfamiliar to readers of the poem. Berceo's chance
to wax symbolic is over the precious gems (one may recall
the prodigious and subtle symbolism of stones in the lapi-

---

40. The metaphor is again echoed in "Estas tres sanctas uirgines en
çielo *coronadas*" (30a). They are already "crowned' 'or receiving their
reward.

41. 77b, 78a, 79b, 89a, 90b, 94a, 96b, 102d, 110c.

daries, not to mention biblical exegetes themselves) . However, the gems are bypassed with the vague "preciosas." As in the case of "bright as the sun," the epithet is admirative rather than descriptive. Further, the gold and precious stones of the throne are the exact echo of Berceo's earlier remark:

> Como era preçiosa mas que piedra preçiada
> Nonbre auja de oro, Oria era llamada.   (9cd)

(Even the same qualifier, "preciosas," is repeated with the "piedras.") However, we learn that the scat is empty and sealed—i.e. reserved for someone. Such naïve tension is also continued on two other occasions. The narrator simply observes that "Bien fue felix la alma para quien estaua" (90d) . Finally it is Oria herself who asks the inevitable (94c) : "Esti tan grant adobo ¿cuyo podria seer?" From this it is clear that the central theme of the throne (as well as its accessories, the "acithara" 78a or "solar" 96b) is symbolic only in the most obvious ways. Rather, its importance seems to be dramatic.[42]

In Orio's second vision, contrary to the other two, the recluse is not transported to higher realms: the whole vision takes place in her cell. Oria is lying on the "cold, hard ground" and, as in the other visions, sleeping. The familiar

---

42. This observation applied also to Oria's frequent questions. It is a commonplace of mystical literature that the candidate for initiation must first ask the proper question before being admitted into the holy of holies (e.g. Perceval) . Oria asks 5 questions in all during her first vision, the first 4 immediately upon rising to a higher level of heavenly contemplation, the fifth upon returning to the level of heaven reserved for her. With the exception of her inquiry concerning her former teacher Urraca (71) , all introduce a *descriptio* of the level of heaven or the object concerned: "¿Que es esto?" (53b) ; "¿Que procession es esta?" (59b) ; "¿Estos que cosa son?" (80d) ; and, concerning the throne destined for her, "¿cuyo podria seer?" (94c) . The formulaic nature of her inquiries suggests a rhetorical function. In short, Oria's questions seem survivals of practices of mystical initiation, but in Berceos' poem they seem to work best as dramatic devices, by enabling descriptions to occur in dialogue form.

three virgins arrive, dressed again in symbolic white, and
announce:

> . . . "Tu que yazes sonnosa,
> Leuantate, reçibi a la Uirgo gloriosa
> Que es Madre de Christo e fija e esposa;
> Serás mal acordada sy fazes otra cosa."   (120)

The strongly admonitory tone is striking—not only in
the fourth verse, which may, after all, be mere padding, but
in the first especially. Of course, Berceo's phrase may simply have adapted itself rhythmically to such familiar biblical utterances as the "O vos omnes qui transistis per viam,
attendite et videte." But this very selection of a biblical
pattern suggests that in this context "sleep" is to be read
symbolically. In addition to being the mere condition or
backdrop of visions, sleep is meant to imply a possibility
or even an actual condition of the soul. Perhaps the "earth"
on which Oria is lying is also to be taken symbolically as
well as literally. Such an interpretation gains in plausibil-
ity through the reproachful tone of the following: " 'Sy
te ffalla en tierra abrá de ti rencura' " (128d). Interspersed
with claims of Oria's great merit, it is possible to find further admonitions as well. Berceo speculates that eleven
months had elapsed since Oria's first vision of the saints:
"But Oria had not yet forgotten them" (114d). The possible disparity between normal chronological time and the
subjective duration of suffering notwithstanding, it seems
unnecessary to insist that Oria remained faithful to her
powerful visions for a mere eleven months. Another detail: Mary, in announcing herself, stresses an aspect of her
protection that is surprising in context:

> "Yo so Sancta Maria la que tu mucho quieres,
> Que saque de porfazo a todas las mugieres."   (125ab)

It is appropriate that she be of special help to women, but is she especially needed to "sacar de porfazo" Oria, to save her from shame?

Oria remained true to her ascetic practices, asserts Berceo in *Santo Domingo,* regardless of what anyone says: "biuia en grant lazerio *qui quier qui al uos diga"* (329d). This suggests the possibility that in writing the second vision of *Santa Oria* Berceo had in the back of his mind, without bothering to make it more explicit, the attacks of the Devil against Oria, such as those described in the Oria episode of *Santo Domingo* (327–33). If so, then it is indeed justified to read "sonnosa" and possibly also "tierra" symbolically as well as literally. Of course, in *Santa Oria* protection of the girl is naturally transferred from Santo Domingo to the Virgin Mary.

At any rate, Mary's protection and comfort is represented symbolically by a "noble lechiga" (*SOr* 127a) or "lecho" (128b). Like the throne, it has some kind of covering ("adobos," one of the words used in reference to the cloth covering the throne), and, also like the throne, it is described only in general terms, such as *noble, real,* and *preciosa.* All one knows is that it is soft and comfortable.

The allegorical setting for Oria's third and final vision, the Mount of Olives, reminds one again of the *locus amoenus* of the *Milagros.* The Mount of Olives is of course the scene of the agony of Christ and prefigures Oria's own imminent death. Around the mountain there is a plain, thick with olive trees. I can find no specific referent for these trees, and their presence seems warranted by the mere realistic necessity that, after all, it *is* the Garden of— Olives. Such verbal relationship—almost verbal causation —is entirely understandable to a countryman of Isidore of Seville and to one who places such meaning on the secret connection between *oro* and *Oria.* As may be expected, these trees are laden with olives. But here the allegorical

is breached, for these olives provide "sonbra," shade of
such a kind that "podria beujr so ellos omne a grant
folgura" (141d), says the author, recalling the language
of the *Milagros* (5d).

In telling her vision to Munno, Oria elaborates the scene
and adds the fresh elements of the flowers and their odor:

> Vidi y logar bueno, sobra buen arbolado,
> El fructo de los arboles non seria preçiado,
> De campos grant amchura, de flores grant mercado,
> Guarria la su olor a omne entecado.   (155)

The rhythmic balance of the verses brings the heartbeat
into harmony with the peace and tranquility of the im-
agery. No specific meanings are given for each element,
and the reader may seek help in the *Milagros* allegory, or,
better yet, find his own.

4. Realism in *Santa Oria*

As a reaction against the didacticism of much medieval literature and its accompanying tendency toward generalization and idealistic distortion, many modern critics have been pleased to regard Berceo's art as an imitation of everyday reality, in all its sensuousness and individuality. For M. Menéndez y Pelayo, for example, Berceo's realism is of the popular sort, unsubtle and not without a certain innocent malice.[1] Guerrieri Crocetti is fond of noting any sense of the sublime or supernatural in Berceo.[2] Joaquín Artiles feels the need to show that the poet's realism is not of the bloody or macabre sort that may be found in the epics of his day and in *Fernán Gonzalez* and the *Libro de Alexandre*.[3] Yet, while evading those excesses which we today more readily associate with naturalism, Berceo's art, he believes, is nevertheless "realistic." If his world is the simple one of the convent, his characters are not for that reason less alive: "en una palabra: *viven* muchas pobres gentes del retablo humano de los días de Berceo." Having made this tempered observation, however, the critic reverts

1. . . . . cierta socarronería e inocente malicia" (*Historia de la poesía castellana en la Edad Media, I,* [3 vols. Madrid, 1911–16], 193. In illustration of this, Menéndez y Pelayo's single example is well chosen. Of the pregnant abbess Berceo writes: "Fol creciendo el vientre en contra las terniellas, / Fueronseli faciendo peccas ennas masiellas" (*Milagros* 508b).
2. C. Guerrieri Crocetti, *Gonzalo de Berceo* (Brescia, 1947). The poet's manner is one of "tocchi vivaci, pittoreschi, di duro e plebeo realismo" (p. 65.). His characters are everyday folk from the lower classes of society, full of common sense and with "temperamento bonaccione e grossolono" (p. 63). Berceo's expression, like theirs, is frank but crude. His world is familiar, a "richiamo alla più umile vita, alla più semplice realtà, alla buona terra" (p. 122).
3. Joaquín Artiles, *Los recursos literarios de Berceo* (Madrid, 1964), pp. 191–98.

to the curious assumption that realism or life is somehow
more real and alive in direct proportion to quantity or
dramatic exaggeration. Life is confused with the lively.
Thus the examples selected are for the most part "graphic"
("la desesperación y el dolor suelen expresarse con grafismo
violento").[4]

The inadequacy of such notions of realism becomes obvious when applied to *Santa Oria,* for the simple reason
that this poem differs considerably in content from Berceo's
previous works.[5] As we have seen, Jorge Guillén's observa-

4. Ibid., p. 195.

5. Thus, in an entire chapter on realism, Artiles makes not a single
reference to *SOr.* Crocetti's examples are more randomly selected, but his
readings and taste are often so arbitrary as to cast doubt on his conclusions. His more serious misreadings are the following:

(a) Somehow the critic thinks that Oria's heavenly "siella" or throne
is a horse (!) : "La stupenda cavalcatura," "un bel cavallo magnificamente
bardato," "il mirabile e lussuoso palafreno" (pp. 119–20). Certainly on
the basis of such readings of "siella" it is possible to speak of a "tono di
realismo" (p. 119).

(b) Crocetti states (p. 120) : "Ma ad una visione segue un'altra, perchè
la fanciulla torna alla realtà, per essere subito avviata verso un altro
mondo di sublime bellezza." The critic is speaking of Oria's first two
visions. It is true that one vision follows the other, but the setting of the
second vision is hardly a "mondo di sublime bellezza." In fact, it is the
virgins and, later, Mary who descend to Oria. The scene takes place in
the recluse's own cell.

(c) Discussing the death scene, the critic states (p. 122) : "Anzi il
narratore diventa uno dei protagonisti, il buon vicino di casa, al quale
si ricorre nel momento del bisogno, per avere un consiglio ed un aiuto."
The reverse is true. It is not Berceo who becomes an active participant,
thus furnishing yet another example of "intimità paesana" or a "senso
practico delle cose." Rather, Berceo has subtly removed himself completely from the narration. In this crucial scene it is the original author,
Munno himself, who speaks: "Yo Munno e don Gomez" (163a). And the
sense of things is anything but practical.

Beyond this, however, it seems to me that Crocetti's general assumptions
need revision. Concerning strophes 57–59 (the description of the bishops),
for example, he notes: "Un mondo solido, un mondo rude" (p. 119). Or
the following (pp. 119–20) : "Passa una scorta di martiri ed il poeta, con
quel suo tono paesano si affretta a riconoscervi qualcuno familiare al
culto della sua terra e dei suoi affetti (str. 84–85) , e lo solleva sulla cima
della più alta gerarchia, *a cui può arrivare la sua immaginazione di*

tion that "Berceo's world shelters more sinners than saints," [6] though valid as a consensus based on all the poet's works, is inapplicable to *Santa Oria*. Here not a single sinner appears in an active role, and only one is even mentioned: a bishop, characterized only by his absence (62). Again, the Devil, such an active and lively figure in some of the earlier works, is merely alluded to, and only in the first half of the poem. This orientation of the poem toward supernatural beings and events accounts for the absence of the more exaggerated and crude kinds of realism. Indeed, the fact that five-eighths of the poem takes place in a visionary and allegorical world, one that is not our own and that is not "real" by ordinary standards, will require a special sense of "realism," for which our study of symbolism will be seen to be useful.

As a nucleus, however, the usual definition will do nicely. Narrative realism means simply that the author succeeds in making his characters live, in "humanizing" them. In *Santa Oria* there is a marked preference for the more tender situations and emotions, resulting in a distinctive warmth and delicacy of feeling. For example, Berceo evokes Oria's age with a single diminutive:

Con ambos sus *labriellos* apretaua sus dientes
Que non salliessen dende palabras desconuenjentes.

(16cd)

---

povero chierico di campagna" (italics mine). As a corrective to these rigid criteria of "sublime and low," or "cultivated" and *grossolano*, cf. Guillén, "Prosaic Language: Berceo," in his *Language and Poetry*, p. 7. As to the myth of Berceo's "naïveté," the time, one hopes, is past when one can hold with a condescending amazement which itself can only be termed naïve, that Berceo allegorizes "como en un juego para niños"; that he "no obra ni tampoco piensa; tan solo siente y siente" (Agustín del Campo, "La técnica alegórica en la introducción a los 'Milagros de Nuestra Señora,'" *RFE, 28* [1944], 15–57). The truth is that Berceo's world-view is highly thought out and coherent, but it works within a framework of sacramental symbolism inaccessible to modern positivistic mentality. Cf. Lorenz, *RJ, 14*, 255–68.

6. Guillén, p. 7.

What a charming, plastic touch: the youth is portrayed as
"squeezing her teeth" with *"both* of her little lips"! In a
related image the poet gives the age at which Oria enters
the convent: [7]

> *Desque mudó los dientes* luego a pocos annos
> Pagauase muy poco de los seglares pannos.   (20ab)

Berceo's tenderness toward the young girl is taken up by
the heavenly visitors. The three virgins counter Oria's
protestations of humility with the comforting words:

> "Fija, dixo Ollalia, tu tal cosa non digas,
> Ca as sobre los çielos amigos e amjgas."   (36ab) [8]

The tenderness and frailty of the young girl is repeatedly
conveyed through the diminutive, this time through Oria's
own mouth. God has told her that her time has not yet
come to remain in heaven, and she replies:

> "Los cielos son mucho altos, yo peccadriz mezquina
> Sy una uez tornaro en la mj *calabrina,*
> Non fallaré enel mundo sennora njn madrina
> Por quj yo esto cobre njn tardi njn ayna."   (104)

The Father gives his comforting promise, adding the en-
dearing "la mj fija querida," and concludes: " 'Torna a tu
casiella, reza tu matinada.' " Again the dual function is
obvious: Oria's house, like her young lips, is small; she
lives "enparedada." But coupled with the physical small-
ness is a suggestion of frailty and tenderness.

---

7. In his selection of expressive detail Berceo shows special preference
for a small number of bodily features: hands, mouth or teeth, and, less
frequently, eyes. Dominic's *taciturnitas* is also expressed pictorially: "los
labros dela uoca tenjalos bien cosidos" (*SDom* 12c). Millán's miracle of
the multiplication of the loaves of bread is described as food that "grows
between the teeth": "Agora el conducho cresçió entre los dientes" (*SMil*
259d). Further examples from *SOr* are given below.

8. This idea is formulaic, however. Dominic's parents are "del Criador
amigos" (*SDom* 6a). Cf. also *SDom* 151a and passim.

In the second vision Mary addresses the recluse as "fija" (125d) or, again with a diminutive, as "fijuela mja." Oria feels she does not deserve such a fine bed; she prefers one that is "aspero, de sedas aguijosas" (130a), for "such precious things are for very great men" (130d). This remark, better than all her other protestations, represents her own type of humility: naïve and without rancor, properly respectful before the great of this world as well as of the other. The virgins, however, will not accept Oria's refusals. With a playful familiarity:

> Tomaron la las uirgines dandol grandes sossannos,
> Echaron la a Oria en essos ricos pannos;
> Oria, con grant cochura, daua gemjdos estrannos,
> Ca non era uezada de entrar en tales vannos.   (131)

The brief scene has a bitter-sweet flavor of friendship and good-natured fun, on the one hand, and of pain, on the other. Of course, Oria is receiving a great honor. And yet, like the humble girl she is, she cannot immediately accept it as such: "For she was not accustomed," the poet explains. Her "strange groanings" ring true as the authentic reaction of a frail and worn youth (it is repeatedly emphasized that she is "muy lazdrada"), totally unable to cope with the new and miraculous experience.

Berceo's art of evoking a whole personality or scene with one or two brief touches may be seen throughout. Take Oria's illness:

> En cuita yazia Oria dentro en su casiella;
> Estaua vn grant conuento de fuera de la çiella
> Rezando su salterio cada uno en su siella,
> E non tenja njnguno enxuta la maxiella.   (137)

This dramatic scene is conceived spatially: Oria lying in her cell, the great crowd outside, "each one in his seat" reading the psalter. The emotions are equally visible: Oria in pain, and everyone else in tears, expressed by a popular

kind of litotes that jars the otherwise perfect economy of
the strophe but which is required by the quite successful
rhymes: "And no one had dry cheeks." To represent Oria's
weakness and great pain, Berceo reverts once more to the
detail of her teeth:

> Yaziendo la enferma en tal tribulaçion,
> Maguera entre dientes fazia su oraçion.   (138ab)

> Dizia entre los dientes con vna uoz cansada:
> "¡Monte Oliueti, Monte Oliueti!" ca non dizia al nada.
> Non gelo entendia nadi de la posada,
> Ca non era la uoz de tal gujsa formada.   (147)

She is in such a state that she cannot even open her mouth
enough to pronounce and must speak indistinctly, "between her teeth."

Berceo also takes care to note the reactions of the "good
ladies" who are sitting next to Oria. They see her mur-
murs but are unable to hear or understand ("entendian").
However, they are sufficiently impressed with the gravity
of the situation, and they probably know enough of Oria's
past visions to suspect some kind of supernatural workings:
"Por vna maraujlla esta cosa aujan" (148c). But the crucial hour of death and eternal salvation or damnation, as
well as their naïve superstitions, cause them to wonder:
"Estauan en grant dubda si era mal o bien" (148d). After
all, as the reader of the Oria episode in *Santo Domingo*
(316–33) will recall, the Devil is also able to cause such a
"maraujlla."

Berceo's immediate literary reaction is identical with
the first thought of all the "good ladies." The next verse
is spoken by Oria's confessor Munno: "La madre de la
duenna fizo a mj clamar" (149a). The dialogue that follows between Oria and her confessor is of exquisite beauty
and artistic concentration. In a four-strophe monologue
Oria tells of her final vision. The gentle landscape and

rhythmic balance of the verses suggest tranquillity. Her tone rises in summary, and her inability to say anything but empty commonplaces results in some kind of artistic merit, as if, after her description, this is all that can be said:

> "Tal era la conpanna, tal era el logar,
> Omne que y morasse nunca ueria pesar.
> Sy oujesse mas vn poco y estar,
> Podria muchos bienes ende acarrear." (157)

Munno's question is superfluous but not inappropriate to a confessor under such circumstances: "Do you desire to go there?" The ensuing dialogue is a model of economy and concentration:

> Dixol Munno a Oria: "¿Cobdiçias alla yr?"
> Dixol a Munno Oria: "Yo si, mas que ujujr;
> E tu non perdrias nada de comjgo venjr."
> Dixol Munno: "¡Quisiesse lo esso Dios consintir!"
> (158)

These few examples must suffice to illustrate the most accessible kind of realism in Berceo: the feel of authentic life. Working within the broad factual limitations of the source Book, the poet's creativity arises in the concrete visualization and dramatization of individual scenes and characters, although the goal is not so much to individualize as to vivify. This is achieved artistically through the expressive detail,[9] which summarizes or typifies a whole scene and impresses it on the mind. Such interpretive details are usually spatial and occur in the foreground, resulting in the familiar "close-up" that is so common in the best medieval authors.[10] It is perhaps inaccurate to regard

9. The term "réalisme expressif" has been used by Georges Cirot in discussing works of Berceo other than *SOr*. See "L'expression dans Gonzalo de Berceo," *RFE*, 9 (1922) , 154–70.

10. The best discussion of this aspect of medieval literature is in C. S. Lewis' *The Discarded Image* (Cambridge, Eng., 1964) , pp. 206 ff.

such notations as creative in the modern sense, however. They are merely one reading of the story and arise, almost in spite of the author, from his intense absorption in the life of the narrative.

Such expressive realism may be more fully understood through the poet's use of space and time, since the usual domain of literary realism is the everyday world we live in, the one limited precisely by space and time.[11] In *Santa Oria*, even in the earthly scenes, indications of time are curiously absent.[12] To begin with, despite the author's constant pledge of historical authenticity, there is not the slightest attempt to indicate the dates of Oria's birth or death, or even the century in which she lived. Only the *places* of birth (4b) and burial (180) are given. Similarly, her age is never stated except in its early stages, and then imprecisely: *"De njnnez* fazia ella fechos muy conue-njentes" (7c) .[13] We learn that she was at some time baptized (9b) and that she entered the convent "when her teeth changed at a young age" (20a) . How long she stayed in the convent and her age at death are left vague. The second vision occurred "probably" eleven months after the first:

11. Jorge Luis Borges has imagined the fictitious planet Tlön, where the inhabitants are congenitally idealists: "The world for them is not a concourse of objects in space; it is a heterogeneous series of independent acts. It is successive and temporal, not spatial" ("Tlön, Uqbar, Orbis Tertius," in his *Labyrinths* [New York, 1962], p. 8. Of special relevance to our study is the interdependence—oversimplification notwithstanding—of time and idealism, on the one hand, and of space and realism, on the other.

12. There is to date no good study of the notion of time in Berceo. The most recent attempt (Artiles, *Berceo*, pp. 222–26) is merely a statistical survey of the most obvious temporal vocabulary ("años, meses, semanas y dias") , along with the hypothesis that the measurement of time by the liturgical hours must have been common in monastic life in Rioja. No meaning of time is attempted.

13. This is merely the traditional topos of the wise youth, the *puer-senex*. See Curtius, *European Literature and the Latin Middle Ages*, pp. 98–101. Similarly, San Millán is "Ançiano de seso, mançebo de edat" (39b) .

"Onze meses senneros *podria* auer passados" (114a). It is during the second vision that the Virgin Mary announces the imminent illness (135b) and death (136b). Thus the maximum possible time between the first vision and the death is about two years. However, the impression that Oria died young—reinforced by the frequent diminutives suggesting tender age—is rendered less certain by Mary's remark that Oria had lived an ascetic's existence for a considerable time ("tan luengos tienpos," 134b) before her first vision.

Other indications of time have a use analogous to those of space and place. For example, the date that occurs formulaicly at the beginning of each vision:

> Terçera noche era despues de Naujdat
> De Sancta Eugenia era festiujdat.   (25ab)

Here time is used merely to *localize* a holy or important event. In just the same way, Berceo is sure to give, whenever possible, the "logar" in which such events occurred. In such cases time is purely functional and static; it can never be an integral part of any action or experience.[14]

There is also a dramatic use of time in *Santa Oria*. Following Oria's ardent oration, the Creator speaks, but not before a pregnant pause: "Dixol *avn de cabo* la uoz del Criador" (105a). Again, after the vision has run its course, the virgins conduct Oria back to earth:

14. A more dynamic view is possible by observing that in *Santa Oria* events are localized according to their position in any one of the traditional or natural *cycles* of time: the seasons, the ages of man ("desque mudó los dientes"), the liturgical year (saints' feast days). There is little interest in locating events in terms of the linear development of human affairs, which, since the 18th century, we have come to know as history or progress. The difference between the two concepts of time, the cyclical versus the linear, could be suggestive in elaborating a poetics of some medieval or "primitive" poets. One may consult the interesting remarks of the poet Peter Viereck (*The Tree Witch* [New York, 1960], pp. 12–13), who, in his choice of poetic mood and symbol, prefers the signs of "season,

> *En muy poquiello rato* al cuerpo la tornaron,
> Esperto ella *luego* que ellas la dexaron.   (108cd)

The indication of time here, however vague, renders the
narrated experience more lively. These two words, *rato*
and *luego,* are frequently used in similar situations; they
are important linking devices in the narration, serving to
join otherwise disconnected scenes. In the second vision
three virgins appear. Then, "Ende *a poco rato* ujno Sancta
Maria" (119a). Oria is laid in the symbolic couch:

> *Luego que* fue la freyra enel lecho echada,
> Fue de bien grandes lunbres la çiella alunbrada.
> Fue de uirgenes muchas *en vn rato* poblada.   (132a-c)

> *Luego que* oyo este mandado Oria.   (151a)

As in Strophe 108d, Berceo has the habit of pointing out
that, preceding or following a vision, the Saint falls asleep
or awakens "immediately"; "Quanto fue acostada fue *luego*
adormjda" (164a) ; "Despertó *luego* ella, moió los lagremales" (201d). The limited number of such words, as
well as the restricted type of situation in which they are

---

cycle, circle (as opposed to straight-line mechanical progress) ." The "pro-
gressive" view, it seems to me, would emphasize individual, nonrecurrent
events and situations, necessarily so because of the relentless and irreversi-
ble flow of time or, more optimistically, because of the perpetual newness
of the world and human experience. The cyclical view, on the other hand,
seems more congenial to ethics than to knowledge, to didacticism rather
than to discovery or experience for its own sake. For the didactic is based
on the notion of type, of the essential and periodic recurrence of experience and moral patterns. That such cyclical views are especially prevalent in so-called primitive or preconceptual mentality, see Philip Wheelwright, *The Burning Fountain: A Study in the Language of Symbolism*
(Bloomington, 1954) , p. 182: "The primitive starting-point . . . is time as
experienced: in the succession of day and night and the cycle of the
seasons, in the progress from childhood to maturity and from maturity to
old age and death, and in the tribal calendar of ceremonies of planting,
reaping . . . and the like. Nature, in rituo-mythic perspective, is cyclical."
See also Mircea Eliade, *Cosmos and History: The Myth of the Eternal
Return* (New York, 1954) .

used, suggest an unconscious stylistic trait or at least a convenient way of filling out a verse. This, of course, may be noted with no prejudice to their dramatic and narrative functions.

There is, however, a more central use of time in *Santa Oria*. Consider the following examples:

> Dixolis: "Piense Oria de ir a su logar,
> Non ujno aun *tiempo* de aquj habitar;
> Avn aue vn poco el cuerpo a lazrar,
> Despues uerna el *tiempo* de la siella cobrar." (102)

> Mas aun essi *tiempo* non era allegado
> Para recevir soldada del lazerio passado. (66cd)

> Dixol la Gloriosa: "Oria la mj lazrada,
> Que de tan luengos *tienpos* eres enparedada,
> Yo te dare vn signo . . ." (134a-c) [15]

This is the time of human suffering, the time still left to live before final relief and salvation. As can be seen, it is most insistently portrayed. Moreover, it is a highly personal experience of time, one for which chronological or more standard measurements can give only the crudest idea. For Berceo is well aware that a day can seem longer than a whole year: "Façíeseli el dia mas luengo que un anno" (*SMil* 12). It is striking in Berceo how often indications of time are associated with suffering. Time operates on a bipolar axis of present suffering and future relief or salvation. The two liturgical delimitations of time noted by Artiles in *Santa Oria* occur in the following contexts: [16]

> *Despues de las matinas, leyda la lection,*
> Escuchola bien Oria con grant deuoçion;
> *Qujso dormir vn poco, tomar consolaçion.* (26ac)

15. Cf. also 98 cd, 142.
16. Artiles, *Berceo*, p. 223.

> *Cantadas las matinas, la liçençia soltada*
> Que fuesse quis quisiesse folgar a su posada,
> *Acostosse vn poco Amunna bien lazrada.*   (189a-c)

Similarly, Berceo's remarks about his own life or age are inevitably linked with weariness and effort:

> Quiero en mj uegez, *maguer so ya cansado.*   (2a)

> Los dias son non grandes, anochezrá priuado,
> *Escriujr en tinjebra es vn mester pesado.*   (10cd)

At one crucial point, the death of Oria, time and suffering become metaphorically fused: "Fuesse mas aquexando, a boca de noche era" (176b) .[17] How effectively the oral complaints are extended and deepened by the approaching "night," itself seen through its "mouth"!

By contrast, Berceo finds space a more congenial artistic medium. His art is often a succession of plastic scenes in which the visual predominates. This tendency reaches an extreme in *Santa Oria,* where action is reduced to a minimum and things are seen in vision (the etymology should provide a clue). Even the author's own "actions," his personal interventions into the narrative, are reduced in number during the visions, and at one point, for a span of 37 strophes, he seems to be in a sort of visual ecstasis; like Oria herself, he merely watches.[18] However, the tendency toward the visual is general in Berceo, limited neither to visions nor to *Santa Oria.*

Jorge Guillén has noted this fact and borrowed Hazlitt's remarks on Chaucer to describe it:

17. Incredulous before the image, Sánchez suggested the punctuation: "Fuesse mas aquexando a boca, de noche era." But such an emendation, in addition to being redundant (how else does one complain except by mouth?) is contrary to Berceo's intentions.

18. The statistical predominance of the verb "to see" over other verbs of action has already been noted, above, pp. 106–07.

> His words point as an index to the object, like the
> eye or finger . . . he was obliged to inspect things for
> himself, to look narrowly and almost to handle the ob-
> ject, as in the obscurity of morning we partly see and
> partly grope our way; so that his descriptions have a
> sort of tangible character belonging to them, and
> produce the effect of sculpture on the mind.[19]

Sculpture is the right word. Berceo's art consists of a series
of statues, of sculpted gestures, of actions petrified in space
—"things done," as the medieval exegete said of actions.[20]
And, as we have already seen, such artistic development
consists in placing in the foreground single, expressive details. Grief is portrayed by tears on the cheek (*SOr* 137d).
The poet pictures himself as writing his work "en su
portaleio" (184b). To convey indecision or sorrow: "Estando los maestros todos *man a maxiella*," with their hands
on their cheeks.[21]
   The poet's fondness for impressive gestures of the hands
is especially noteworthy:

> Estas tres sanctas uirgines en çielo coronadas
> Tenjan sendas palonbas *en sus manos alçadas.*
>
> (30ab)

> Salieron recivirla con responsos doblados,
> Fueron abraçarla *con los braços alçados.*   (64ab)

The same idea is obviously present in the appearance of
the bishops ("siniestras" and "diestras" refer to the unex-
pressed upraised hands, *las manos*) :

---

19. Guillén, *Language and Poetry*, p. 8.
20. See Robertson, *A Preface to Chaucer*, p. 300. It was common to
contrast historical *res facta* to the *res ficta* of poetry. See De Bruyne,
Historia de la estética medieval, 2, 527.
21. *SMil* 209, 229; *Duelo* 34. Cf. also the *Libro de buen amor* 179.

> Todos vestian casullas de preciosos colores,
> Blagos en las siniestras como predicadores,
> Caliçes en diestras de oro mui meiores.   (58a-c)

God the Father appears as in the Final Judgment on a
romanesque tympanum:

> El Rey de los reyes, Sennor de los sennores,
> En cuya mano yazen justos e peccadores.   (113ab)

Oria's death is without doubt the best example of this, so
much so that G. Cirot compared it to a gothic painting: [22]

> Fuel ujnjendo a Oria la hora postremera;
> Fuesse mas aquexando, a boca de noche era.
> Alçó la mano diestra de fermosa manera,
> Fizo cruz en su fruente, santiguó su mollera.
>
> Alçó ambas las manos, juntólas en igual
> Como quj riende graçias al buen Rey spirital;
> Cerró oios e boca la reclusa leal,
> Rendió a Dios la alma, nunca mas sintió mal.
>
>   (176-77)

The interest of such a scene is increased when compared
with the deaths of St. Millán and St. Dominic, where the
similarities extend to entire hemistichs. St. Millán:

> Desent alzó a suso la sue mano denosa,
> Bendissólos a todos la sue boca preçiosa,
> Commendólos a Dios, a la Virgo gloriosa
> Que ellos los guardassen de tacha periglosa.
>
> Sanctigó a si mismo por fer buen complimiento,
> Tendió ambas sues palmas, iuntólas muy a tiento,
> Cerró ambos sos oios sin nul conturbamiento,
> Rendió a Dios la alma, fizo so passamiento.   (300-01)

22. Cirot, *RFE, 9,* 168.

Likewise, St. Dominic:

> Fue cerrando los oios el sancto confessor,
> apretó bien sus labros, nunca ujestes mejor,
> alçó ambas las manos a Dios nuestro Señor,
> rendió a El la alma a muy grant sabor.   (521)

Such gestures, in their solemn conformity,[23] symbolize spiritual states or truths and, because the Saint has approximated the ideal way of dying (or living), are meant to be inspirational. Oria's life is a moral model which it is the job of the *vida* to reproduce and of Christians to emulate. In consequence, in seeming to portray ideal and general situations rather than concrete particulars, such timeless and simplified plastic scenes have led some to question their effectiveness as "realistic" or mimetic representation. Speaking of similar literary trends in France, Erich Auerbach has noted that

> the urge to establish connections and pursue developments is feeble. Even within an individual scene, the development, if any, is halting and laborious. But the gestures of the scenic moment are simply and plastically impressive in the highest degree. . . . The various phases of the story . . . are concretized in gestures to such an extent that the pictured scenes, in the impression they produce, closely approach the character of symbols or figures, even in cases where it is not possible to trace any symbolic or figural signification.[24]

In practice, this figural tradition, continues Auerbach, reduces the range of reality in art to "that portion which the

23. The stylized or formulaic nature of these descriptions may be seen further by comparing the death of Christ (*Duelo* 108) or of a man named Estevan (*Milagros* 269). Berceo's great love of *hands* is echoed by the Virgin Mary at the foot of the Cross. She laments over being able to kiss neither the feet nor the mouth of her Son, "Nin . . . *las manos que io mas cobdiçiaba*" (*Duelo* 138d).

24. Auerbach, *Mimesis*, p. 101.

crystallized idioms of the established categories are able
to convey." When this occurs, the figures represented "no
longer have any reality, they have only signification." At
least in theory, however, the concept of pictorial or spatial
realism need be restricted only with reference to that
portion of reality that can assume visual plasticity, a less
serious limitation than the linguistic one. Oria's death
scene may serve as an illustration. Despite formulaic composition, the pronounced visibility of the scene, dominated
by impressive gestures of great plastic beauty, is alone sufficient claim to some kind of realism.[25] Moreover, the gestures themselves, though stylized and of epic dimension,
are not unbecoming to such a saint as Oria; nor is their
figurative meaning so abstruse as to distract from the scene
itself. Thus Auerbach, after noting the limiting effects of
visual plasticity alone (p. 101), goes on to point out that
it is precisely in such isolated pictures that there can be
discerned in Western literary art a new tendency toward
a fuller mimetic representation of reality.

The larger problem raised by Auerbach, however—to
what degree mimetic representation is necessarily limited
by both symbolism and didacticism—becomes especially
acute in *Santa Oria,* since its didactic symbolism is conveyed through superterrestrial visions that transcend the
boundaries of our normal experience. The point is that
the world of visions is not considered miraculous in any
ontological sense—at least by Berceo. Being a real experience, its phenomenal surface is capable of both realistic
treatment and symbolic profundity. Like our own physical
world, it is but another occasion for revealing meaning
beneath external immediate appearance, the difference
being that visions are usually reserved for the elect and

25. I mean in the sense suggested above (p. 122 and n. 11) through the
association of realism and space (as opposed to idealism and time).
Spatial reality is that world of physical objects apprehended through that
faculty of external perception par excellence, the eyes. Time, by contrast, is not perceived but rather intuited through the inner sense.

are intended to reveal important truths relating to their
own personal destinies. This explains why the vision is
traditionally so important an allegorical medium: it is a
privileged area of the irruption of the divine into the human, of the hidden into the literal. Thus, as Jorge Guillén
has observed, "miracles do not break in in order to throw
things out of order, but rather to restore them to their
own being." [26] In the same way, symbolic visions do not
disrupt our normal understanding of things but rather expand it.

The distance between human and divine is reduced even
further in Berceo through the almost total anthropomor-
phization of heaven. Jorge Guillén has noted that in
Berceo there is no line between heaven and earth, that the
world is "organically divine." [27] The complementary way
of looking at the matter, I suppose, is that heaven is organically human. At least this is the way it happens in *Santa
Oria*.[28] If only by analogy, one "hears" conversations and
"sees" colors. The relationship between Oria and heavenly
creatures is "friendly" (36b), and she is a "good friend of
God" (127c). Saints retain their human forms, and angels
("*cosas* angelicas," 47b, a revealing phrase) appears in
"humanas figuras" (47d). To ascend to heaven the virgins use a column or ladder. Magical in any way? No, says
Berceo:

> Veer solemos tales en las torres obradas,
> Yo sobi por algunas, esto muchas uegadas. (39bc)

"I myself have ascended such towers." In heaven the saints
wear clothes and are said to live in a house or castle. Now

26. *Language and Poetry,* p. 8. Or, as the Scholastics put it: "Gratia
naturam non tollit sed perficit" (quoted in G. Saitta, *Filosofia italiana e
umanesimo* [Venezia, 1928], p. 9).

27. Ibid., p. 7.

28. Guillén goes on to note (ibid., p. 13) that "everything is natural,
prodigiously natural, even in that Heaven visited by Santa Oria during a
pause in her earthly existence."

this metaphor is traditional enough,[29] but Berceo's variations are charming: the hermits live in an "apartamjento"
(83a) ; the house has windows (46c) , a door (195d) , and,
of course, a doorkeeper ("portera," 196c) . When the
chorus of virgins comes out to receive Oria, one must
imagine them as emerging from their own quarters of the
divine mansion ("salieron," 63d) .

In the latter examples one may discern, beyond that
tendency toward pictorial representation already noted, a
concern for the coherence of the literal or visible level as
such. Berceo visualizes a total context and tries to remain
faithful to it, even if this means using allegorical objects
for simply "realistic" purposes. For example, while the
four virgins are speeded up to heaven by grace, Berceo
adds: "Non li fazia enbargo njn el sol njn la luna" (50b) .
It is hardly possible to read this allegorically, since the sun
is God and the moon the Virgin Mary, and one could not
imagine why Berceo would stop to assert that God did not
impede their ascent. After all, it is precisely through His
grace that they are making the journey in the first place.
Similarly, to ascend to heaven Oria follows the Holy Spirit
up the ladder of humility. But certainly Berceo does not
mean that Oria also descends that allegorical ladder at any
time when he specifies:

> Tomaron la las martires que ante la gujaron
> Por essa escalera por la que la leuaron.   (108ab)

This is simply another case of fidelity to the established
context. Berceo *sees* the scene and narrates it in its spatial
authenticity.

29. Alfonso X (*Cantiga* No. 241) has a boy brought back to life by the
Virgin Mary refer to heaven by saying to Mary: "What a beautiful mansion you took from me!" (quoted in F. Callcott, *The Supernatural in
Early Spanish Literature*, p. 34) . In *Santa Oria* Berceo calls heaven a
"palaçio" (196b) or "posada" (49d) . Celestial inhabitants are designated
as "morador" (Urraca, 73c) or "essa sancta mesnada" (63a, 69c) . This is
the home that Oria will "inhabit" ("habitar," 102b) .

There is in fact an instance—unique in Berceo—where this tendency is carried to the point of functioning as a kind of *anti*allegorical device. It happens that, once within the celestial palace, Oria remembers her former spiritual guardian Urraca and looks for her. When the virgins call her name and Urraca answers, Oria recognizes the voice but cannot "see" her. This is strange because Oria is permitted to see everyone else except God himself. One suspects a secret meaning; and, to be sure, the explanation follows immediately:

> La az era muy luenga, esso la enbargaua,
> Que non podia ueerla ca en cabo estaua.   (76ab)

The line of virgins is so long and Urraca is of such high merit that she is simply out of sight over the horizon. Even everyday rules of causality and visibility are operative in Berceo's heaven.

In summary, the term that best characterizes the realism of *Santa Oria* has been supplied by the poet himself. While Oria delights in the mystical meadow, she sees three angels emerge through the windows of the divine palace:

> Salieron tres personnas por essas auerturas,
> Cosas eran angelicas con blancas uestiduras,
> Sendas uergas en manos *de preçiosas pinturas.*
>
> (47a-c)

Again, of course, there is the gesture of the hands. But it is the final phrase that justifies Cirot's "gothic painting" and that deserves to stand as a permanent testimonial to the breadth of Berceo's kind of realism: plastic, stationary, with bright colors and impressive gestures, like a loosely connected series of precious paintings (pictorial realism), capable of pointing to higher meanings of a moral and spiritual order (symbolism), while still retaining the warmth of personal emotion and lived experience (expressive or dramatic realism).

While it is quite proper, then, to speak of both expressive and pictorial representation in *Santa Oria,* one should not go on to imagine that Berceo's prime artistic concern is "realistic" in any sense. As for the pictorial, it is clear that the stylized solemnity of such scenes as Oria's death point beyond realistic observation and suggest ritualistic or liturgical reenactment. Even Berceo's great flair for the expressive, one suspects, is more for didactic effectiveness than "for its own sake." [30]

To be sure, Berceo uses the normal world of sensual experience with great effect. In the famous Introduction to the *Milagros,* for example, he begins with a lengthy description of a lush meadow before passing on to an exegesis of its deeper meaning. But this is no naturalistic description of a real meadow; it is an ideal construction based on deeply religious desires and experiences symbolically apprehended.[31] By apparent contrast, Oria's visions are sup-

30. The comparison already drawn between Berceo's spatial scenes and sculpture is suggestive in yet another way of the poet's antirealism. Like a statue, Berceo's scenes are cold and self-contained; they remain removed from the spectator, who is moved to approve or disapprove but never to "identify" with the character. Although one is invited to emulate Oria's *vida* and to view her death with admiration, the scene keeps its distance from the viewer and never attempts to lure him into the pleasurable illusion of vicarious participation in its own life. Though Oria's death may prefigure our own, the artifice is not maintained wherein *art* and *life* may be confused. On these differences between medieval and post-Romantic sensibility, cf. Robertson, *A Preface to Chaucer,* pp. 9ff. The historical origins, in Schiller, Goethe, and Kant, of such theories of "Erlebniskunst" have been drawn by H. G. Gadamer, "Simbolo e allegoria," *Archivio di Filosofia* (Roma, 1958), pp. 29–33.

31. That Berceo's meadow is ideal rather than "real" may be seen in his frequent insistence that it is in all respects better than anything earthly: "Nunqua trobé en sieglo logar tan deleitoso . . ." (6a); "Nunque udieron omnes organos más temprados" (7c); "Semeia esti prado egual de paraiso" (14a). Similarly, though Berceo speaks frequently of flowers, he rarely specifies either their kind or their concrete relation to their environment: "diuersas flores" (*SOr* 43d), "las flores de mayo" (*SOr* 53d), "caeçí en un prado . . . de flores bien poblado" (*Milagros* 2). Artiles remarks that such flowers "son más bien un objeto bello, esencialmente

posedly "realistic" in the further sense of actual historical experience; but Berceo's concern is again precisely that they can point beyond the realm of pure sense. This may be seen in the frequent comparisons between this world and heaven. Things are compared to paradise (and not vice versa). The perspective begins in heaven; and "contra los sus bienes el mundo non es nada."

The truth is, however, that from the symbolic-sacramental perspective of Berceo, realism and symbolism are inseparable. Spiritual meaning is immanent in sensual appearance, which, like all true metaphor, is able to evoke higher truths but never exhaust their richness.[32] Thus the world is not denied before the spiritual; it is, to use a Hegelian word, *aufgehoben,* synthetically incorporated into it in its upward motion.[33] This results in a necessarily ambiguous attitude toward the created world. For if, in comparison to heaven, the world is as nothing, it is no less important for human thinking and expression that this world does exist as a basis for comparison. Indeed, the very possibility of its being so employed is an indication of its worth.[34] The resulting unity of physical and spiritual

bello, sin conexión con el huerto o el prado, que viene muy bien para exaltar la hermosura de la Virgen" (*Berceo,* p. 177). It is therefore wrong to assert, with Agustín del Campo (*RFE, 28, 52*), that "todo el mundo alzado ante sus ojos enciende su fervor"; or that Berceo is concerned with "un conjunto de atracciones físicas, quietas o móviles, pero exteriores y cercanas" (p. 20). Rather, as we have already shown, it is a question of "ein ursprünglich im Mythologischen und abgeleitet im Theologischen wurzelndes Naturbild" (Lorenz, *RJ, 14,* 257).

32. In such instances the poet's formulaic assertion that he is unable to relate one-tenth of the Virgin's "bondades" (*Milagros* 10) acquires special force.

33. "Out of the reality of creation, without the latter's existence being denied or annihilated, the inexpressible mystery of the Godhead becomes visible. . . . The infinite shines through the finite and makes it more and not less real." Scholem, *Major Trends in Jewish Mysticism,* p. 28.

34. Thus, provided they be properly used, earthly goods and creatures are devalued by comparison, not intrinsically. A somewhat analogous attitude may be seen in *La Vie de Saint Alexis,* where the Saint leaves his

realities—the paradox of sacramental immanence—[35] was
thought to be based on a divinely ordained similitude between hidden truths and their material symbols. For example, water, according to Hugh of St. Victor, is an image
of the grace of the Holy Spirit, and this through its own
natural quality, *ex naturali qualitate*.[36]

Such ways of thinking are pervasive in Berceo and extend far beyond his liturgical works and visions. For example, in many of Millán's and Dominic's miracles it
happens that physical and spiritual blindness are mutually
symptomatic and usually coexist. The cure, absolution and
return to Christ, also relieves the sinner of his physical infirmity.[37] Similarly, famine is the result of "mal pecado"

new bride neither because he despises her nor because he rejects love
itself as false, but rather because neither perfect love nor the perfect beloved can be found on this earth. See Curtius' remarks in *ZRP, 56,* 123:
"Nicht weil er die Liebe verleugnete . . . hat Alexius die Gattin verlassen;
sondern weil er die vollkommene Seelenliebe, welche freiwillige Virginität
fordert, über das irdische und leibliche Band stellt."

35. Walter Benjamin speaks of "die Einheit von sinnlichem und
übersinnlichem Gegenstand, die Paradoxie des theologischen Symbols."
Ursprung des deutschen Trauerspiels (Frankfurt, 1963) , p. 175.

36. "Habet autem omnis aqua ex naturali qualitate similitudinem
quamdam cum gratia Spiritus Sancti . . . et ex hac ingenita qualitate omnis aqua spiritalem gratiam representare habuit, priusquam etiam illam ex
superaddita institutione [i.e. baptism] significavit" Hugh of St. Victor, *De
sacramentis fidei,* 1.9.2, in *PL, 176,* 318) . C. S. Lewis glosses this passage
as follows: "For Hugo, the material element in the Christian ritual is no
mere concession to our sensuous weakness and has nothing arbitrary about
it. . . . *Quod videtur in imagine sacramentum est*" (*Allegory of Love,* p.
46) .

37. Two thieves who try to steal Millán's donkey "Fueron mal con-
fondidos por sos graves peccados: / Ovieron sendos oios de las caras
quebrados" (*SMil* 273bc) . Two *ciegos* who live "en tiniebra oscura" pray
to Millán "Que de toda la tierra eres *salut* e manto, / Por estas *pecadores*
ruega. . . ." Their sight is restored and they again see "the light which
they had misused [*que avien desusada*]" (*SMil* 323–29) . For no apparent
reason Berceo calls a blind man a "çiego porfidioso" (*SDom* 611b) . The
general principle is that physical cure and spiritual salvation are part of
the same process: Dominic has a reputation of "sanar los enfermos, la
salut les render" (551b) .

and can be remedied only through prayer to Christ, "que
eres pan de ujda clamado" (*SDom* 449–51). In narrating
Millán's wanderings in the desert, Berceo is especially
emphatic concerning the correspondences between the
Saint's real, concrete experiences and their symbolic counterpart:

> Por las montannas yermas las carnes martiriando
> Iba enna Cogolla todavia puiando,
> *E quanto mas puiba mas iba meiorando.*   (54b-d)

Millán's physical and spiritual ascent is made difficult:

> Subió en la Cogolla en somo del otero,
> Alli sufrió grant guerra el sancto caballero
> *De fuertes temporales, e del mortal guerrero.*
>   (56b-d)

Such juxtaposition emphasizes the independent truth of
both the "temporales" and the Devil, as well as the immanence of one in the other. In the same way, while Millán was on the mountain, he fought real snakes. He is
therefore known as he who "echó al diablo e venció las
serpientes" (*SMil* 133d).[38] And it should not be assumed

38. Hugh of St. Victor provides a clear explanation of the workings of
this kind of figure: "The Scripture says: 'Watch, because your adversary
the Devil goeth about as a roaring lion.' Here, if we should say that the
lion stands for the Devil, we should mean by 'lion' not the word but the
thing. For if the two words 'devil' and 'lion' mean one and the same
thing, the likeness of that same thing to itself is not adequate. It remains,
therefore, that the word 'lion' signified the animal, but that the animal in
turn designates the Devil" (*Didascalicon,* 5.3, trans. Taylor). For further
discussion of the idea of all creatures as both creatures in themselves and
also signs or mirrors, see De Bruyne, *Historia de la estética medieval,* 2,
579–80. Gershom Scholem's compact observations on this matter may be
applied to Berceo. Concerning that kind of allegory found in the Introduction to the *Milagros:* "That which is expressed by and in the
allegorical sign is in the first instance something which has its own meaningful context, but by becoming allegorical this something loses its own
meaning [e.g. 'lo de fuera dessemos'] and becomes the vehicle of some-

that such modes of perception are peculiar to Berceo; they are part of the whole tradition, and the poet often merely copies them from the source Book.[39]

Thus it may be said, by way of summary, that in Berceo symbolism is a way of thinking, essentially religious, whereas realism is a convenience of perception and expression, which, however, neither mystic nor didactic poet can do without.

---

thing else. Indeed the allegory arises, as it were, from the gap which at this point opens between the form and its meaning. The two are no longer indissolubly welded together; the meaning is no longer restricted to that particular form, nor the form any longer to that particular meaningful content" (*Major Trends,* p. 26) . Radically different from allegorization is that kind of symbolism characterized by the immanence of sign and meaning (e.g. the wolves that attack San Millán in the wilderness) : "In the mystical symbol a reality which in itself has, for us, no form or shape becomes transparent and, as it were, visible, through the medium of another reality which clothes its content with visible and expressible meaning, as for example the cross for the Christian. The thing which becomes a symbol retains its original form and its original content. It does not become, so to speak, an empty shell into which another content is poured; in itself, through its own existence, it makes another reality transparent which cannot appear in any other form" (ibid., p. 27) . The wolves that attack San Millán are both wolves and obscure but meaningful symbols of the great adversary, the Devil.

39. Dominic cures a man of blindness and warns him of the dangers of falling into sin a second time (i.e. he had already sinned once, and this sin was the cause of his blindness, or rather, the physical infirmity was an image of his interior "blindness"): "curia te que non peques e non fagas folia, / ca sera por tu tidio sy fazes recadia" (350cd) . The corresponding passage from Berceo's source book by Grimaldus (ed. Vergara, pp. 352-53; reprinted in J. Fitz-Gerald, *La vida de Santo Domingo de Silos* [Paris, 1904], p. xlvii) reads as follows: "Igitur totum hominem sanat. qui interiorem hominem ab omni viciorum sorde. & exteriorem ab omni infirmitatum labe lavat."

5. Style as Recurrence

Ernst Robert Curtius holds the merit of documenting the important fact of recurrence in medieval literature, at the levels of both form and content.[1] The medieval author works with a given number of traditional themes or *topoi,* which he casts in molds formed not so much by immediate meaning as by preexistent patterns of expression. The study of such formulaic speech, of long interest to critics,[2] received a decisive impetus in the 1930s from Milman Parry's work on oral tradition in Yugoslav poetry.[3] Although Homer was the first beneficiary of such studies, they were subsequently applied to the Spanish *romancero,*[4] Anglo-Saxon poetry,[5] the medieval epic,[6] and the Old Testament.[7] By focusing on formulaic composition as the best way of coping with the pressures of spontaneous creation during oral performance, the Parry school plausibly explained such phenomena as metrical irregularity, absence of enjambement, recurrent epithets, and stock phrases or formulas.

1. In *European Literature and the Latin Middle Ages.*

2. See, for example, Henry R. Lang, "Contributions to the Restoration of the *Poema del Cid," BH, 66* (1926) , 1–509. Formulaic parallels between Berceo and the *Libro de Apolonio* have been pointed out by C. C. Marden, in his edition of the poem (Paris, 1917) , p. lvi.

3. A good summary and synthesis of Parry's work may be found in Albert B. Lord, *The Singer of Tales* (Cambridge, Mass., 1960) .

4. Ruth House Webber, *Formulistic Diction in the Spanish Ballad* (Berkeley-Los Angeles, 1951) .

5. F. P. Magoun, Jr., "Oral-Formulaic Character of Anglo-Saxon Poetry," *Speculum, 28* (1953) , 446–67.

6. Stephen G. Nichols, Jr., *Formulaic Diction and Thematic Composition in the "Chanson de Roland"* (Chapel Hill, 1961) .

7. William Whallon, "Formulaic Poetry in the Old Testament," *CL, 15* (1963) , 1–14.

Berceo's use of so-called formulaic discourse has been amply documented throughout this study: "in *cuaderna vía* Berceo uses formulaic composition as much as any epic minstrel." [8] To be sure, important differences exist. In contrast to the rapid oral composition of the illiterate epic poet, Berceo worked slowly and patiently (cf. *SOr* 184b) from a printed source. The results show far greater metrical perfection. The similarities that persist (use of formula and absence of enjambement) are to be accounted for, first of all, precisely by the metrical demands of the *cuaderna vía*. The difficulties of quick oral composition are simply replaced, and the new and more intricate poetic form favors certain ways of shaping content: "La forma se crea un contenido." [9] This is why, as Lord also found, any discussion of formula must begin with the study of versification. [10]

First, a word about terminology. Although formulaic composition has been a valid focal point for the study of oral poetry, the plausible hypothesis that one implies the other is of little use in the context of Berceo's poetry. For example, it has been claimed that formulaic composition *proves* its oral nature. [11] Similarly, such poetry has been

8. Brian Dutton, review of J. Artiles, *Los recursos literarios de Berceo,* in *BHS, 42* (1965), 185. Parry defines formula as "a group of words which is regularly employed under the same metrical conditions to express a given, essential idea" (*Harvard Studies in Classical Philology, 41* [1930], 80). Prominent examples of formulaic discourse already studied above include Berceo's introduction to his visions and his narration of death. I also call formulaic his many narrative formulas (cf. above, Chap. 1, pp. 25 ff.), although these may not always seem to express "essential" ideas.

9. Victor Shklovski, *O teorii prosy* (Moscow, 1929), pp. 36–37; quoted in Eugenio Asensio, *Poética y realdad en el cancionero peninsular de la edad media* (Madrid, 1957), p. 89.

10. Lord, *Singer of Tales,* p. 31.

11. Nichols, *"Chanson de Roland,"* p. 9. The actual context has richer implications. The author studies the *Chanson de Roland* "from the point of view of formula, enjambement, and thematic composition, in order to demonstrate the textual characteristics that argue its oral rather than literary character."

explained as due to mnemonic necessity on the part of the poet.[12] However, it is virtually certain, on the contrary, that Berceo wrote his poems down and that these were literally "read" in performance. Although the formula does have an important function in Berceo's style, it seems more profitable to consider it as but one aspect of a larger tendency toward repetition, which we have termed the *principle of recurrence.* Now there are basically four levels on which recurrence may occur: metrical, verbal, syntactical, and conceptual. Obviously, in any given instance more than one kind may be, and usually is, operative, and the likelihood of such overlapping must be borne in mind. Eugenio Asensio has sounded the proper note of caution in these matters:

> La repetición puede afectar a las palabras (paralelismo verbal), a la estructura sintáctica y rítmica (paralelismo estructural), a la significación o concepto (paralelismo mental o semántico o de pensamiento) . . . Entre estos tipos teoricamente diferenciados hay una zona indecisa en que la nomenclatura depende del arbitrio.[13]

VERSIFICATION

We shall begin, at the most fundamental, preverbal level, with Berceo's versification in its two main aspects: as repetition of both rhythm and sound.

ACCENT AND HYPERBATON

Rhythm is a characteristic recurrence of three phenomena: accent, syllabic number, and pause. In regard to the first, as Fitz-Gerald found to be the case in *Santo Domingo,* the only fixed or completely *metrical* accent in our poem falls invariably on the sixth syllable of the hemistich.[14]

12. Webber, *Spanish Ballad,* p. 175.

13. Asensio, *Poética y realdad,* p. 79.

14. John D. Fitz-Gerald, *Versification of the Cuaderna Vía as Found in Berceo's Vida de Santo Domingo de Silos* (New York, 1905), pp. 35–39.

Other accentuation is customary and coincides with the
tonic and secondary accents in the normal pronunciation
of words. Fitz-Gerald calls them *rhetorical* accents, thus
emphasizing their difference of kind and flexibility of position within the hemistich.[15]

An outstanding achievement of the *cuaderna vía* form is
the absolute regularity of the metrical accent, an effect that
is cumulative and that is best apprehended by sustained
(and preferably oral) reading. Bello has noted this well:

> Fácil es ver que los versos en que no se pide más
> acento que la cláusula final, no tienen apariencia
> alguna de ritmo, si se considera cada uno por sí. Para
> que se perciba ritmo, es necesario oír una serie de
> versos, porque solo entonces se hace sentir la recur-
> rencia de un acento a espacios iguales de tiempo.[16]

Moreover, this regular metrical accent usually coincides
with a syntactical pause at the end of each hemistich and
especially at the end of each verse, thus separating and
isolating, as it were, each hemistich. The result is a structure of parallel and independent blocklike units (further
accentuated by the strong terminal and even internal
rhymes), reproducing themselves in a series of larger rhythmic blocks or strophes. Monotony may be avoided by the
wide range of possible variation in the secondary or rhetorical accents. For example: "Que Diós por el su ruégo
. . ." (2c), accented on the second as well as the sixth
syllable; " (E) stáuan marabilládas . . ." (7d), accented on
the first; "Essa Uírgen preciósa . . ." (4a), accented on

15. Different terminology has been used by Carlos Barrera, "El alejandrino castellano," *BH, 20* (1918), 4: "La mayor parte de los versos que nos
ocupan, además de dicho acento *tónico,* tienen otros *rítmicos* en el cuerpo
de los hemistiquios, lo que les da un ritmo constituido por sus cuatro
acentos, de los cuales dos siempre caen en las sextas sílabas; los otros dos
varían entre la primera y la cuarta."

16. Andrés Bello, *Opúsculos gramaticales, 1: Ortología. Arte métrica*
(Madrid, 1890), p. 164.

the third. Such variation in Berceo, however, seems natural or accidental rather than contrived.[17]

Closely related to accentual structure is the grammatical device known as hyperbaton (inversion or alteration of the logical or normal syntax), for its use is to place a word in a position of emphasis or to adjust a series of words to the demands of accent and rhyme. This can best be done in the *cuaderna via* system by making the word to be emphasized coincide with the metrical accent. As Artiles puts it: "lo que importaba a Berceo era colocar las palabras más importantes . . . al final de los hemistiquios, cn la cresta misma de los acentos, para llamar atención sobre ellas." [18] Examples are abundant, and our list is but a sampling:

De vna sancta uirgen quiero *uersificar.*	(1d)
De esta sancta uirgen romançar su *dictado.*	(2b)
Como dize *del apostol* Sant Pablo *la lection.*	(8a)
De Sancta Eugenia era *festiujdat.*	(25b)
Que *de don Iesu Christo* qujso seer *esposa.*	(28b)
Era *de la maestra* Oria muy *querida.*	(70d)
De sanctos hermjtannos vn preçioso *conbiento.*	(83b)
Que *de Ualuanera* fue *abbat consagrado.*	(84d)
Pero *de los reclusos* fue la mayor *partida.*	(92c)
Ca es *del tu serujçio* el Criador *pagado.*	(95d)
Oria, *del poco merito* non ayas [nul] *temor.*	(105b)
Fablaron li a Oria *de Dios buena amjga.*	(127c)
Lecho quiero yo *aspero* . . .	(130a)

17. Artiles (*Berceo*, pp. 103–06) has claimed artistic merit in Berceo's use of the rhythmic accent, which is said to occur in patterns derived from Latin metrics, although it is obvious that such terms as "iamb" and "trochee" no longer designate long and short syllables but rather tonic and atonic ones. Brian Dutton has observed, however, that "Berceo appears to be aware only of the stress on the sixth syllable of each hemistich, and to develop intuitively the musicality of his lines" (*BHS*, 42, 185).

18. Artiles, p. 65.

Fue *de bien grandes lunbres* la çiella *alunbrada.*
Fue *de uirgines muchas* en vn rato *poblada.*   (132bc)
Es *de las sus iornadas* esta *la postremera.*   (167d)
De la su sancta graçia en mj mucha metió.   (198d)

For purposes of emphasis the poet may exploit rhetorical rather than metrical accents. This may be done effectively by placing words requiring emphasis at the two ends of the verse, in symmetrical fashion:

De piedras muy preçiosas toda *engastonada.*   (77c)
Del duelo de la fija estaua muy *lazrada.*   (162b)

Or hyperbaton may be used for emphasis by using the first rhetorical accent of each hemistich, thus achieving a parallel effect: "*Sanctos* fueron sin dubda *e iustos* los parientes" (7a) . Of course it is obvious from some of the examples seen that hyperbaton has uses other than emphasis: rhyme and meter, to name but two.

Finally, several cases of rather extreme hyperbaton may be noted:

Auemos en el prologo mucho detardado.   (10a)
Mas en esto culpados nos seer non deuemos.   (89c)
Cerca anda del cabo Oria de la carrera.   (167b)

LENGTH OF VERSE

Although the regular metrical accent is the dominant rhythmic device, its effect may be varied by alternating the length of the hemistich. For the metrically accented syllable need not coincide—and indeed seldom does—with the final syllable of the hemistich. Fitz-Gerald has succinctly summarized the workings of Berceo's system of versification:

The *cuaderna vía* consists of coplas of four verses in monorime. Each verse consists of two hemistichs. Each hemistich contains seven syllables if the hemi-

stich is grave, or paroxytone (this is the normal hemistich) ; six syllables if the hemistich is acute, or
oxytone; and eight syllables if it is *esdrújulo,* or
proparoxytone.[19]

In *Santa Oria* there are no *esdrújulo* verses (i.e. *esdrújulo* rhymes at the end of the verse) .[20] However, there are
43 first hemistichs that end in an *esdrújulo* word and hence
have 8 syllables. These are the following: *prologo* (10a) ;
catholicos (12a) ; *sopieremos* (19c) ; *virgines* (27a, 29a,
30a, 32a, 41a, 48a, 63c, 66b, 67a, 69c, 73a, 77a, 81a, 119b,
127a, 131a, 197c) ; *martires* (27b, 59c, 62a, 81b, 108a, 109b) ;
reçibiessedes (35c) ; *angeles* (42b, 143c) ; *angelicas* (47b) ;
pennolas (48b) ; *merito* (68a, 105b, 199d) ; *discipula* (73d) ;
disçipulo (84c) ; *apostolos* (86a) ; *talamo* (97c) ; *huespeda*
(122d); *aspero* (130a) ; *arboles* (155b) ; *Dominj* (192b) ;
clerigos (193b) .

Out of 205 strophes, 55 are acute *(i.e.* their second hemistich has only six syllables) and 9 are indeterminable.[21]
The rhymes are as follows: *-ar,* 14 times; *-at,* 9 times; *-on,*
9 times; *-al,* 7 times; *-ir,* 6 times; *-or,* 5 times; *-er,* 3 times;
-az, once; *-ó(io),* once. At the first hemistich there are 15
indeterminables [22] and 23 clear cases of acute endings: 2a,

19. Fitz-Gerald, *Versification,* p. 1.
20. Following Fitz-Gerald (ibid., pp. 10–33) , I exclude as indeterminable words ending in postaccentual *-ia* or *-io,* such as *gracia, Oria, servicio,*
since there is evidence that these endings may have been either mono-
syllabic *(gracia)* or dissyllabic *(graci-a)* and hence could have been either
grave or *esdrújulo.* In *Santa Oria* there are 7 such strophes or 28 verse
endings. At the end of the verse, strophes 35, 97, 111, 151, 172, end in
postaccentual *-ia;* strophes 13 and 112 end in *-io.*
21. Again following Fitz-Gerald *(Versification,* pp. 10–33) . Verses or
hemistichs ending in an accented *-ia* (or, only once in our text, *-io*) may
apparently have been pronounced in either of three different ways: *di-a,
dia, diá.* In the first case the verse or hemistich would be regular or grave;
in the second or third alternatives the result would be acute or oxytone.
The following strophes have indeterminable rhymes: 3, 57, 85, 110, 119,
124, 133, 148, 166. All are in accented *-ia.*
22. The 15 indeterminables at the hemistich are as follows: *yazia* (31a) ,
reluzia (42c) , *Maria* (125a) , *dias* (135b and 136b) , *entendia* (147c) ,

14b, 22c, 24d, 28d, 31b, 41c, 42a, 53c, 81c, 90c, 99b, 110a, 117a, 147d, 151a, 155d, 157c, 189d, 191b, 200c, 204a, 205d.

The total number of "irregular" (either *esdrújulo* or acute) first hemistichs is thus 72 out of a possible 747, or at least 675 regular seven-syllable hemistichs. The total number of irregular (acute) second hemistichs is 220 out of a possible 756, or 556 regular seven-syllable hemistichs. Although the regular seven-verse hemistich is by far the most prevalent, the poet was obviously free to vary the length of his line by either acute or *esdrújulo* words.

PAUSE AND OVERFLOW

As already seen in the previous discussion of accentuation, the metrical accent usually coincides with a syntactical pause in the normal reading of the verse. This is true not only at the end of the strophe [23] and the verse but at the hemistich as well (although the latter is quite understandably not always possible). The infringement of this rule of practice is known as overflow or *encabalgamiento*.[24] It is naturally more frequent between hemistichs of the same verse:

E non quiera uengança tomar del mj peccado.	(2d)
Ruegue a la Gloriosa Madre Sancta Maria.	(3c)
Podrian ualer pocos dineros los sus peannos.	(20d)
Alla ujdieron muchas honrradas proçessiones.	(48d)
Aparesçiolis otra asaz grant compannia.	(57c)
Aquelli que non qujso segujr nulla follia.	(85d)

---

comja (162d), *Garçia* (165a, 167a, and 168a), *tenja* (175b), *Dios* (183c). I also list as indeterminable the conditional *querria* (193c), the ending of which may be either mono- or dissyllabic in our text. Also indeterminable are *dende* (16d) and *ende* (81d), usually but not always apocopated.

23. Artiles, *Berceo*, p. 98: "Entre estrofa y estrofa se levanta siempre, señalando fronteras, la pausa prolongada de un punto final."

24. Defined by Rafael de Balbín, *Sistema de rítmica castellana* (Madrid, 1962), pp. 202–18: *encabalgamiento* "consiste fundamentalmente en el desajuste entre pausa rítmica y pausa sintáctica."

Fasta que sea toda tu ujda acabada.	(98d)
Fasta que a su casa mjsma la traxieron.	(99d)
Espertó ella luego que ellas la dexaron.	(108d)
Que eran bien bestidas todas, e bien calçadas.	(156b)
Todas eran en vna uoluntat acordadas.	(156d)
Avn assaz tenja cosas que uos dezir.	(175b)
Desque murió la fija sancta enparedada.	(186a)
Reçebir Corpus Dominj sagrado enel altar.	(192b)
Vido syn estas otras muy grandes ujsiones.	(202a)

By contrast there is in *Santa Oria* not a single example
of necessary overflow between verses, and hence none between strophes. The end of each verse coincides with a syntactical pause, itself made more emphatic by the metrical
accent and heavy rhyme.[25]

ALLITERATION

We shall now consider the content of these rhythmic
patterns. The most elementary kind of sound repetition is
that of individual letters. Two kinds occur in *Santa Oria:*
(a) Repetition of consonants:

Porque daban al pueblo bever de buen castigo,
Por ende tienen los calices cada uno consigo.   (60ab)

Con sabor de la cosa qujso se leuantar,
Como omne que quiere en carrera entrar.   (159ab)

Double alliteration with "k" and "s":

25. The absence of necessary overflow is also characteristic of the oral
epic tradition, although the tendency is even more pronounced in Berceo.
The difference between the two occurs in the area of so-called unperiodic
overflow—i.e. one which is syntactically unnecessary. In oral epic, connec-
tions between verses are frequently paratactic; verses which are syntactically independent are strung together by free association of ideas. By
contrast, although Berceo's verses can usually stand alone, further additions
within the same sentence are linked by some kind of grammatical device,
such as subordinate or coordinate conjunction. Cf. the discussion of this
problem in the *Chanson de Roland,* in Nichols, pp. 20–24.

> *Q*ue fue*ss*e *q*ui*s q*ui*s*ie*ss*e folgar a *s*u po*s*ada.   (189b)
> *C*on *s*abor de la *c*osa *q*uj*s*o *s*e leuantar.   (159a)

Artiles points out the exquisite sleeping quality of the *n* sound in:

> En*s*o*nn*o esta due*nn*a vn *s*ue*nn*o desseado.   (188c)

(b) Parallelism of vocalic patterns. A sequence of sounds may be echoed in the following verse.

> *En el* no*n*br*e* del padre qu*e n*o*s* qu*i*so cri*a*r,
> *Et* d*e* d*on* I*e*su Christo qu*e n*o*s* u*j*no salu*a*r.   (1ab)

> Non se part*ia* Dios d*ella en* nj*n*gu*n*a *sa*z*o*n
> Ca siempre ten*ja ella en* El *s*u cora*ç*on.   (115cd)

> *Nunca tan* blanca uj*d*o *njn* toca *njn* cam*j*sa,
> *Nunca ta*l cosa ouo *njn* Genua *njn* Pisa.   (118cd)

Such examples, it seems to me, show a sensitivity to musical effect.

RHYMES

This is the most consistent and important kind of sound repetition in the poem. As Fitz-Gerald found in *Santo Domingo*, "from, and including, the rhyme vowel to the end of the verse we must always have full rhyme."[26] Double use of the same word within the single strophe is prohibited, although it does happen three times in our text: *podedes* (6ac), *entrar* (159bd), *oyestes* (197cd). Of course, the same word with different meanings seems to have been permissible. There are six such examples in our text: *contadas* (46ad), *claridat* (93bc), *ujno* (116cd), *entrar* (149bd), *pasada* (169ac), *soffrir* (175cd).

By the same token, the rhyme was supposed to change from strophe to strophe. However, some interesting patterns can be noted. Strophes 157–60 all end in acute

26. Fitz-Gerald, *Versification*, p. 97.

rhymes: *-ar, -ir, -ar, -ar,* as do strophes 191–95: *-al, -ar, -ar, -ir, -ar.* Only once is an identical grave rhyme continued for eight consecutive verses: *-ado* (95–96). Berceo also achieves musical effect by reproducing only the assonance in consecutive strophes (or the assonance and only part of the consonance), with an effect much like the epic poets: *-ado* and *-ada* (9–10), *-enda* and *-ientes* (15–16), *-on* and *-ones* (23–24), *-ana* and *-ada* (62–63), and so on.

From his thorough study of *Santo Domingo,* Fitz-Gerald observes that "the rhyme is not at all concerned with the vowel, semivowel, or consonant that may *precede* the accented rhyme vowel." [27] However, Berceo often does resort to this in our poem, and with luxuriant results. To give but a sampling: *razones, cabazones, sazones* (202b-d); *mortal, por tal* (135cd); *casiella, çiella, siella, maxiella* (137); *tribulaçion, oraçion* (138ab).

Imperfect rhymes are rare in our text. I have found the following: *digas, amjgas, agujsas, predigas* (36); *njnguna, luna, alguna, Amunna* (50 [presumably the last rhyme is pronounced *ñ*]); *lazerio, mjnjsterio, salterio, Euangelio* (112). Concerning the first, Lida de Malkiel's emendation is probably correct: [28] **ajigas,* a metathesis used by Berceo (cf. mod. ast. *xiga,* "guija") for the better known *aguijas* (cf. "sedas aguijosas," 130a), which the copyists restored and interpreted as *aguissas,* since the phonetic difference between *s* and *j* was slight at that period and led to frequent confusion.[29] Lida de Malkiel does not mention the other two cases of imperfect rhyme, probably because the infringements are really minor and reduced by the like quality of the dissident consonants, *n* and *nn* [*ñ*] being nasals and *r* and *l* liquids. There are but three further examples—all rhymes with *Oria: Oria, gloria, nouja, es-*

27 Ibid., p. 97. His italics.
28. Lida de Malkiel, *RPH, 10,* 30.
29. See Ramón Menéndez Pidal, *Manual de gramática histórica española* (11th ed. Madrid, 1962), pp. 119–20.

coria (97) ; *Oria, gloria, ujctoria, mjsericordia* (111 and not 110, as Lida de Malkiel noted) ; *Oria, memoria, gloria, querimonia* (151). Lida de Malkiel speculates that the poet simply ran out of rhymes. However, this did not prevent Berceo from trying one final time, with better success: *Oria, gloria, istoria, memoria* (172).

Internal rhymes (affecting only the first hemistichs) are frequent in our text, most often involving the repetition of the accented vowel (assonance) but also consonance or even the same word: *padre/madre* (4cd), *fijos/fija* (15ab), *tierra/tierras* (18cd), *poco/pocos* (20bd), *adelante/delante* (57ab), *siniestras/diestras* (58bc), *ella/ellas* (101ab), *tiempo/tiempo* (102bd), *della/ella* (115cd), *plogujesse/podiesse* (121bc), *otras/cosas* (126cd), *oliuos/oliuas* (141bc), *eran/ujdieran* (143bd), *duenna/duenna* (161d-62a), *todo/todo* (170cd).

VERBAL RECURRENCE

The most unsophisticated kind of verbal repetition in Berceo is the simple re-use of the same word, instead of seeking out an adequate synonym. His limited range of descriptive vocabulary, or perhaps his lack of concern for such matters, causes him, for example, to repeat the adjective "precioso" three times within seven verses (*SOr* 58–59), or the verb "querer" ten times in the course of eleven consecutive verses (192c–195a). Such a mannerism finds a parallel in the consistent use of basic ideological terms (*lazerio, carne, merito*), where the author cannot risk being misunderstood. Rather than a major sin against doctrinal clarity, Berceo prefers a venial one against stylistic originality. Or, more likely, he uses the term to which he is accustomed or which happens to emerge in his accoustic memory.

Repetition of the same word, however, was a rhetorical procedure well known to medieval authors. Several kinds may be distinguished.

ANAPHORA

In Nebrija's definition, "anaphora es cuando começa-
mos muchos versos con una misma palabra." [30]

> *Todas* uenjan gradosas a Oria resçebir,
> *Todas* bien agujsadas de calçar e de uestir.   (142bc)

> *Bien* lo decoró esso como todo lo al;
> *Bien* gelo contó ella, non lo aprendió él mal.
>
> (171ab)

> *Aun* non me querria, sennores, espedir;
> *Avn* fincan cosiellas que uos e de dezir.   (185ab)

The verses may be consecutive and within the same
strophe, as here, or they may be consecutive but in different strophes, in which case anaphora acts as a linking force:

> *Trayan* en todas cosas todas tres igualdat.   (126d)
> *Trayan* estas tres uirgines vna noble lechiga.   (127a)
> *Vido* en poca hora vna grant vision.   (26d)
> *Vido* tres sanctas uirgines . . .   (27a)

Or, again within the wide limits of Nebrija's definition,
the verses need not be consecutive, as when Berceo begins
strophes 141, 142, and 144 with "Vido," or, again, strophes
155 and 156 with "Vidi." It will be noted, however, that
although the elements of anaphora are separated by four
verses, they occur in parallel situations.

Departing from Nebrija's definition, we note that anaphora may also occur in consecutive verses at (or near) the
hemistich:

> En esta pleytesia non *qujero* detardar,
> Sy por bien lo tobierdes *quiero* uos destaiar.
> A la fin de la duenna me *quiero* acostar.   (160a-c)

---

30. Nebrija, *Gramática*, IV, 7; quoted in Artiles, *Berceo*, p. 82.

Or it may occur within the same verse, at the beginning of each hemistich:

> Aujalis poco grado a los despertadores,
> *Siquiera* a la madre, *siquier* a las sorores.   (146ab)

> *De* campos grant amchura *de* flores grant mercado.
>   (155c)

> *Tal era* la conpanna, *tal era* el logar.   (157a)

The various possibilities may be compounded:

> *Nunca* tan blanca ujdo *njn* toca *njn* camjsa,
> *Nunca* tal cosa ouo *njn* Genua *njn* Pisa.   (118cd)

PARONOMASIA

This figure is closely related to anaphora.[31] Artiles differentiates them adequately: "Si la anáphora repite una misma palabra sin cambios morphológicos, la paronomasia emplea palabras que pueden ser de distinta morfología, pero que, al menos fonéticamente, guardan entre sí un cierto parentesco o semejanza."[32] Examples are numerous and always occur in pairs:

> *Enparedada* era; yazia entre *paredes.*   (6b)
> Como era *preçiosa* mas que piedra *preçiada.*   (9c)
> *Principes* de los pueblos son omnes *principales.* (87b)
> E ferla *conpannera* de *conpannas* meiores.   (113d)
> *Relunbró* la confita de *relumbror* doblado.   (122c)
> Esto ten tu por *signo,* por çertera *sennal.*   (135a)
> Queredes que uos *fable;* yo non puedo *fablar.*   (174a)
> Vna *ujsion ujdo* . . .   (164b)
> *Ensonno* esta duenna vn *suenno* deseado.   (188c)

31. Curtius, *European Literature and the Latin Middle Ages,* p. 44, points out that it was conventional to regard anaphora as a figure of language rather than a figure of thought. Paronomasia is similarly an "acoustic conceit," a "play on words in the stricter sense," a "figure of sound" (p. 300). Yet, although certainly not a figure of thought, it is an "intellectual product" relying on puns and the like and thus qualifies for a "place in conceptistic theory."

32. Artiles, p. 84.

Paronomasia may affect more than one verse:

> Yo *sobi* por algunas, esto muchas uegadas,
> Por tal *suben* las almas que son auenturadas. (39cd)

In another instance two different groups are used and placed in chiastic order:

> De lo que tu *temes* non seras *enbargada,*
> Non abras nul *enbargo,* non te *temas* por nada.
> (107ab)

Artiles amplifies his definition with the help of Curtius,[33] who speaks not only of "various inflectional forms of the same word and of its derivatives but also of words perfectly or approximately homophonous." Thus we may list under paronomasia the pun on Oria's name: "Nonbre auja de oro, *Oria era llamada*" (9d). Later the figure is expanded both acoustically and metaphorically:

> "Sy como tu me dizes, dixoli Sancta *Oria,*
> A mj es prometida esta tamanna gloria,
> Luego en esti talamo querria seer nouja,
> Non querria del *oro* tornar a la *escoria.*" (97)

Finally, there are several cases of repetition of the same word with different meanings:

> Auja *ujda* lazrada qual entender podedes,
> Sy su *ujda* leyerdes assy lo prouaredes. (6cd)

In the first instance it means the life lived; in the second the reference is to the written life or to a literary genre. Similarly:

> Mas quando no lo quiere el Criador *soffrir,*
> Lo que a el plogujere es todo de *soffrir.* (175cd)

The translations are, respectively, to "permit" and to "suffer."

---

33. Ibid., p. 84; Curtius, *European Literature,* p. 278.

RHYTHMIC PATTERNS AND THE
BINARY EXPRESSION

A rhythmic pattern is a group of words related by position within the metrical structure. Patterns which repeat "a given essential idea" without regard for the specific meaning of the passage in which they occur are known as formulas. Rather than specific words, however, in Berceo it is more often patterns which recur and which relate new ideas in a particular way, both rhythmically and conceptually.[34] It is of course permissible to speak of metrical causation, in the same way that hyperbaton, for example, disrupts the normal order of the verse in order to meet the exigencies of rhyme and accent. In Berceo the six-syllable hemistich and the parallel verse encourage certain patterns of speech. Yet the widespread occurence of such kinds of expression among primitive poets of many nations suggests profound mental habits, of which versification can be regarded as but a manifestation and not a final explanation.

By far the most frequent kind of rhythmic pattern in Berceo occurs in pairs and may be referred to as binary expression, dual construction, bifurcation, bimembration, and the like. Such word-pairs in Berceo have as their basic unit either the hemistich or the single verse. Moreover, their relationship is often emphasized by their coincidence with accent or by some other parallelistic device. The pairs may be either (a) synonymous (strict or, more often, approximate), (b) antithetical or contrastive, or (c) somewhere in between, with distinct and often complementary meanings.

34. Ruth House Webber (*Spanish Ballad*) expresses this distinction by dividing her study of the *romancero* into (1) formulas, and (2) repetition.

PAIRS OF SYNONYMS[35]

In *Santa Oria* these occur only within the hemistich or
in the single verse. In the first case they occur as nouns:
"lazerio e quebranto" (173c) ; as verbs: "resçibir e tomar"
(192c); as adverbs: "de amor e de grado" (66b) ; and as
adjectives: "flaca e muy lazrada" (117c) , "non pobres njn
mendiga" (127b) , "grant amor e conplida" (182b) , "triste
e desarrada" (169d) , "alegres e pagadas" (46b) .[36] Or, just
as they occupy the whole hemistich, they may also require
the entire verse:

Tenja se por *guarida* e por muy *confortada*.   (186d)
Estava *atordida en grant desarramiento*.   (65c)
"Lo que tu tanto *temes, e estás desmedrida,*
Que los çielos son *altos, enfiesta* la subida."   (106ab)

Nouns are frequent in this type of construction:

Ca abian enel *folgura,* enel grant *conplimjento.* (45d)
Cayo vna grant *fiesta,* vn *dia sennalado.*   (188a)
Qual *gloria* reçibiemos e quales *gualardones.*   (34d)
Ca estaua en grant *gloria,* en *sabroso logar.*   (145c)
Ca estaua en grant *gloria,* entre *buenos sennores.*
                                                     (146c)

35. Although Berceo is especially inclined to use his synonyms in pairs,
at one point (191c–192b) , within the space of five verses, he gives no less
than 5 different synonyms for "to take Communion": "prender . . . el
çeuo spirital"; "prender el cuerpo de don Christo"; "comulgar"; "reçibir
Corpus Dominj sagrado"; "essy . . . resçibir e tomar."
36. Binary nouns and adjectives are the most characteristic patterns of
speech in Berceo and always occur in the second hemistich. By far the
most frequent formulas of this kind are the synonymous *alegre e pagada*
(*Signos* 50c, *Milagros* 213d, *SMil* 153a, and passim) and *triste e desarrada*
(*Loores* 138a, *SMil* 381c, and passim) . Other such approximately synonymous patterns are *alegres e gozosos* (*Duelo* 65b) , *precioso e cabdal* (*Duelo*
90b) , *pobre e menguada* (*Duelo* 122d) , *uerde e sano* (*SDom* 621b) ,
sannoso e irado (*Signos* 31a) . Binaries are also common in the *Chanson
de Roland* (*prozdom e vaillant, Rollant e Oliver*) and usually occur in
the second hemistich. Cf. Nichols, p. 18. Ruth House Webber gives a
generous sampling of binary patterns in medieval literature (pp. 218–23) .

Berceo is especially prolific in bimembrations designating
people, usually groups:

Visto este *convento,* esta sancta *mesnada.*   (63a)
Preguntó a las *virgines,* essa sancta *mesnada.*   (69c)
El *coro* de las virgines, *procession* tan honrrada.   (63c)
El *coro* de las virgines una fermosa *az.*   (67a)
Vido grandes *conpannas,* fermosa *criazon.*   (80b)
Conpannera es nuestra e nuestra *morador.*   (73c)
Todos estos son *martires,* vnas *nobles personas.* (81b)
Vidi y grandes *yentes* de *personas* honrradas.   (156a)
Monges e hermjtannos vn general *conujento.*   (178c)

Finally, the poet may use verbal expressions in the forma-
tion of such binaries:

Qujso *dormir* vn poco, *tomar consolaçion.*   (26c)
Fizo cruz en su fruente, santiguo su mollera.   (176d)
Assy *mandas tus carnes* e assy *las agujsas* . . .   (36c)
Martiriaua las carnes, dandolis grant lazerio.   (112a)
Suffria grant astinençia, ujuja ujda lazrada.   (21c)

Under the title of "gemination" (D. Alonso) and following distinctions found in Geoffroi de Vinsauf, Artiles gives
a separate presentation of binary adjectives.[37] However,
there does not seem to be any essential difference in literary
method between, say, the binary adjectives "flaca e muy
lazrada" and the nouns "planto e duelo." Yet there is a
type of synonymous variation that seems to have escaped
the notice of critics and that is yet common in Berceo:
apposition or epithets.

EPITHETS

Aside from such elementary kinds of apposition as "Oria
la seror" or, more picturesquely, "Oria toca negrada"

37. Artiles, *Berceo,* p. 115; G. de Vinsauf, *Poetria nova,* verses 1770–74.

(21a), the exclusive practice in the poem is to herald the proper name at the front of the verse. The appositive expression then follows and occupies the entire second hemistich:

> Todas tres fueron martires en poquiella edat:
> Agatha en Catanna, *essa rica ciudat,*
> Olalia en Melerida, *njnna de grant beltat.*   (27b-d)

Holy people introduced for the first time often receive this treatment, especially if they are only met once and in passing:

> Bartolomeo, *ducho de escriujr passiones;*
> Don Gomez de Massiella *que daua bien raçiones.*
>
> (55cd)

> Don Xemeno terçero, *vn uezino leal*
> Del uarrio de Uellayo fue esti natural;
> Galindo, *su criado, qual el bien otro tal,*
> Que sopo de bien mucho e sabia poco mal.   (56)

> Conosçió la reclusa en essa proçession
> Al obispo don Sancho, *un precioso varon;*
> Con el a don Garcia, *su leal conpannon,*
> Que sirvió a don Christo de firme coraçon.   (61)

> Urraca li dixieron *muger buena conplida.*   (70b)

> Con Iusta su disçipula, *sierua del Criador.*   (73d)

> Alli es Sant Esteuan *el que fue apedreado,*
> Sant Lorente *el que Çesar ouo despues assado,*
> Sant Viçent *el caboso de Ualerio criado.*   (82a-c)

> Don Sancho li dixieron, *baron fue massellano.*   (144b)

El buen abbat don Pedro, *persona de buen tiento.*

(178b)

It is clear that the apposition does not usually add much
knowledge about the person; or if it does, that information
is general and known to all (e.g. the stoning of St. Stephen). Perhaps this was merely a quick way to complete
the line, for Berceo had to whittle out four difficult rhymes
per verse. There are, however, other aspects to consider.
The holy people, about many of whom Berceo probably
received no information from the source except the bare
name, nevertheless receive the consideration of a full verse.
Their name is, as it were, balanced by an epithet of
praise.[38] Perhaps for Berceo this was a matter of devotion
or simple courtesy. Moreover, praise of saintliness served
an important propagandistic or didactic function.

In conversations apposition may form an integral part
of the dramatic situation. Mary announces herself as: " 'Yo
so Sancta Maria *la que tu mucho quieres*' " (125a). This
is the beginning of a vision; perception is unclear and further identification is needed. Similarly, during Oria's agony
Amunna tries to arouse the daughter from her delirium:
" 'Rescibe a don Munno, *el tu amo honrrado*' " (150c).
Moreover, Oria's name is often accompanied by apposition:

Don Oria la reclusa *de Dios mucho amada.*   (49a)
Fablaron li a Oria *de Dios buena amjga.*   (127c)

38. The same technique may be seen in the epic (see *Mio Cid:* "Martín
Antolínez, el Burgalés conplido"), where it seems to serve the same celebrative function as in Berceo. Artiles (p. 242) finds that this practice did
not have much influence on Berceo: "Este caudal de epítetos que inunda
el *Mio Cid* y otras gestas, apenas tiene una escasa presencia en el Mester
de Clerecía." This observation, made only with reference to direct borrowings of content ("una fardida lanza," etc.), is hardly accurate if one
considers the high number of epithets in *Santa Oria* that resemble the
epic formulas in structure or rhythm.

> . . . la reclusa, *que auja nonbre Oria.* (35a)
> Dixol la Gloriosa: *"Oria la mj lazrada . . ."* (134a)

Amunna is also a "cosa de Dios amada" (162a). In the case
of God, the epithet of praise also elaborates an important
aspect of His being:

> . . . don Christo, *de quien todo bien mana.* (33b)
> El Rey de los reyes, *Sennor de los sennores.* (113a)
> Dios nos dé la su graçia *el buen Rey spirital.* (205c)

The opening invocation is especially impressive in this
respect:

> En el nonbre del Padre *que nos quiso criar,*
> Et de don Iesu Christo *qui nos ujno saluar,*
> E del Spiritu Sancto, *lumbre de confortar.* (1a-c)

Berceo's other appositive technique consists in following
the name of the person by a whole verse. This second
verse may follow upon the shorter kind of hemistich apposition just studied:

> Con el a don Garcia, su leal conpannon,
> *Que siruió a don Christo de firme coraçon.* (61cd)

Or it may occur alone:

> Reffirian con los cuentos al mortal enemigo
> *Que engannó a Eva con un astroso figo.* (60cd)

This kind of appositive verse is usually linked by the simple relative "Que" (cf. 28b, 43d, 56d, 83cd, 84d, 87d, 92b,
92d) or by the verb "to be":

> Era de la maestra Oria muy querida. (70d)
> Cosas eran angelicas con blancas uestiduras. (47b)

Berceo consistently places complete appositive verses in the
fourth verse or, much less frequently, in the second. They
never occur in either the first or third verses.

BINARY EXPRESSIONS OF CONTRAST

These approximate synonyms just studied do not greatly expand knowledge of the thing or person named; rather, as it were, they celebratively reaffirm them in their being. However, Berceo's habit of thinking and speaking in binaries may have as a goal the expression not of an entity but rather of a whole class or dimension of things: "de noche e de dia" (3d, 112b, 124d), "durmiendo e velando" (72d). These are more concrete ways of saying "always," of expressing the whole dimension of time by stating two extremes conceived as antonymous. This temporal dimension can be expanded to cosmic proportions (205d) through the contrastive pairs "alla" (heaven) and "aquj" (earth).[39] And the whole universe of men can be evoked by the opposites "justos e peccadores" (113b). A simpler way of doing this, especially when there is no convenient antonym at hand, is to contrast a term with "everything else": "Que para el su serujcio fuesse, que para al non" (14c). All of the possible ways of life are included here, as in the following: "Guarda esta palonba, todo lo al olujda" (37b). The more abstract concept of "everything" is rendered as "que era o que non" (187c).

An important goad to this way of thinking was furnished by the popular medieval Christian ways of conceiving the universe in terms of static, mutually exclusive opposites. The famous dictum from the *Chanson de Roland* is a good example: "Paiens ont tort e Chrestïens ont dreit." Good

---

39. Further examples: "njn tardi njn ayna" (104d), "ever"; "njn poco njn mucho" (193d), "not at all." Medieval Romance literature shows a proliferation of such antithetical locutions. Among those listed for Old Spanish by Ruth House Webber (pp. 222–23) are the following: *paz y guerra, mozos y viejos, cristianos y moros, grandes e chicos, tierra y mar, amigo y enemigo, muchos y pocos.* In Berceo *Loores* 227–29 is constructed on a series of such contrasts: *vivos y passados, pacificos y irados, noches e dias, flacos y valientes, andantes y iaçientes, estantes y dormientes.*

and evil, heaven and hell, these are recurrent didactic patterns of thinking in Berceo: [40]

> Syempre en bien punaron, partieron se de mal. (11c)
> Que sopo de bien mucho e sabia poco mal.   (56d)
> Estauan en grant dubda si era mal o bien.   (148d)

This exclusive kind of thinking may help to explain the
absence of any kind of joy in Oria's earthly existence (her
visions are *super*terrestrial). Heaven is pure joy and this
mortal life is unmitigated pain:

> Vido se alongada de muy grande dulçor,
> Auja muy grande cuyta e sobeio dolor.   (109cd)

> Toujeron en el mundo la carne apremjda,
> Agora son en gloria en letiçia conplida.   (54cd)

> . . . "¡Ay, mezqujna! estaua en grant gloria,
> Por que me despartaron so en grant querimonia."
> (151cd)

> O si sodes en pena o sodes ende salida.   (190d)

Berceo is obviously fond of giving a longer, two-verse development to this important contrast between heaven and
the world. It is really an arbitrary matter whether this kind
of technique be called verbal repetition or structural parallelism or even conceptual parallelism. Obviously all are
operative.

---

40. The close connection between antithesis and didacticism has been
noted in Alain de Lille by G. de Lage (*Alain de Lille,* p. 158), who further relates the two to verbal play and punning: "il semble qu'il y ait
une sorte de connivence entre l'antithèse et l'intention didactique; ce
trope permet à un maître de souligner efficacement sa pensée, d'étayer
fortement l'essentiel avec des oppositions tranchées, de marquer de nettes
distinctions, dans le domaine moral surtout—comme aussi de jouer avec
les mots et de se livrer à toutes les subtilités verbales qu'aimait le XIIe
siècle."

Other binary contrasts are:

> En cuita yazia Oria *dentro* en su casiella;
> Estaua vn grant conuento *de fuera* de la çiella.
>
> (137ab)

> La obra *començada* bien la quiero *conplir*.   (185c)

> Yo *ganaré* y mucho, uos nada non *perdredes*.   (74d)

Finally, while in heaven, it is remarked that Oria can only hear but not see:

> Conosçió la uoz Oria, *entendió* las senneras,
> Mas *ueer* non la podió por njngunas maneras. (75cd)

> *Oyo fablar* a Christo en essi buen conujento;
> Mas non podió *ueerlo* a todo su taliento.   (88bc)

> Fablolis Dios del çielo, la uoz bien la *oyeron,*
> La su maiestat grande, pero non la *ujeron.* (101cd)

COMPLEMENTARY BINARIES

These are pairs of words or expressions neither synonymous nor contrastive; the meanings are simply distinct. Usually some kind of contrast or comparison is implied, but it is relative and not, as above, absolute. They may require only one hemistich: "la hora nj el dia" (110a) ; "njn el sol njn la luna" (50b) ; "grande e preciosa" (59b) . However, the binaries are usually reinforced in their meaning by a parallelistic treatment that extends the length of the verse:

> Sy *ante* fuera buena fue *despues* muy meior.   (18a)
> Sy *ante* fue en cuyta *despues* fue mas coitada. (169b)
> Los martires *delante,* la freyra *en su guia.*   (57b)
> Mucho otra buen *lego,* mucho buen *ordenado.*   (82d)
> Dexemos de la *madre,* en la *fija* tornemos.   (19a)

Nunca lo ouo *ujsto* njl *tanso* de la mano. (144c)
Que nos *salue* las almas, *perdone* los peccados. (183d)

Finally, the binaries may extend to two or more verses, in which case their relationship is again stressed by some kind of parallel position:

Enpeçaron las uirgines lazradas a *sobir,*
Enpeçolas la duenna reclusa a *segujr.* (41ab)

Que *suffrieron* por Christo mucho amargo ujento
Por *ganar* a las almas ujda e guarimjento. (83cd)

Auja en ella nonbres de *omnes de grant ujda* . . .
Pero de los *reclusos* fue la mayor partida. (92a,c)

It is by now obvious that, as in Berceo's earlier works, binary patterns of expression are extremely frequent in *Santa Oria.* Their semantic import may be neatly summarized by Asensio's remark that "la dualidad unas veces es oposición y antítesis, otras veces plenitud complimentaria." [41] Such patterns, he continues, are characteristic of the primitive poetry of all nations. D. Alonso's formulation—especially suggestive when placed within the context of Oria's struggles—may serve to explain such contrasts: "Quien dijo que la vida humana era lucha, dijo que era bimembración: toda la vida es emparejamiento." [42] In Berceo such rhythmic patterns of thought seem prereflective and possibly relate to so-called primitive ritual or liturgy or work or play or dance habits.[43] But it is certain that binary patterns reveal a conscious literary effort based on medieval rhetorical practices: the art of repetition and

41. Asensio, *Poética y realdad,* p. 78.
42. Quoted ibid. In reference to synonymous or complementary pairs, Asensio (p. 78) recalls the biblical commentator who noted that, beginning with Genesis and Noah's ark, "les objets, les végétaux, les animaux, les concepts se présentent en couples solennels."
43. One may consult Asensio, pp. 75 ff.

variation (*amplificatio*) or, better yet, variation within repetition.

PARALLELISM

Recurrence may extend beyond the individual verse and even beyond the strophe. Such instances may involve repetition of specific words, but the essential kind of repetition is conceptual and is often emphasized by some kind of rhythmic or syntactic parallel structure. The following may be noted in *Santa Oria:*

(1) *Synonymous parallelism* (repetition of content in parallel or consecutive position but with distinct snytax) :

> Ponjan toda femençia en fer a Dios seruiçio . . .
> A Dios ponjan delante en todo su offiçio.   (13b,d)

> Que ouo con su carne baraia e contienda,
> Por consentir al cuerpo nunca solto la rienda. (15cd)

> Los pueblos de la tierra fazian li grant honor,
> Salia a luengas tierras la su buena loor.   (18cd)

(2) *Antithetical parallelism* (contrastive context) :

> Si lis dio otros fijos non lo dize la leyenda,
> Mas diolis vna fija de spiritual fazienda.   (15ab)

> O sy uos dieron luego en el cielo logar,
> O uos fizieron ante a la puerta musar.   (195cd)

(3) *Syntactical parallelism* (repetition of the same scheme of composition) :

> En el nonbre del Padre que nos quiso criar,
> Et de don Iesu Christo qui nos ujno saluar,
> E del Spiritu Sancto, lumbre de confortar.   (1a-c)

> Amunna fue su madre, escripto lo tenemos;
> Garcia fue el padre, en letra lo auemos.   (4cd)

Era esta reclusa uaso de caridat,
Templo de paçiençia e de humjldat.   (22ab)

Enpeçaron las uirgines lazradas a sobir,
Enpeçolas la duenna reclusa a segujr.   (41ab)

Salieron recivirla con responsos doblados,
Fueron abraçarla con los braços alçados.   (64ab)

Las letras de los justos de mayor sanctidat
Paresçian mas leybles, de mayor claridat;
Los otras mas so rienda de menor claridat,
Eran mas tenebrosas, de grant obscuridat.   (93)

Todas eran iguales de vna calidat,
De vna captenençia e de vna edat.   (126ab)

The unity of the Garden of Olives description is assured
by the parallel (but not synonymous) statements:

Ca estaua en grant gloria en sabroso logar.   (145c)
Ca estaua en grant gloria entre buenos sennores.
                                                     (146c)

The syntax may be chiastically ordered:

Estos son los nuestros padres, cabdiellos generales,
Principes de los pueblos son omnes principales.
                                                     (87ab)

The syntactical arrangement may be symmetrical:

Cantadas las matinas, la liçençia soltada . . . (189a)

Other repetitions are less difficult to achieve but important nevertheless. We shall call them:

(4) *Morphological parallelism* (mere repetition of
units, usually verbs, that are morphologically identical or
similar) *in parallel positions:*

Moujósse la polonba, *començó* de uolar,
Suso contra los çielos *començó* de pujar.   (40ab)

Abrió ella los oios, *cató* enderredor,
Non *ujdo* a las martires, *ouo* muy mal sabor.   (109ab)

Bien *conosçió* a Oria, *sopo* su poridat,
En todo quanto *dixo dixo* toda verdat   (204cd)

"Ante de pocos dias *enfermarás* muy mal,
Serás fuerte enbargada de enfermedat mortal,
Qual nunca la oujste *terrásla* bien por tal."   (135b-d)

"*Veráste* en grant quexa, de muerte *serás* cortada,
Serás a pocos dias desti mundo passada;
Irás do tu codiçias . . ."   (136a-c)

This is the controlling device for the famous death scene:

Alcó la mano diestra de fermosa manera,
Fizo cruz en su fruente, *santiguó* su mollera.

Alçó ambas las manos, *juntólas* en igual
Como quj riende graçias al buen Rey spirital;
Cerró oios e boca la reclusa leal,
Rendió a Dios la alma, nunca mas *sintió* mal.

                                    (176c–177d)

(5) *Conceptual parallelism* (repetition of thought content). Several examples of this have already been noted. However, this kind of repetition has a special and frequent function in Berceo: the linking of strophe to strophe.[44]

44. Artiles (*Berceo*, p. 98) makes an important observation concerning the grammatical and syntactical independence of each strophe: "Los tetrástrofos de Berceo nunca se unen por nexos gramaticales. Cada estrofa, y con frequencia cada verso, se cierra sobre sí misma en unidades sintácticas completas, con sentido cabal. Los nexos interestróficos de Berceo no son gramaticales. Entre estrofa y estrofa se levanta siempre, señalando

The following variations of this procedure may be found in *Santa Oria:*
(a) Repetition of the first hemistich of the final verse in the first hemistich of the following verse:

El coro de las virgines, procession tan honrrada,
Salieron rescivirla de volumtat pagada.

Salieron recivirla con responsos doblados.   (63d–64a)

Yo so la que tu ruegas de noche e de dia.

Yo so Sancta Maria la que tu mucho quieres.
    (124d–125a)

Vidi y tales cosas por que so muy pagada.   (154d)

Vidi y logar bueno . . .   (155a)

Vidi y grandes yentes . . .   (156a)

Recontógelo todo a Munno su querido;
El decoró lo todo como bien entendido.

fronteras, la pausa prolongada de un punto final. Berceo recurre a otros nexos que no tienen nada que ver con la gramática." The ways of linking may vary in form, but they all involve essentially the repetition or recapitualation of content. Artiles continues: "Pudiera describirse como un trasiego de contenido, como un trasvasamiento de elementos de una a otra estrofa. Parece como si la estrofa primera, manteniendo su independencia sintáctica, rebosara sobre la siguiente vertiendo parte de su caudal." This usually happens in the following ways: "El trasvasamiento se detiene siempre en el primer verso del secundo tetrástrofo; pero la materia trasvasada puede afectar, preferentemente, al último o al penúltimo verso del tetrástrofo primero, pero, a veces, también a otras verso o a toda la estrofa. Este trasiego de una estrofa a otra se verifica repitiendo en la segunda algunos elementos de la primera, unas veces con repetición literal y exacta; otras, con algún leve cambio de palabras o, simplemente, de orden" (pp. 98–99). S. Nichols shows ("*Chanson de Roland,*" p. 17) how such a "hesitation-step" progression of ideas caracteriza the linking process between sentences as well as *laisses.*

> *Bien lo decoró esso* como todo lo al;
> Bien gelo contó ella, non lo aprendió el mal.
>
> (170c–171b)

(b) The repetition may affect only the first hemistich of the *penultimate* verse:

> *Vido a su marido* omne de sancta ujda,
> Padre de la reclusa que yazia mal tenjda.
>
> *Vido a don Garçia* qui fuera su marido.
>
> (164c–165a)

(c) The *entire* penultimate verse may be repeated in the first hemistich of the following strophe:

> *Bien conosçió a Oria, sopo su poridat,*
> En todo quanto dixo, dixo toda uerdat.
>
> *Dello sopo de Oria,* de la madre lo al.
>
> (204c–205a)

(d) Or the entire penultimate verse may be repeated in the entire first verse of the following strophe:

> *"Todo esto que uees a ti es otorgado,*
> Ca es del tu serujçio el Criador pagado.
>
> *Todo esti adobo a ti es comendado."*   (95c–96a)

(e) Or, extending Artiles' observation, the repetition may flow beyond the first verse of the second strophe:

> *De vna sancta uirgen quiero uersificar.*
>
> *Quiero* en mj uegez, maguer so ya cansado,
> *De esta sancta uirgen romançar* su dictado.   (1d–2b)
>
> *"Que non abras enbargo* en toda tu uenjda.

De lo que tu temes *non seras enbargada,*
Non abras nul enbargo, non te temas por nada."

(106d–107b)

Conosçio la uoz Oria, entendio las senneras,
Mas ueer non la podio por njngunas maneras.

La az era muy luenga, esso la enbargaua,
Que non podia ueerla ca en cabo estaua.   (75c–76b)

(f) The repetition may affect only the first verse of each strophe:

> *En cuita yazia Oria* dentro en su casiella.   (137a)
> *Yaziendo la enferma* en tal tribulaçion . . .   (138a)

(g) The repetition, as in many examples already cited, may be of only one or two identical words:

> Non fazia a sus *carnes* nulla mjsericordia.
> Martiriaua las *carnes,* dandolis grant lazerio.

(111d–112a)

However, it will be noted that the repetition involves not only the word "carne" but also the whole idea of asceticism. The final step in this direction may be referred to as:

(h) Synonymous linking. Here the repetition is that of content and involves no reproduction of specific words or phrases. Berceo simply stops to recapitulate before taking another step forward:

> Desque mudó los dientes luego a pocos annos
> Pagauase muy poco de los seglares pannos;
> *Vistió otros uestidos de los monges calannos,*
> Podrian ualer pocos dineros los sus peannos.

> *Desemparó el mundo Oria toca negrada.*   (20–21a)

En muy poquiello rato al cuerpo la tornaron,
Espertó ella luego que ellas la dexaron.

Abrió ella los oios, cató enderredor.   (108c–109a)

Though the expression is different, the meanings are obviously synonymous. Berceo's habit of summarizing a situation before continuing with the progress of the narration
may be seen in the following:

Estando enel arbol estas duennas contadas,
Sus palomas en manos alegres e pagadas,
Vieron enel çielo . . .   (46a-c)

Visto este convento, esta sancta mesnada,
Fue a otra comarca esta freyra levada.   (63ab)

In conclusion, Berceo's is a style in which repetitive
patterns govern the arrangement of speech at all levels:
metrical, verbal, syntactical, and semantic. Within this
framework two principles are operative, one static and the
other kinetic. On the one hand, verbal expression is characterized by a series of syntactically and semantically independent units, rendered further immobile by infrequent
overflow and strong accentual and rhyme patterns, as well
as by a pronounced tendency toward pictorial realism. On
the other hand, the narrative must move ahead, if only to
"interest" the audience: whereas the Latin source was a
simple record or history, the Romance version must tell a
story. But movement progresses step by step, with deliberate and frequent recapitulations, like a wave that gathers
its full weight before advancing. Variation and change of
content, by being always cast into increasingly impressive
molds of sound and rhythm, thus seem echoes or reaffirma-
tions of all that has gone before.

6. Lyricism and Epic Celebration

"El bien que esperamos esso versifiquemos." (*Signos* 48d)

Every work of art represents a "compromise" between external influences and individual creativity, between communal and personal or lyrical forms of expression. Indeed, critics have often understood as their supreme task the description of the peculiar balance that exists between these opposing tendencies in a given author or work.[1] Since originality obviously cannot be assessed except against a broad background of fact, the separate findings of the present study may now be taken as a descriptive basis for considering the most delicate of critical problems: the uniqueness of the poem and the personal concerns it reveals.[2]

Our investigation is complicated, however, by the frequent neglect of the artistic role of traditional elements, itself due to oversimplified views of the opposition between traditional and originality. The problem may be stated as follows: To what degree does didacticism (traditional religious content) and rhetoric (traditional formal devices) inhibit artistic expression, which critics seem determined to interpret as originality or invention or the spontaneous expression of emotion? The general feeling is that they are

1. In Dámaso Alonso's words, the work of art has always been a "compromiso entre tradición y expresión individual" ("Berceo y los *topoi*," in *De los siglos oscuros al de oro*, p. 82). This opposition forms the basis of Pedro Salinas' *Jorge Manrique: Tradición y originalidad* (Buenos Aires, 1947).

2. Alonso (p. 85) admits—but without enthusiasm—that *topoi* and other traditional elements must be studied. For him the true concern of literary study can only be "lo 'único,' lo 'personal' del escritor, lo 'peculiar' de su obra, y su efecto sobre mí."

opposites and that one precludes the other—whence Curtius' dictum that "a constant literary formula must not be regarded as the expression of spontaneous sentiment." [3] Solalinde reaches similar conclusions concerning the religious subject matter of the *Sacrificio:* "del estudio del simbolismo resalta . . . la confirmación de que Berceo nada inventó, sino que se limitó a traducir en romance las enseñanzas teológicas." [4] In other words, a religious and didactic art, especially elaborated within a strong rhetorical tradition, strikes most modern readers as impersonal, uninteresting, nonartistic. The personality of the artist is lost under the welter of traditional themes and may express itself only by variation on well-known formulas—itself usually viewed as a mere school exercise *(amplificatio)* .

My intention is not so much to call into question at this point the general validity of Curtius' principles but rather to claim immunity for certain works of art which may make use of such formulas even in their most undisguised or traditional form but which use them with such effectiveness, which set them within a context of such congenial tonality, that the formula is transformed into a highly effective, organic, intensely *personal* part of the whole work. The same may be true of so-called didactic content. This usually pejorative term means simply that the poem teaches something, but the practice among critics is to emphasize the teaching aspect, on the assumption that the poet stands in more or less objective or impersonal relation to the "something" he preaches. It may happen, however, that the poet's subjective commitment to the subject matter is quite different.

In short, there is a suspicion that art or originality or spontaneous feeling, on the one hand, and rhetoric or didacticism, on the other, are not simply mutually exclu-

3. Curtius, *European Literature and the Latin Middle Ages,* p. 412.
4. Antonio Solalinde, review of T. C. Goode's study, in *HR, 3* (1935) , 177–78.

sive and that these supposed opposites can in fact collabo-
rate toward the same end. As early as 1926 J. M. Manly
raised the problem: "that some of Chaucer's freest and
most delightful work should contain twice as much rhetoric as some of the least inspired compositions is a puzzle
that demands investigation." [5] But for the time being let
us modestly assume, on the basis of this striking example,
that rhetoric at least need not hamper artistic endeavor.
Its positive aesthetic role may best be seen only after
Berceo's originality has been more clearly defined.

Generally speaking, Berceo criticism has been preoc-
cupied with two theses: the poet's aestheticism and his
self-expressionism. Concerning the first, Berceo's originality is seen in his desire to create a beautiful poem:
"Estamos ante un escritor con voluntad de belleza." [6] To
this end, critics have studied a wide range of stylistic traits,
attitudes, and topics, from which they have inferred
Berceo's "primitivism," intimacy, picturesque imagination,
and religious simplicity. In all such cases the emphasis is
not so much on what is said as on how it is said, and the
method is eclectic: relevant verses are selected and ab-
stracted from context.

Another mood among critics has led them to inquire
into the personality behind this poem. Berceo writes not
only about subjects or people that may or may not hold
an interest for the modern reader; he also writes about
himself—or at least his presence is felt: inconspicuous,
humble, but real nevertheless. This "penetración en el

5. J. M. Manly, "Chaucer and the Rhetoricians," *Proceedings of the British Academy, 12* (1926) , 108.
6. Artiles, *Berceo,* p. 123. The critic is speaking here of style: "Queramos o no, hay un buscado artificio en estos ejemplos de Berceo, una dis-tribución intencionada de palabras y de conceptos, una búsqueda de ritmos y contrastes, un propósito estético. Estamos ante un escritor con voluntad de belleza." Similarly, Carmelo Gariano writes that in the *Milagros* "el móvil principal es artístico" (*Análisis estilístico de los "Milagros de Nuestra Señora" de Berceo* [Madrid, 1965], p. 27) .

cuadro del escritor y de su oficio," [7] says Dámaso Alonso, is common in the Middle Ages: "se producen con frecuencia rompimientos en la tela de la creación estética, y por el roto aparece la faz humilde del escritor con su ingenuidad, con su oficio, con sus dolamas o su vejez, en fin, con sus necesidades." [8] In other words, even rhetorical authors or versifiers of didactic subjects "tienen su corazoncito," and there is some sense in which their poems are autobiographical—at least sections of their poems. Dámaso Alonso's metaphor is taken from painting: "le place meterse en el cuadro mismo . . . en cualquier parte, en un rinconcito." [9] Because of technical expediency as well as humility, the author appears only on the fringes of his poem: "estas penetraciones del autor en el cuadro ocurren en los extremos mismos del poema o de sus partes principales. Tenía que ser así: servían para señalar bien—en época de mera comunicación manuscrita—el comienzo y la terminación. Este uso . . . sirve, a la par, para una necesidad técnica y para la expresión personal del autor." [10]

In analyzing the essays of Dámaso Alonso, Jorge Guillén, Américo Castro,[11] and others, we learn that this distinctive autobiographical tone of Berceo is achieved through one simple stylistic device: the personal intervention in the first person singular. Now we have seen that this must be distinguished from the rhetorical "I" studied in Chapter 1. The first person cannot be sufficiently explained by traditional practices or artistic necessity; it signifies the irruption into the poem of the poet's intimate personality.

Due to their extraordinary frequency and intimacy, such passages in Berceo have been often quoted and greatly

7. Alonso, *De los siglos*, p. 83.
8. Ibid., p. 78.
9. Ibid.
10. Ibid., pp. 82–83.
11. See esp. his *Structure of Spanish History* (Princeton, 1954) , pp. 351–61.

admired. From *Santa Oria* two, perhaps three, are always mentioned. The first is the most famous of Berceo's utterances:

> Quiero en mj uegez, maguer so ya cansado,
> De esta sancta uirgen romançar su dictado,
> Que Dios por el su ruego sea de mj pagado,
> E non quiera uengança tomar del mj peccado.   (2)

In the second he must hurry on with his task because the days are short:

> Aucmos en el prologo mucho detardado;
> Siguamos la estoria, esto es agujsado.
> Los dias son non grandes, anochezra priuado,
> Escriujr en tinjebra es un mester pesado.   (10)

Finally, the poet wants to close his work:

> Gonçalo li dixieron al uersifficador
> Que en su portaleio fizo esta lauor,
> Ponga en el su graçia Dios el nuestro sennor,
> Que uea la su gloria en el regno mayor.   (184)

Curtius has attempted to account for the second as a traditional topos, though unsuccessfully.[12] It is true that the third can be so explained, since it was common for the *jongleur* to give his name at the outset or the end, along with a petition for a glass of wine or a good reward. However, Berceo's variation distinguishes itself by its appeal for a *supernatural* reward and especially by its touching plastic evocation of the author busy at work in his "portaleio." These three examples, then, are original; they cannot be reduced to topoi, and they also fulfill the two functions of the personal "I" noted by Alonso. They are an authentic expression of the poet's intimate personality and at the same time serve a rhetorical function. The first marks the

---

12. Curtius, *European Literature,* p. 91 and n.; answered by Dámaso Alonso, *De los siglos,* pp. 74–85.

opening of the poem; the second, the transition between prologue and "estoria"; the third, the projected end of the poem.

Thus Berceo maintains, especially at predictable intervals, a personal but humble contact with both his poem and his audience. This is his most distinctive feature and has been widely studied and praised. Here again, the critical method is eclectic: passages containing the personal "I" are removed from context and appreciated in isolation, with the result that one might say, paradoxically, that there is considerable interest in Berceo but very little in his works [13]—at any rate, not in the poems as poems, as unities characterized by a single intention or complex of intentions and to which artistic invention and autobiographical elements are related as parts to a whole.

Our concern thus cannot be with Berceo the individual, but is rather with the poem, which expresses his total intention. The error of Berceo criticism, to repeat, has been to divorce the poet from the poem, on the assumption that since the subject matter is didactic, the real Berceo must be sought elsewhere. In consequence, critics have somewhat impressionistically concentrated on those instances of direct intervention where the narrator lays his heart bare, reveals a delicate sensibility, and so forth. It seems hardly

13. Despite new criticism allegations on the part of critics. For example, in his Introduction to *Los recursos literarios de Berceo,* Artiles is still fighting battles long won when he militantly announces that his study will be concerned only with "the work itself": "sólo las obras mismas justifican todo nuestro interés . . . por todo el proceso de la literatura" (p. 7). It should be realized, however, that Artiles' book is certainly not concerned with the works themselves—with the texts, yes (this in itself is an important advance), but always with verses and examples necessarily extracted from context, precisely *from* the works to which they belong. Of course such an eclectic method can reveal interesting facts about the continuity and development of stylistic and thematic materials, and in this way furnish a new perspective for studying the work. The important point is that such a study is a necessary preparation—but only a step—toward the final critical effort: the study of the individual poem as a unity in itself.

to have occurred to anyone that there is a vital connection between Berceo's *obiter dicta* or charming asides to his audience and the very subject matter he is treating, that the subjective resonances are echoed and developed in the so-called didactic stories themselves. Yet it must not be forgotten that there are other ways of expressing one's intimate personality besides the obvious address in the first person. Even the didactic author usually had the freedom to choose both the general subject matter and the more minor themes, manner of development, tonality, shading, comparisons, intensity, and the like. The final result is a unity in which the author completely invades the subject matter and is possessed by it. Such at least is the case of *Santa Oria*. In the final word Berceo is Oria.

It is therefore necessary to retain the notion of autobiography as the basic critical criterion, provided it be expanded in two ways. First, Berceo not only hovers about the fringes of the poem; he can be sensed in all of its parts. Secondly, the autobiographical passages have been seen so far only in a local sense: Berceo is old; he has to write quickly because the days are short; he gives his name and shows us the place where he works. These atomic elements must be related to the larger context, itself defined as the profound unity of poet and poem.

Although a purely statistical approach to Berceo can yield good results, the meaning can only be seen by an intuitive plunge into the poet-poem. Our critical method at this point can be well stated by a slight adaptation of Unamuno's text:

> Si quieres buscar, lector, por la crítica, personas reales . . . no acumules detalles, no te dediques a observar exterioridades de los que contigo conviven, sino trátalos, excítalos si puedes, quiérelos sobre todo y espera a que un día—acaso nunca—saquen a luz y desnuda el alma de su alma, el que quieren ser, en un

grito, en un acto, en una frase, y entonces toma ese
momento, métalo en ti y deja que como un germen
se te desarrolle en el personaje de verdad, en el que
es de veras real.[14]

As readers of Berceo, we shall take only passing interest
in his specific problems of composition, in the picturesque
allusion to his workshop, in Oria herself. We must seek
the basic intention, the "cry of the heart" that sponsors
the poem in all of its parts.[15]

Santa Oria is the most intensely autobiographical of
Berceo's poems, and it is fortunate that the essential personal facts are stated at the outset and in such an explicit
manner. Berceo is old and tired, and the days are short. To
this double twilight of the day and old age, already pointed
out by Guillén,[16] may be added a third dimension. "Los
dias son non grandes . . ." Winter is fast approaching.
"Escriujr en tinjebra es vn mester pesado." The poet is
writing in November, concludes Dámaso Alonso (p. 83),
and must "aprovechar la luz del día." But we have seen
that Berceo's mind functions in accordance with biblical
patterns of exegesis and often with the ease of a simple
reflex. He can entertain two or more levels of meaning
simultaneously as a normal manner of consciousness: the
literal and immediate, on the one hand; the spiritual and

14. *Tres novelas ejemplares y un prólogo*, prólogo iv. Unamuno's text
begins as follows: "Si quieres crear, lector, por el arte, personas, agonistas
trágicos, cómicos o novelescos, no acumules detalles." The rest is exact
quotation.

15. Such a critical position is treated with slight irony by Northrop
Frye in *Anatomy of Criticism*, p. 81: "According to this the literal core of
poetry would be a *cri de coeur*, to use the elegant expression, the direct
statement of a nervous organism confronted with something which seems
to demand an emotional response, like a dog howling at the moon." In
contrast to the sentimentalism ridiculed by Frye, however, Berceo is trying
to describe not a personal emotion but a religious and historical event
to which he is emotionally committed. Whatever uniqueness his feelings
may have is humbly concealed, as we shall see.

16. Guillén, *Language and Poetry*, p. 4.

more personal, on the other. San Millán's temptations in the desert are described uniquely in terms of physical desolation and ferocious wolves, but Berceo and his audience were thinking also and especially of that other "wolf" as well, the "mal enemigo": ". . . anochezrá privado." He is old and weary, in the autumn of his life; "night" is approaching soon ("privado"). And to the three impending nights of day, season and life must yet be added a fourth, the most important and terrifying "night" of all, really the only one that matters:

> Que Dios por el su ruego sea de mj pagado,
> E non quiera uengança tomar del mj peccado. (2cd)

Perhaps we are now beginning to see the impossibility of quoting the more obvious autobiographical material out of its full context, or of disregarding the rest because it is mere formula. This is the heart of the poem, the cry of desire that organizes all of the parts into a meaningful autobiographical pattern under the sign of a definite and consistent tonality: salvation from the night of death, both the fact itself and especially what may follow. For:

> Luengo será *el dia* a los bien aventurados,
> Ca nunca avran *noche* que sean embargados.
> *(Signos* 68ab)

Berceo's emotion is bipolar: fear of "night" and desire for eternal "light." Each of these opposing forces sponsors its own "associative cluster" (Kenneth Burke), a consistent set of affective resonances which, incidentally, gain in power by their mere opposition. The relative strengths of these two elements is suggested by the proportions of the poem: five-eights of the verses narrate supernatural concerns; *Santa Oria* is a poem of heaven. Yet there is a tone of anxiety throughout. First of all, there is a strong sense of the pain of living. All the inhabitants of heaven have had to suffer "lazerios muy granados" (183b). The poet

views his own task as a "lauor" (184b) and describes the
Saint's death as a triumphant release from pain: [17]

> Rendió a Dios la alma, *nunca mas sintió mal.*
>
> (177d)

Oria is saved, and yet the poet is anxious about the details;
he feels the need to return in the final section to this same
matter. When Oria appears to her mother, Amunna's first
question is: " 'O si sodes en pena o sodes ende salida' "
(190d). Oria reassures her, but this is still not enough.
Berceo (or rather, Amunna) detains the Saint for one final
question; and although Oria is eager to return to heaven,
the narrative takes up four strophes (195–98) :

> "Mas, fija, vna cosa uos quiero demandar;
> Sy en el passamjento resçibiestes pesar,
> O sy uos dieron luego en el cielo logar,
> O uos fizieron ante a la puerta musar."   (195)

What happened to her in the "night" (196a, 197a) of
death? What pain ("pesar") did she receive? Did she have
to undergo the whole experience unaided?

The intense human solitude of death and pain is especially acute in Berceo, until it is finally overcome by divine
presence:

> La Virgo gloriosa lo que me prometió,
> Ella sea laudada, bien me lo guardó.
> En el mj passamjento de mj non se partió.
>
> (198a-c)

Similarly, during visionary experiences:

> Non se partia Dios della en njnguna sazon
> Ca siempre tenja ella en El su coraçon.   (115cd)

17. This may be compared in intensity with the parallel scene in *San
Millán*, where the fact of death is merely stated:
> Cerró ambos sos oios sin nul conturbamiento,
> Rendió a Dios la alma, *fizo so passamiento.*   (301cd)

Even the dead body is granted appropriate companionship. The monks "non se partieron delli fasta fue soterrado" (179d).

The minor chord tonalities of night and winter are sustained during Oria's visions, though this may be coincidental and due to the source. For the first, "Terçera noche era despues de Naujdat" (25a). The second occurs also at night (116a), in November. Oria's final vision and death take place in late evening ("a boca de noche," 176b). Perhaps significantly, it is no longer winter but spring: "El mes era de março" (161a).

The first associative cluster, then, is a group of negative metaphors. Verbally, it may be written by a series of hyphenated words indicating simultaneous experience and interdependence of each component, something like the following: "darkness-night-devil-death-pain." The central positive metaphor, by contrast, is light, itself such a complex experience that a new word must also be improvised such as "light-whiteness-dove-God-grace-comfort-sun-heaven." One would have to regroup the disparate findings of this study in order to see the metaphor of light as yet another element in the autobiography of our poet.

In the very opening invocation there is an important clue. The Father created, and the Son came to save us, both in the past. Only the Holy Spirit is viewed as active in the present. Now He is described as "lumbre de confortar," His symbol is the white dove, and His function is to lead souls to heaven. His light is reflected in Oria:

> *Luz* era e *confuerto* de la su uezindat.   (22d)

One then recalls that light always accompanies divine creatures, indeed that it is a dominant tonality throughout the poem. Moreover, light is only the visible aspect of a higher reality—divine grace:[18] "luzían como estrellas"

---

18. The beautiful hymns attributed to Berceo (*BAE*, 57, 144) all begin with metaphors of light: "Veni Creator Spiritus pleno de dulçe lumne"; "Ave Sancta Maria estrella de la mar"; "Tu Christe que luz eres, que alumnas el dia."

(29d), "lumbres" from heaven (46d, 132b), "claridat" (86d, 93bc), "cosa . . . clara" (78b), "reluzir" (42c), "rayos del sol" (90c), "Relunbró la confita de relumbror doblado" (122c). The metaphor of light is extended in the color white, which, in addition to its symbolic meaning of purity, is also its visual synonym: "mas blancas que las njeues" (30c), "personas . . . tan blancas" (168b), "blancas uestiduras" (47b), "bestiduras albas" (52b), "blanca frisa" (118bc), "blancos çiclatones" (143b). The white dove is the light of comfort, of heaven: "Omne que y morasse nunca ueria pesar" (157b).

In a felicitous phrase Fitzmaurice-Kelly has said that Berceo fathers Oria.[19] We interpret this by saying that Oria is a child of the poet's creative desire; he wishes to be like her, to share her destiny. The reader should therefore not be reluctant to see further autobiographical material of the poet spoken by Oria herself. A case in point is that tender scene where Mary appears to the ascetic in her cell and comforts her with the symbolic soft couch:

> "Lieuate de la tierra que es fria e dura,
> Subi en esti lecho, yazras mas en mollura."
>
> (128a-b)

Oria is embarrassed and, with characteristic humility, says that she does not deserve such a couch:

> "Duennas, dixolis Oria, non es esso derecho;
> *Para ujeio e flaco* conbiene esti lecho." (129a-b)

---

19. James Fitzmaurice-Kelly, *Some Masters of Spanish Verse* (Oxford, 1924), pp. 10–11. The full statement deserves to be quoted for its interesting reportage of Berceo's own literary opinions—opinions for which I, unfortunately, can find neither textual nor historical documentation: "He himself valued most highly his life of Santa Oria; but his taste was not infallible, and the judgment of authors on their works is not to be blindly followed. As the *Vida de Santa Oria, Virgen* was, as Berceo tells us, the child of his old age, we perhaps ought to make some deduction for parental partiality."

Is it possible not to recall Berceo's opening autobiographical remark: "Quiero en mj uejez, maguer so ya cansado . . ."? Oria is apparently talking about herself, and her comment here is an aside that contrasts rhetorically with the following verse: " 'Yo ualiente so e njnna por soffrir todo fecho.' " (129c) Yet the ideas and their order of presentation are identical with Berceo's own earlier words: "spiritual comfort and rewards are more suitable to an old and weary [cansado or flaco] man!"

Or take the dialogue between Oria and her confessor shortly before her death. The Saint tells of her vision of the Mount of Olives (death), and he then questions her:

> Dixol Munno a Oria: "¿Cobdiçias alla yr?"
> Dixol a Munno Oria: "Yo si, mas que ujujr;
> E tu non perdrias nada de comjgo venjr."
> Dixol Munno: "¡Quisiesse lo esso Dios consintir!"
>
> (158)

This is but one more instance of the persistent *contemptus mundi* theme. Yet the focused brevity of the exchange is almost painful. Berceo has never cried out so intensely. Note also how the purely topological prayer, so frequent in the final verse position, is completely transmuted through its dramatic use. We have already seen in another context how Munno is the poet's narrative *alter ego*. This provides Berceo with yet another way of integrating himself subtly in the narrative, as well as, in the present instance, heightening the dramatic intensity.

Or consider the following situation. As Oria is about to embark on her journey to heaven, she looks up and sees a column that reaches up and out of sight. Berceo describes the column and adds a delightful personal observation:

> Auja en la colunpna escalones e gradas,
> Veer solemos tales en las torres obradas,
> *Yo sobi por algunas,* esto muchas uegadas.   (39a-c)

The use of the first person is neither rhetorical nor autobiographical in any of the senses already examined. Américo Castro suggests that this is an instance of Spanish "in-
tegralism": the author integrates himself into the narrative
through "consciousness of fulfilling a holy mission as he
writes." Berceo "incorporates his own process of writing
into his writing." [20] The examples can be multiplied. He
says in *Santo Domingo:*

> Conpuso la iglesia, esto bien lo creades . . .
> Yo Gonçalo, que fago esto asu honor,
> *yo la ui,* assy uea la faz del Criador.   (108b, 109ab)

Likewise, in *San Millán:*

> Dues campaniellas pienden sobre el so altar . . .
> Assi pueda la gloria del Criador aver
> Commo por mis oreias *las oy yo tanner.* (485a, 487a-b)

Américo Castro's commentary is mainly concerned with
one aspect of the poet: we are asked to consider, throughout Berceo's poems, the presence of the author *as author;*
the primary fact is that "the author includes within the
poem his consciousness of himself making his poem." [21]
And yet we are asked to understand that this consciousness
functions in such a way as to divorce Berceo from his subject matter, to turn the author into an "extra-literary"
person, "positively heterogeneous to the poetic matter."
This literary approach is likened to the autobiographical
confession, where "the writer presents himself as existing
in the privacy of his own consciousness." [22] In other words,
on the pretext of trying to understand how the subject

---

20. Castro, *Spanish History,* p. 352.
21. Ibid., p. 358.
22. Ibid., pp. 360–61.

matter exists in Berceo,[23] the critic has, on the one hand, disregarded what the subject matter is, and on the other, reduced the poet to that curious modern abstraction called "the author." Thus, for example, when Berceo's personal intrusions are described as the consciousness of "fulfilling his holy mission as he writes," [24] this holy mission is narrowly understood as precisely the writing itself.

However, literature was not always considered such a self-contained activity, nor is Berceo's consciousness primarily explained in isolation from the *object* of consciousness. The truth is that Berceo can only be understood in terms of his subject matter, and this subject matter is an integral expression of his innermost desires. The way to see this is, once again, not to isolate phrases and verses from context but rather to consider the complete unit (usually the strophe). Let us quote once again the *Santa Oria* passage, this time emphasizing not the third verse (Castro) but rather the fourth:

> Auja en la colunpna escalones e gradas,
> Veer solemos tales en las torres obradas,
> Yo sobi por algunas, esto muchas uegadas,
> *Por tal suben las almas que son auenturadas.*   (39a-d)

Similarly, whereas in the *Santo Domingo* and *San Millán* texts quoted above the critic would signal out "yo la vi" and "las oí yo tanner," we suggest that the emphasis is rather on the remarkably parallel (and equally personal) utterances that follow:

> . . . asy uea la faz del Criador.   (*SDom* 109b)
> Assi pueda la gloria del Criador aver.
>   (*SMil* 487a)

23. Ibid., p. 354.
24. Ibid., p. 352.

It is now obvious that these passages in which the author reveals his alleged consciousness as an author are always coupled with an ardent wish for salvation. It seems rather that Berceo's separate consciousness is of himself as a person with an eternal destiny and that the personal comments hitherto considered so important are only incidental and preparatory to deeper things. The *Santa Oria* passage is exactly parallel to these other two texts, with the slight difference that here the poet is perhaps less explicit: "Por tal suben las almas que son auenturadas" (39d).

Let us follow the thought or desire process. Oria ascends to heaven on a column described concretely ("escalones e gradas") in its supernatural setting and which may be read symbolically as the ladder of humility or transcendence. Suddenly the level of reference changes:

> Veer solemos tales en las torres obradas.   (39b)

Berceo can never go too far from the earth or from his audience. This is a real ladder with no symbolic referent:

> Yo sobi por algunas, esto muchas uegadas.   (39c)

The poet is still discussing the purely physical "torre," he himself has ascended such ladders. But he then adds, in the fourth and concluding verse, the heaviest of the *cuaderna vía* form:

> Por tal suben las almas que son auenturadas.   (39d)

This is the point at which it is meaningful to speak of Berceo's naïveté or primitivism. The poet has artlessly and quite imperceptibly reverted to the symbolic level and the celestial setting, with an unconscious ease that is perhaps apt to pass unnoticed. Here symbolism and realism, heaven and earth, are fused or, rather, flow freely into the other. But there is one further element. The poet has modestly intruded himself into the picture, but not only as an author composing the poem or as a picturesque monk climbing a fancy tower in Old Castile.

Santa Oria is a fitting final work. Berceo's other poems have been those of a good pastor: preaching, chastizing, painting worthy exempla for the faithful, and glorifying God and the Virgin Mary. The *Sacrificio,* for example, is purely doctrinal, and the personal intrusions of the poet are rare. In *Santa Oria* the emphasis has shifted; the tone is more personal, more self-centered, if you will: "E non quiera vengança tomar del mj peccado." The traditional topos of *contemptus mundi* has taken on a poignant personal relevance. The sermon is also a prayer.[25]

So far as we know, *Santa Oria* is Berceo's final work. He wants to finish, but not in order to begin quickly and enthusiastically another Book as, for example, in *Santo Domingo:* "Esti libro finamos, en otro contendremos" (288d). Rather he wants to "ir a folgar" (160d) in a soft couch such as is reserved for the weary.[26] Like the medieval Everyman, the poet is aware that man lives with and for others but dies alone. When the day's work is done, the weary laborer must finally think of his own soul. The old *joglar's* thoughts turn to death, and many fears and desires well up in him. His basic affective reactions are re-

25. If the spirit of Romanesque art may be likened to a "prayer" and that of Gothic art to a "sermon," Berceo's art may be said to partake of both. See J. Gantner, *Romanische Plastik* (Vienna, 1948), p. 54.

26. "Folgar" is of course another instance of personal intervention with formulaic status. Berceo uses it as merely another way of saying: "I want to finish this work":

> Sennores, Deo graçias, contadovos avemos
> Del sancto solaterio quanto saber podemos,
> E de las sues andadas secund lo que leemos:
> Desaqui, si quisieredes, *ora es que folguemos.*   *SMil* 108

In another context it may mean "to rest" or "take a nap" (*SOr* 140a, 189b). But its metaphorical extension suggesting the final "rest" is suggested in the very same poem:

> Fue a Monte Oliueti en ujsion leuada,
> Vido y tales cosas de que fue saborgada,
> Sy non la despertassen cuidó seer *folgada.*   (139b-d)

peated with slight variation. Winter is approaching
and his days are short. "La tierra es fria e dura," the
dominant colors are white (as snow), alternating with the
spring flowers which he hopes to see again soon. He is
old and weary but perhaps not alone. In the night of death
("la noche primera") perhaps the Virgin will watch over
him: "En el mj passamjento de mj non se partió" (198c).
Life is harsh, but heaven is a "logar bueno" with "folgura," comfort and light: I am tired and so, if you don't
mind (160b), I shall "accompany" Oria to her throne and
then go to rest (160d) —a touching ambiguity when one
realizes that *Oria* is probably the last of his writings.

Yet the aged cleric regains a second wind, and the narrative toward the end takes on the rhythm of the final
strides of a wearisome pilgrimage. He stops (184), then
starts again, feeling that perhaps he can go a little farther
(185). But his strength is worn and he ends his poem with
a strange excuse, perhaps the vaguest or most veiled personal statement in all of Berceo:

> Tengo otras priessas de fer mjs cabazones.   (202c)

A mind given to more fanciful interpretations would almost suspect, if not a "sennal" of the sort given by the
Virgin to Oria (134), at least a premonition of the approaching end.

Santa Oria is thus autobiographical to an extent not
previously suspected. The concourse of the diverse elements are simply too many and too intensely narrated to
overlook: thematic materials, stylistic peculiarities, and
what little is known of the author through his own remarks. The very structural fact of dedicating five-eighths
of the poem to visions of heaven is appropriate to the
dreams of an old and weary Christian: his thoughts have
already left the world. The visions of the ascetic reflect the
poet's own deepest desires: a "good place" with rest and

comfort, the company of heaven and old personal acquaintances, the Virgin Mary in the image of a lovely tree in flower, and the Trinity God who rewards the worthy with love, as a Father.

Berceo invades his poem in all of its parts; he can be confined to a "rinconcito" of his work only by abstracting from the work the explicit indications of his presence (the personal "I"). Yet Berceo is so delicately integrated into the thematic materials as to merit fully the epithet so aptly supplied by Jorge Guillén: humble.[27] Indeed, it is safe to say that the profoundly autobiographical structure of the poem was neither planned nor consciously portrayed. It depends—to repeat—not on narrow aesthetic criteria but rather on Berceo's intensely personal involvement, accentuated by old age, in his own salvation. This, it seems to us, is the fundamental unity of the poem.[28]

Yet this is only half of the picture. Berceo is alone in

27. Guillén, *Language and Poetry*, p. 3. D. W. Robertson has pointed out that "no poetic is as alien to the notion of 'poesia-confessione' in the modern sense as was the medieval poetic." *A Preface to Chaucer*, p. 14.

28. Carmelo Gariano has excellently sought the artistic unity of the *Milagros* in Berceo's underlying attitude of charity directed especially toward the Virgin. The artistic values of the work, says Gariano, are to be found in "ese amor cristiano dotado de sencillez e iluminado de humilde nobleza, en que la luz de la caridad tiene un poder catártico no sólo sobre los pecadores sino hasta los traviesos de los demonios. Esa caridad bondadosa adquiere su signo poético en el amor por una mujer divina, lo cual da la unidad espiritual más íntima al poema. Según se señaló con detalle, en ese amor se concentra mucho del valor artístico de la obra." (*Análisis*, pp. 194–95). In view of this it is disappointing to see the critic revert in the very next paragraph to the position of Dámaso Alonso (see above, p. 174, nn. 8–11), according to which artistic merit is to be sought in "breves descansaderos líricos de exquisito encanto," thus resulting in the fragmentation of artistic unity: "En resumidas cuentas, la esencia artística de los *Milagros de Nuestra Señora* consiste en la emoción lírica en ellos depositada, y por eso se trata de un valor discontinuo, fragmentario" (*Análisis*, p. 195). The author has reverted to the conception of an absolute cleavage between personal emotion, on the one hand, and of a "fondo hagiográfico y desenvolvimiento narrativo," on the other, despite his previous effort to bridge these through Berceo's implicit but continuous and real emotion of love throughout the poem.

death before God. But as artist and living Christian (one must insist on the inseparability of the two), he is but one of many: "Todos somos romeos que camino andamos" (*Milagros* 17c). His desire for salvation is also shared with all other Christians: Oria's "pilgrimage" is also their own. To relate Oria's heroic deeds is thus to renew themes vital to the happiness of the community. Moreover, the dominant rhythm of recurrence at all levels of style, the majestic solemnity of movement and scene, the similarity with the *cantares de gesta* in the use of laudatory epithet, all of these suggest ritualistc and celebrative reenactment.[29] Berceo's artistic creation is thus a re-creation. Rather than beauty or self-concern, the poet of *Santa Oria,* like the epic *joglar,* celebrates the hero, but his warriors fight for God.[30]

Such a perspective requires a new evaluation of the artistic status of traditional speech patterns. For, like the priest or *joglar* celebrating the hero-god, Berceo performs his task in formulaic and repetitive discourse. One example can suffice for many—the closing invocation:

> Dios nos dé la su graçia el buen Rey spiritual
> Que alla njn aquj nunca ueamos mal.   (205cd)

This prayer has two focal points: keep us from the harm of sin here on earth and give us eternal life—a mere repetitive formula, one might observe. And, to be sure, Berceo is extremely fond of concluding his poems with such topoi.

---

29. This is the real explanation of recurrent style: not aesthetics but religious celebration of traditional themes. As in primitive epic, repetition was "not for the sake of metre, nor for the sake of convenience in building in line, but for the sake of redoubled prayer in its hope of surer fulfillment." Lord, *The Singer of Tales,* p. 67; cf. also pp. 220–21.

30. Battle metaphors are frequent in Berceo's *Vidas.* Millán is "el bon campeador," and Domingo is "el adalit caboso" (441a). Artiles (*Berceo,* p. 242) lists Berceo's borrowings from the epic but neglects to point out the transference of such profane epithets *a lo divino.* Cf. Dutton, *BH, 42,* 184.

But it must be remembered, first of all, that what seems to us students of the letter mere formula can also contain the most poignant spiritual plea. The *Pater* and *Ave* are also formulas. The truth is that prayer is—or is not—in the mind of the sayer, but this does not remove the essential distinction between "saying" one's prayers and praying. In the literary context the authenticity of such formulas can be tested only against other aspects of the poem. Taken in themselves, they are aesthetically neutral. But— and this is the important point—they may not be discounted as irrelevant to the total effect of the work of art merely because of their formulaic or traditional nature.

Secondly, it may now be observed that the final prayer in *Santa Oria* is not the same as in Berceo's other poems. Concluding invocations in Berceo may be classified thematically into two groups. In the first the plea is for protection from sin:

> Gonzalvo fue so nomne que fizo est tractado . . .
> Dios guarde la su alma del poder del peccado.
>
> > (*SMil* 489a,d)

> Tu aguisa, sennora, pora mi tal mercado,
> Porque nungua me vea en premia del pecado.
>
> > (*Duelo* 210cd)

Or, as in *Santa Oria,* to protection from sin may be added the plea for eternal salvation:

> Guýanos en tal guysa por la vida mortal
> Commo en cabo ayamos el regno çelestial.
>
> > (*Loores* 233cd)

> Guardanos de mal colpe e de mala caida,
> Que las almas en cabo ayan buena essida.
>
> > (*Milagros* 911cd)

> Por el su sancto merito nos guarde Dios de mal,
> e nos lieue las almas al Regno Çelestial.
>
> > (*SDom* 777cd)

All of these are quoted so that the slight but extremely significant variation in *Santa Oria* may be put into bold relief. The first two are focused only on man's earthly existence: save us from sin. In the other three examples, although the themes are identical with those in the *Santa Oria* invocation, they differ in the order of presentation, and this reversal of order suggests a parallel shift of emphasis: may we fall into harm *neither in heaven* nor on earth. The poet's perspective has shifted; his primary focus is no longer on the long daily struggles and their dangers. His first concern, stylistically and existentially, is with heaven.

It is evident from this that topoi and other traditional means of expression cannot properly be appraised without assessing their tonal compatibility with the rest of the work in which they occur, and without diachronic comparisons on a stylistic level with the author's other works. Even the slightest formulaic variation may become heavy with meaning, although such practices may require a sensitivity quite undeveloped in the modern reader. But this failure does not refute either the existence of such practices or their effectiveness in promoting the central intention of the work of art. And if this intention consists in the communal celebration of the hero (whether god or warrior or saint), mankind from earliest tribal records, at least to Péguy, has often preferred a formulaic speech characterized by strong rhythm and repetitiveness and in which originality is of little value.

Appendix I

Prudencio de Sandoval's Version of the
Vida de Santa Oria [1]

*VIDA DE LA BIENauenturada virgen santa
Auria, monja de san Benito, sacada de un
libro antiquissimo, escrita por un monge,
de san Millan, llamado Munno, que la vió,
y trató.*

XX.

Fve Santa Auria natural de Villauelayo, junto a Mansilla, seis
leguas de San Millan, hija de Garcia Nunno, y Amuna, nobles
y principales, santos y virtuosos, que es la verdadera nobleza,
y como a tales dió el Sennor tal hija, pidiéndosela a Dios con
muchas oraciones. La qual desde su ninnez amó la virtud y
despreciando el regalo de los padres, galas, y hermosura, ves-
tíase de pannos muy asperos, y humildes. Era continua en la
lecion, y oracion, y tan encendida en ella, que sus ojos eran
fuentes: los ayunos notables. Hazia las limosnas que podia, no
le yendo en nada los padres a la mano, por ser ellos tales qual
fue el fruto que de si dieron santo y bueno, que como a tal,
no sin orden del cielo, le dieron el nombre de Auria, pues la
conuirtió en oro el calor ardiente del verdadero Sol de justicia,
que desde su ninnez la abrasaua. Y pareciéndole a la santa
virgen, que estando en casa de sus padres no podia tener el
rigor que desseaua en la vida, tomó el abito de monja con
perpetuo encerramiento y clausura en el monesterio de San
Millan de Suso, segun la costumbre de aquellos tiempos, que
estauan los monesterios de monges y monjas juntos. La fama

1. *Primera parte de las fundaciones de los monesterios del . . . padre
san Benito que los reyes de España fundaron y dotaron . . . , 2* (3 vols.
Madrid, Luis Sánchez, 1601) , folios 39–41.

de su vida y milagros, que Dios por sus ruegos obraua, se
estendió por la tierra desuerte, que quando más encerrada, y
apartada del mundo, se veia en él, como la ciudad en el monte,
y lucia, como la hacha encendida en el candelero. Eran grandes
los regalos que el diuino esposo le hazia, y estando en Maytines
tercero dia de Nauidad, que en aquel tiempo se celebraua la
fiesta de Santa Eugenia, dichos los Maytines, se quedó en oracion, y dióle vn gran suenno; en el qual vió tres hermosas
virgenes que le dixeron que eran Agata, Olalla, Cecilia, todas
vestidas de vn panno, y con soberana hermosura, echando de
sí más luz que las estrellas: y cada vna destas virgenes tenia en
la mano vna blanca paloma. Causó algun pauor en Santa
Auria la repentina vision, mas esforçándose lo que pudo, les
preguntó quienes eran. Dixeronlo las virgenes, y que por el
amor que la tenian, auian hecho tan largo camino solo a
visitarla, y ofrecerle su conpannía, que ya Dios en el cielo le
tenia sennalada, donde veria el premio de sus trabajos, y lo
que ante Dios valian los cilicios, ayunos, encerramientos, la-
grimas, y oraciones, y le dieron las gracias por el gusto que
recebia leyendo sus vidas, y martyrios, y le ofrecieron mostrarle
el premio de gloria que se les auia dado. Respondióles Santa
Auria, que ella no lo merecia. Santa Olalla le dixo, que no
dixesse tal cosa, que en los cielos tenia amigos y amigas: Que
el castigo que hazes (dixeron) en tu persona, y rigor de vida,
está muy bien recebido en el acatamiento diuino, auiéndole
Dios sennalado eterno y glorioso premio. Toma de mí este consejo que te doy como amiga, que recibas esta paloma, y te guies
por ella los dias que biuieres: guia te por nuestro consejo, que
Iesu Christo te llama por suya. Oyendo esto Santa Auria, le-
uantó los ojos, y vió vna hermosa coluna, que desde el suelo
llegaua al cielo, y al derredor della vna escalera, como la
suelen tener algunas torres antiguas: y dixeronle, Esta es la
escala por donde las almas bienauenturadas suben al cielo,
y la paloma que santa Olalla auia ofrecido a santa Auria,
començó de bolar para el cielo. Mirándola con atencion santa
Auria donde iria a parar, perdióla de vista: y luego las tres
virgenes, tomando consigo a santa Auria, subieron por aquellas
gradas, y entraron por lugares amenos, llenos de flores y hermosura, donde la gloriosa virgen vió celestiales compannías.
Tal fauor, y tal consuelo recibió esta virgen del Sennor de las

virgenes santas, con que començó santa Auria a annadir rigor
a su penitencia, y hazer más aspera su vida, desseando verse
libre de la carga del cuerpo, para gozar de los bienes que en
esta vision, suenno, o arrobamiento le mostró el Esposo.

Regaló el Sennor a la virgen Auria dentro de onze meses
despues de lo dicho, noche de san Saturnino, primero de Di-
ziembre: estando la virgen en su continua oracion, se la apare-
ció la Reyna del cielo, con la magestad y gloria que en esta
vida no se alcança ni imagina, acompannada de muy hermosas
donzellas, y dixo a santa Auria, Hija el rigor de tu vida es
bien que se temple, y que salgas de la aspereza de la cama en
que duermes, y reciba tu cuerpo tan fatigado algun aliuio. Con
esto acudieron las virgenes, que acompannauan a la Reyna del
cielo, y tomaron a santa Auria (aunque lo resistia, diziendo
con humildad, que bastaua para ella la cama que tenia, y que
no merecia otros regalos) y echáronla en vna riquissima y
regalada cama, siendo grande la luz y hermosura que aquella
celestial conpannía de sí daua. Dixo la Virgen a santa Auria,
como ya se le acercaua el fin de sus dias: y que dentro de breue
tiempo enfermaria, y passaria desta vida al descanso eterno,
como fue, y la enfermedad larga y penosa, mas no sin grandes
consuelos y fauores del cielo, con que el Sennor consolaua a
su esposa: y a onze dias del mes de Marzo, dia de nuestro padre
san Gregorio, hallándose presentes Munna madre de santa
Auria, y don Pedro Abad de san Millan, Munno monge que
escriuió esta historia, y don Gomez cillerero, y el conuento de
monges y ermitannos de S Millan, dió el alma a Dios, con
grandissimas muestras y sennales de su gloria. Sepultaron su
santo cuerpo en S Millan de Suso, como al presente se muestra
su sepultura, cauada en la penna biua de aquella montanna,
que con la humidad está muy gastada; y dentro de pocos dias
lleuó Dios a su madre Munna al descanso eterno, y la sepultaron junto a su hija. Otras reuelaciones hechas a Santa Auria,
y otras que la santa despues que passó al cielo hizo, consolando
a su madre, cuenta esta historia, que las déxo por el mal estilo
con que las dize el poeta. Pusieron en la piedra de la sepultura
de santa Auria los versos siguientes.

> *Hunc quem cernis lapidem scultum,*
> *sacra tegit membra*
> *Beata, simul Auria virgo cum matre*

Amunna quiescunt
In vrna, et quia pro Christo arctam
    duxerunt vitam,
Simul cum eo cum beatis laetantur, in
    coelestia regna.

Que es: Debaxo desta piedra yaze el cuerpo de Santa Auria, y
el de su madre Amunna, muger de buena memoria. Fueron de
gran abstinencia en esta vida transitoria: por lo qual son
coronadas en el cielo de gloria, y se gozan con los bienauen-
turados. Y en vna memoria de mucha antigueded se dize:
B. Auria, quae fuit reclusa in coenobio S. AEmiliani superioris,
requiescit ibi in quadam specu post basilicam eiusdem loci:
quae multa vidit mirabilia et secreta, ante corporis sui finem;
quae habentur scripta in transitu vitae suae.
Que es: La bienauenturada santa Auria, que fue monja encerrada deste monesterio de san Millan de Suso, descansa allí en vna
cierta cueua, debaxo de la Yglesia del mesmo lugar. La qual
Santa vió en esta vida cosas marauillosas y secretas: las quales
están escritas en el transito, o discurso de su vida.

El nombre de Auria, es lo mismo que Oria, y fue muy vsado
entre gente principal en los tiempos muy antiguos, y por
auerse poblado la ciudad de Soria en vn lugar donde estaua
vna Yglesia dedicada a esta Santa, que llamauan san Oria, le
quedó el nombre de Soria.

El lugar donde está la sepultura de santa Auria, y su madre
Amunna, es a la entrada de la Yglesia de Suso, y se baxa a él
por vna escalera muy estrecha de treinta y cinco passos, y al fin
dellos está socauada la penna, y en ella quatro sepulturas muy
antiguas, las tres más pequennas, la otra es de Santa Auria. No
se sabe qué huessos sean los de las tres sepulturas, si de Santos,
o algunos Reyes, o grandes caualleros, de los muchos que por
tener esta tierra por santa, excogieron con deuocion en ella sus
sepulturas.

Appendix II

The Text of Berceo's *Vida de Santa Oria* According to Tomás Antonio Sánchez [1]

1. EN el nombre de el Padre que nos quiso criar,
   Et de Don Jesu Christo que nos vino salvar,
   Et del Spiritu Santo lumbre de confortar,
   De una santa Virgen quiero versificar.
2. Quiero en mi vegez, maguer so ya cansado,
   De esta santa Virgen romanzar su dictado,
   Que Dios por el su ruego sea de mi pagado
   E non quiera venganza tomar del mi pecado.
3. Luego en el comienzo è en la primería
   A ella mercet pido, ella sea mi guia,
   Ruegue à la Gloriosa Madre Santa Maria,
   Que sea nuestra guarda de noche è de dia.
4. Essa Virgen preciosa de quien fablar solemos,
   Fue de Villa Vellayo, segunt lo que leemos:
   Amunna fue su madre, escrito lo tenemos,
   Gracía fue el padre, en letra lo avemos.
5. Munno era su nombre, ome fue bien letrado,
   Sopo bien su facienda: él fizo el dictado,

---

1. *Colección de poesías castellanas anteriores al siglo XV*, 2 (4 vols. Madrid, 1779–90), 435–61. This was the first edition of *Santa Oria* and, along with Marden's edition of manuscript *A* used in the body of our study, is the basis of all modern versions of the poem. For example, the texts of the poem published by Eugenio de Ochoa, (*Colección de los mejores autores españoles* [Paris, 1842]) and Florencio Janer (*Poetas castellanos anteriores al siglo XV* [Madrid, 1864]) are mere reproductions of Sánchez, with emendations that do not always seem consistently motivated. I reprint Sánchez' text here rather than Marden's because its modernized lettering renders it more readable, and because it seems based in part on a slightly different manuscript tradition. On this latter problem the reader may consult Sánchez, *1*, 121, and especially Brian Dutton's forthcoming book on the *Vida de San Millán* (London, Támesis Ltd.).

Havíagelo la madre todo bien razonado,
Que non quiera mentir por un rico Condado.

6. De suso la nombramos, acordarvos podedes,
Emparedada era, yacia entre paredes,
Havia vida lazrada qual entender podedes,
Si su vida leyerdes, asi lo probaredes.

7. Santos fueron sin dubda è iustos los parientes,
Que fueron de tal fixa engendrar merescientes:
De niñes facia ella fechos muy convenientes,
Estaban maravilladas ende todas las gentes.

8. Como dice del Apostol Sant Paulo la lection,
Fue esta santa Virgen vaso de *oracion*,
Ca puso Dios en ella cumplida bendicion,
E vido en los Cielos mucha grant vision.

9. Bien es que vos digamos luego en la entrada
Qual nombre li pusieron quando fue baptizada:
Como era preciosa mas que piedra preciada,
Nombre habia de oro, Oria era llamada.

10. Havemos en el prologo mucho detardado,
Sigamos la estoria, esto es aguisado,
Los dias son non grandes, anochecerá privado,
Escribir en tiniebra es un mester pesado.

11. Fue de Villa Vellayo Amunna natural,
El su marido santo Gracía otro tal,
Siempre en bien puñaron, partieronse de mal,
Cobdiciaban la gracia de el Rey celestial.

12. Omes eran catolicos, vivian vida derecha,
Daban à los Sennores à cada uno su pecha,
No fallaba en ellos el diablo retrecha,
El que todas sazones à los buenos acecha.

13. Nunca querian sus carnes mantener à grant vicio,
Ponian toda femencia en fer à Dios servicio,
Esso avian por pascua è por muy grant delicio,
A Dios ponian delante en todo su officio.

14. Rogaban à Dios siempre de firme corazon
Que lis quissiese dar alguna criazon,
Que para el su servicio fuese, que para al non,
E siempre meiorase esta devocion.

15. Si lis dió otros fixos non lo dice la leyenda;

Mas diólis una fixa de spiritual facienda,
Que hovo con su carne baraia è contienda,
Por consentir al cuerpo nunca soltó la rienda.

16. Apríso las costumbres de los buenos parientes,
Quanto li castigaban ponia en ello mientes,
Con ambos sus labriellos apretaba sus dientes,
Que non saliessen dende palabras desconvenientes.

17. Quiso seer la madre de mas aspera vida,
Entró emparedada de celicio vestida,
Martiriaba sus carnes à la mayor medida,
Que non fuese la alma del diablo vencida.

18. Si ante fuera buena, fue despues muy meyor,
Placia su servicio à Dios nuestro Sennor,
Los pueblos de la tierra facianli grant honor,
Salia à luengas tierras la su buena loor.

19. Dexemos de la madre, en la fixa tornemos,
Essas laudes tengamos cuyas bodas comemos:
Si nos cantar sopieremos, grant materia tenemos,
Menester nos será todo el seso que avemos.

20. Desque mudó los dientes, luego à pocos años
Pagabase muy poco de los seglares pannos:
Vistió otros vestidos de los Monges calaños,
Podrian valer pocos dineros los sus peaños.

21. Desamparó el mundo Oria toca negrada,
En un rencon angosto entró emparedada,
Sofria grant astinencia, vivia vida lazrada,
Por onde ganó en cabo de Dios rica soldada.

22. Era esta reclusa vaso de caridat,
Templo de paciencia è de humildat,
Non amaba oir palabras de vanidat,
Luz era e confuerto de la su vecindat.

23. Porque angosta era la emparedacion,
Teniala por muy larga el su buen corazon:
Siempre rezaba Psalmos è facia oracion,
Foradaba los Cielos la su devocion.

24. Tanto fue Dios pagado de las sus oraciones
Que li mostró en Cielo tan grandes visiones
Que debian à los omes cambiar los corazones:
Non las podrian contar palabras ni sermones.

25. Tercera noche era despues de Navidat,
De Santa Eugenia era festividat,
Vido de visiones una infinidat,
Onde parece que era plena de santidat.

26. Despues de las matinas leida la leccion
Escuchóla bien Oria con grant devocion:
Quiso dormir un poco, tomar consolacion,
Vido en poca hora un grant vision.

27. Vido tres santas virgines de grant auctoridat,
Todas tres fueron martires en poquiella edat:
Agata en Catanna essa rica ciudat,
Olalia en Melerida ninna de grant beldat.

28. Cecilia fue tercera, una martir preciosa
Que de Don Jesu Christo quiso seer esposa:
Non quiso otra suegra sino la Gloriosa
Que fue mas bella que ni lilio ni rosa.

29. Todas estas tres virgines que avedes oidas,
Todas eran iguales de un color vestidas:
Semeyaba que eran en un dia nacidas,
Lucian como estrellas, tanto eran de bellidas.

30. Estas tres santas virgines en Cielo coronadas
Tenian sendas palombas en sus manos alzadas,
Mas blancas que las nieves que non son coceadas:
Parescia que non fueran en palombar criadas.

31. La niña que iacia en paredes cerrada
Con esta vision fue mucho embargada;
Pero del Spiritu Santo fue luego conortada:
Demandólis qui eran, è fue bien aforzada.

32. Fablaronli las virgines de fermosa manera,
Agatha è Eolalia, Cecilia la tercera:
Oria, por ti tomamos esta tan grant carrera:
Sepas bien que te tengas por nuestra compañera.

33. Combidarte venimos, nuestra hermana,
Embianos Don Christo, de quien todo bien mana,
Que subas à los Cielos, è que veas que gana
El servicio que faces è la saya de lana.

34. Tu mucho te deleitas en las nuestras passiones,
De amor è de grado leies nuestras razones,
Queremos que entiendas entre las visiones

Qual gloria recibiemos, è quales galardones.

35. Respondió la reclusa que avia nombre Oria:
Yo no seria digna de veer tant grant gloria;
Mas si me recibiesedes vos en vuestra memoria,
Alla seria complida toda la mi estoria.

36. Fixa, dixo Ollallia, tu tal cosa non digas,
Ca as sobre los Cielos amigos è amigas:
Asi mandas tus carnes, è assi las aguissas
Que por subir à los Cielos tu digna te predigas.

37. Rescibe este conseio, la mi fixa querida,
Guarda esta palomba, todo lo al olvida:
Tu ve do ella fuere, non seas decebida,
Guiate por nos, fixa, ca Christus te combida.

38. Oiendo este conseio que Olalia li daba,
Alzó Oria los oios, arriba onde estaba,
Vido una coluña, à los Cielos pujaba,
Tanto era de enfiesta que aves la cataba.

39. Avia en la coluna escalones è gradas:
Veer solemos tales en las torres obradas:
Yo sobi por algunas, esto muchas vegadas,
Por tal suben las almas que son aventuradas.

40. Moviose la palomba, comenzó de volar,
Suso contra los Cielos comenzó de pujar:
Catabala Don Oria donde iria à posar,
Non la podia por nada de voluntat sacar.

41. Empezaron las virgines lazradas à sobir,
Empezolas la dueña reclusa à seguir:
Quando Don Oria cató, Dios lo quiso complir,
Fue puia[da] ensomo por verdat vos decir.

42. Quando dormia Jacob cerca de la carrera,
Vido sobir los Angeles por una escalera:
A esta relucia ca obra de Dios era,
Entonce perdió la pierna en essa liz vecera.

43. Ya eran, Deo gracias, las virgines ribadas,
Eran de la columpna ensomo aplanadas,
Vieron un buen arbol, cimas bien compasadas,
Que de diversas flores estaban bien pobladas.

44. Verde era el ramo de foyas bien cargado,
Facia sombra sabrosa è logar muy temprado,

Tenia redor el tronco maravilloso prado,
Mas valia esso solo que un rico regnado.

45. Estas quatro doncellas ligeras mas que viento
Ovieron con este arbol placer è pagamento:
Subieron en el todas, todas de buen taliento,
Ca avian en el folgura en el grant cumplimiento.

46. Estando en el arbol estas duennas contadas,
Sus palomas en manos alegres è pagadas,
Vieron en el Cielo finiestras foradadas,
Lumbres salian por ellas, de duro serian contadas.

47. Salieron tres personas por essas aberturas,
Cosas eran Angelicas con blancas vestiduras,
Sendas vergas en manos de preciosas pinturas,
Vinieron contra ellas en humanas figuras.

48. Tomaron estas virgines estos santos varones
Como à sendas peñolas en aquellos bordones:
Pusíeronlas mas altas en otras regiones,
Alla vidieron muchas honrradas processiones.

49. Don Oria la reclusa de Dios mucho amada,
Como la ovo ante Olalia castigada,
Catando la palomba como bien acordada,
Subió en pos las otras à essa grant posada.

50. Puyaba à los Cielos sin ayuda ninguna,
Non li facia embargo, ni el Sol ni la Luna,
A Dios havia pagado por manera alguna,
Si non, non subria tanto la fixa de Amunna.

51. Entraron por el Cielo que abierto estaba,
Alegrose con ellas la corte que y moraba,
Plógolis con la quarta que las tres aguardaba,
Por essa Serraniella menos non se preciaba.

52. Apareciolis luego una muy grant companna,
En vestiduras albas fermosas por fazanna:
Semeioli à Oria una cosa estranna,
Ca nunca vido cosa de aquesta su calanna.

53. Preguntó à las otras la de Villa Vellayo:
Decitme, qué es esto por Dios è Sant Pelayo?
En el mi corazon una grand dubda trayo:
Meior parescen estos que las flores de Mayo.

54. Dixeronli las otras: oye, fixa querida,

Colonges fueron estos, omes de santa vida;
Tuvieron en el mundo la carne apremida,
Agora son en gloria en leticia complida.

55. Conosció la fixa buenos quatro varones,
Los que nunca vidiera en ningunas sazones:
Bartolomeo ducho de escribir passiones,
Don Gomes de Masiella, que daba bien raciones.

56. Don Xemeno tercero un vecino leal,
De el barrio de Vellayo fue esti natural:
Galindo su criado, qual el, bien otro tal,
Que sopo de bien mucho è sabia poco mal.

57. Fueron mas adelante en esa romeria,
Las martires delante, la freira en su guia,
Aparesciolis otra asaz grant compannia,
De la de los Colonges avia grant meioria.

58. Todos vestian casullas de preciosas colores,
Blagos en las siniestras como predicadores,
Calices en las diestras de oro muy meiores,
Semeiaba ministros de precioso Sennores.

59. Demandó la Serrana, qué eran esta cosa?
Qué procesion es esta tan grande è tan preciossa?
Dixeronli las martires respuesta muy sabrosa:
Obispos fueron estos siervos de la Gloriosa.

60. Porque daban al pueblo beber de buen castigo,
Por ende tienen los calices cada uno consigo:
Refirian con los quentos al mortal enemigo
Que engañó à Eva con un astroso figo.

61. Conoció la reclusa en essa processon
Al Obispo Don Sancho, un precioso varon:
Con el à Don Garcia su leal compannon
Que sirvió à Don Christo de firme corazon.

62. Dixeronli las martires à Oria la Serrana:
El Obispo Don Gomez non es aqui, Hermana:
Peroque trayo mitra fue cosa muy llana,
Tal fue como el arbol que florece è non grana.

63. Visto este convento, esta santa mesnada,
Fue à otra comarca esta freyra levada:
El coro de las Virgines procesion tan honrrada
Salieron rescibirla de voluntat pagada.

64. Salieron recibirla con responsos doblados,
    Fueron abrazarla con los brazos alzados:
    Tenian con esta novia los corazones bien pagados,
    Non ficieran tal gozo annos havia passados.

65. Embargada fue Oria con el recibimiento,
    Ca tenia que non era de tal merecimiento:
    Estaba atordida en grant desarramiento;
    Pero nunca de cosas ovo tal pagamiento.

66. Si del Rey de la gloria li fuese otorgado,
    Fincaria con las Virgines de amor è de grado:
    Mas aun esi tiempo non era allegado
    Para recibir soldada de el lazerio passado.

67. El coro de las Virgines una fermosa az
    Dieronli à la freyra todas por orden paz:
    Dixeronli: contigo mucho nos plaz:
    Para en esta companna digna eres assaz.

68. Esto por nuestro merito nos non lo ganariemos,
    Esto en que somos, nos non lo mereciemos;
    Mas el nuestro Esposo à quien voto ficiemos
    Fizonos esta gracia porque bien lo quisiemos.

69. Oria, que ante estaba mucho embergozada,
    Con estos dichos buenos fizose mas osada,
    Preguntó à las Virgines esa santa mesnada.
    Por una su maestra que la ovo criada.

70. Una maestra ovo de muy santa vida,
    Urraca li dixeron muger buena complida,
    Emparedada vísco una buena partida,
    Era de la maestra Oria muy querida.

71. Preguntolis por ella la freyra que oydes:
    Decitme, mis Sennoras, por Dios, à qui servides,
    Urraca es en estas las que aqui venides?
    Grant gracia me faredes, si esto me decides.

72. Mi ama fue al mundo esta por quien demando,
    Lazrró conmigo mucho, è à mi castigando,
    Querria yo que fuesse en esti vuestro vando,
    Por su deudor me tengo durmiendo è velando.

73. Dixeronli las Virgines nuevas de grant sabor:
    Esa que tu demandas, Urraca la Seror,
    Compannera es nuestra è nuestra morador:

Con Justa su discipula sierva del Criador.

74. Ruegovos, dixo Oria, por Dios que la llamedes:
Si me la demostrardes, grant mercet me faredes:
Yo por la su doctrina entré entre padredes,
Yo ganaré y mucho, vos nada non perdredes.

75. Clamaronla por nombre las otras companneras,
Respondiolis Urraca à las voces primeras:
Conoció la voz Oria, entendió las senneras;
Mas ver no la podio por ningunas maneras.

76. La az era muy luenga, eso la embargaba,
Que non podia veerla, ca en cabo estaba:
Levola à delante la voz que la guiaba,
Pero à la maestra nunca la olvidaba.

77. En cabo de las Virgines, toda la az pasada,
Falló muy rica siella de oro bien labrada:
De piedras muy preciosas toda engastonada,
Mas estaba vacia è muy bien seellada.

78. Vedia sobre la siella muy rica acitára,
Non podria en este mundo cosa ser tan clara:
Dios solo faz tal cosa que sus siervos empara,
Que non podria comprarla toda alfoz de Lara.

79. Una duenna hermosa de edat mancebiella
Voxmea havia nombre, guardaba esta siella:
Daria por tal su Reyno el Rey de Castiella,
E seria tal mercado que seria por fabliella.

80. Alzó Oria los oios escontra Aquilon,
Vido grandes compannas, fermosa criazon:
Semeiaban vestidos todos de vermeion,
Preguntó à las otras: estos que cosa son?

81. Dixeronli las virgines que eran sus guionas,
Todos estos son martires, unas nobles personas,
Dexaronse matar à golpes de azconas,
Jesu Christo por ende diolis ricas coronas.

82. Alli es Sant Estevan el que fue apedreado,
Sant Lorente el que Cesar ovo despues asado,
Sant Vicente el caboso de Valerio criado:
Mucho otro buen lego, mucho buen ordenado.

83. Vido mas adelante en un apartamiento
De santos hermitannos un preciosso conviento,

Que sufrieron por Christo mucho amargo viento
Por ganar à las almas vida è guarimiento.

84. Conosció entre todos un Monge ordenado:
Monio li dixeron, como diz el dictado:
A otro su discipulo, Munno era llamado,
Que de Valvanera fue Abat consagrado.

85. Y vido à Galindo en esa compannia,
Ladrones lo mataron en la hermitannia:
Y vido à su padre que llamaban Garcia,
Aquelli que non quiso seguir nulla folia.

86. Vido à los Apostolos mas en alto logar,
Cada uno en su trono en que debia jusgar:
A los Evangelistas y los vido estar,
La su claridad ome non la podrie contar.

87. Estos son los nuestros padres cabdiellos generales,
Principes de los pueblos, son omes principales,
Jesu Christo fue Papa, estos los Cardenales,
Que sacaron de el mundo las serpientes mortales.

88. Como asmaba Oria à su entendimiento,
Oió fablar à Christo en esse buen conviento;
Mas non podio veerlo à todo su taliento,
Ca bien lieve non era de tal merecimiento.

89. Dexemos lo al todo, à la siella tornemos,
La matiera es alta, temo que pecaremos;
Mas en esto culpados nos seer non debemos,
Ca al non escribimos, sí non lo que leemos.

90. De suso lo dixiemos, la materia lo daba,
Voxmea avia nombre la que la siella guardaba:
Como rayos de el Sol, assi relampagaba:
Bien fue felix la alma para quien estaba.

91. Vistia esta manceba preciosa vestidura,
Mas preciosa que oro, mas que la seda pura;
Era sobresennada de buena escritura.
Non cubrió ome vivo tan rica cobertura.

92. Avie en ella nombres de omes de gran vida,
Que sirvieron à Christo con voluntat complida;
Pero de los reclusos fue la mayor partida
Que domaron sus carnes à la mayor medida.

93. Las letras de los Justos de mayor sanctidat

Parecian mas leybles de mayor claridat:
Los otros mas sorienda de menor claridat
Eran mas tenebrosas de grant obscuridat.

94. Non se podia la freyra de la siella toller:
Dixole à Voxmea que lo querria saber:
Este tan grant adobo cuyo podria ser?
Ca non seria por nada comprado por haver.

95. Respondioli Voxmea, dixoli buen mandado,
Amiga, bien has fecho è bien has demandado:
Todo esto que vees à ti es otorgado,
Ca es del tu servicio el Criador pagado.

96. Todo esti adobo à ti es comendado,
El solar è la siella, Dios sea ende laudado,
Si non te lo quitare conseio del pecado
El que hizo à Eva comer el mal bocado.

97. Si como tu me dices, dixoli Santa Oria,
A mi es prometida esta tamanna gloria,
Luego en esti talamo querria ser novia;
Non querria de el oro tornar à la escoria:

98. Respondioli la otra como bien razonada:
Non puede seer esto, Oria, esta vegada,
De tornar as à el cuerpo, yacer emparedada,
Fasta que sea toda tu vida acabada.

99. Las tres martires santas que con ella vinieron
En ninguna sazon de ella non se partieron;
Siempre fueron con ella, con ella andidieron
Fasta que à su casa misma la tragieron.

100. Rogó à estas Santas de toda voluntat
Que rogassen por ella al Rey de meiestat,
Que gelo condonase por la su piedat
De fincar con Voxmea en essa heredat.

101. Rogaron à Dios ellas quanto meior supieron,
Mas lo que pedia ella ganar non lo podieron:
Fabloles Dios de el Cielo, la voz bien la oieron,
La su Majestad grant; pero non la vieron.

102. Dixolis: piense Oria de ir à su logar,
Non vino tiempo aun de aqui habitar:
Aun ave un poco el cuerpo à lazrar,
Despues verná el tiempo de la siella cobrar.

103. Señor, dixo è Padre, peroque non te veo,
     De ganar la tu gracia siempre ovi desseo:
     Si una vez salliero del solar en que seo,
     Non tornare y nunca segun lo que yo creo.

104. Los Cielos son mucho altos, yo pecadriz mezquina
     Si una vez tornaro en la mi calabrina,
     Non fallare en el mundo sennora nin madrina,
     Por qui yo esto cobre nin tarde nin ayna.

105. Dixoli aun de cabo la voz del Criador:
     Oria, del poco merito non ayas temor:
     Con lo que has lazrado ganesti el mi amor,
     Quitar non te lo puede ningun escantador.

106. Lo que tu tanto temes è estás desmedrida,
     Que los Cielos son altos, enfiesta la subida,
     Yo te los faré llanos, la mi fixa querida,
     Que non havrás embargo en toda tu venida.

107. De lo que tu temes non serás embargada,
     Non abrás nul embargo, non te temas por nada:
     Mi fixa, benedicta vaias è santiguada,
     Torna à tu casiella, reza tu matinada.

108. Tomaronla las martires que ante la guiaron
     Por essa escalera por la que la levaron:
     En muy poquiello rato al cuerpo la tornaron,
     Espertó ella luego que ellas la dexaron.

109. Abrió ella los oios, cató enderredor,
     Non vido à las martires, ovo muy mal sabor;
     Vidose alongada de muy grand dulzor,
     Havia muy grande cuita è sobeio dolor.

110. Non cuidaba veer la hora ni el dia
     Que podiese tornar à essa confradia:
     Doliase de la siella que estaba vacia,
     Siella que Dios ficiera à tan gran maestria.

111. Por estas visiones la reclusa Don Oria
     Non dió en si entrada à nulla vanagloria:
     Por amor de la alma non perder la victoria
     Non facia à sus carnes nulla misericordia.

112. Martiriaba las carnes dandolis gran lacerio,
     Complia dias è noches todo su ministerio:
     Jeiunios è vigilias è rezar el Psalterio,

Queria à todas guisas seguir el Evangelio.

113. El Rey de los Reyes, Señor de los Señores,
En cuya mano iacen justos è pecadores,
Quiso sacar à Oria de estos baticores,
E ferla compannera de compannas meiores.

114. Once meses, Sennores, podrie haber pasados
Desque vido los pleitos que avemos contados:
De Sanctos è de Sanctas conventos mucho onrrados,
Mas no los havia Oria encara olvidados.

115. En esi mes onceno vido grant vission,
Tan grande como las otras las que escritas son:
Non se partia Dios de ella en ninguna sazon,
Ca siempre tenia ella en el su corazon.

116. Tercera noche ante de el Martir Saturnino
Que cae en Noviembre de Sant Andres vecino,
Vinoli una gracia, meior nunca le vino,
Mas dulce è mas sabrosa era que pan nin vino.

117. Seria la meatat de la noche pasada,
Avia mucho velado, Oria era cansada,
Acostose un poco flaca è muy lazrada,
Non era la camenna de molsa ablentada.

118. Vido venir tres virgines todas de una guisa,
Todas venian vestidas de una blanca frisa,
Nunca tan blanca vido nin toca nin camisa,
Nunca tal cosa ovo nin Genua nin Pisa,

119. Ende à poco rato vino Santa Maria,
Vinolis à las Virgines gozo è alegria,
Como con tal Sennora todas havian buen dia,
Alli fue adonada toda la confradria.

120. Dixeronli à Oria: tu que yaces sonnosa,
Levantate y recibe à la Virgen gloriosa,
Que es Madre de Christo è fixa è esposa:
Serás mal acordada si faces otra cosa.

121. Respondiolis la freira con grant humildat:
Si à ella ploguiesse pora la su piadat
Que yo llegar podiesse à la su maiestat,
Cadria à sus piedes de buena voluntat.

122. Aves avia Don Oria el vierbo acabado
Plegó la Gloriosa: Dios tan buen encontrado!

       Relumbró la confita de relumbor doblado:
       Qui oviese tal huespeda seria bien venturado.

123. La Madre benedicta de los Cielos Sennora
       Mas fermosa de mucho que non es la Aurora,
       Non lo puso por plazo nin sola una hora,
       Fue luego abrazarla à Oria la Serora.

124. Ovo en el falago Oria grant alegria:
       Preguntola si era ella Santa Maria:
       Non ayas nulla dubda, dixol, fijuela mia:
       Yo so la que tu ruegas de noche è de dia.

125. Yo so Santa Maria la que tu mucho quieres,
       Que saqué de porfazo à todas las mugieres:
       Fixa, Dios es contigo: si tu firme estovieres,
       Irás à grant riqueza, fixa, quando morieres.

126. Todas eran iguales de una calidat,
       De una captenencia è de una edat:
       Ninguna à las otras non vencia de bondat,
       Trahían en todas cosas todas tres igualdat.

127. Trahían estas tres virgines una noble lechiga,
       Con adobos reales non pobres nin mendiga:
       Fablaronli à Oria de Dios buena amiga:
       Fixa, oy un poco, si Dios te bendiga.

128. Lievate de la tierra que es fria è dura,
       Subi en este lecho, yazrás mas en mollura:
       E aqui la Reyna, de esto sei segura,
       Si te falla en tierra avrá de ti rencura.

129. Dueñas, dixolis Oria, non es eso derecho,
       Para vieio è flaco conviene este lecho:
       Yo valiente so è niña por sofrir todo fecho:
       Si yo y me echase, Dios avria ende despecho.

130. Lecho quiero yo aspero de sedas aguijosas,
       Non merecen mis carnes iacer tan viciosas:
       Por Dios que non seades en esto porfidiosas,
       Para muy grandes omes son cosas tan preciosas.

131. Tomaronla las virgines dandol grandes sosannos,
       Echaronla à Oria en esos ricos pannos:
       Oria con gran cochura daba gemidos estrannos,
       Ca non era vezada de entrar en tales bannos.

132. Luego que fue la freira en el lecho echada,

Fue de bien grandes lumbres la ciella alumbrada,
Fue de virgenes muchas en un rato poblada,
Todas venian honrrarla à la emparedada.

133. Madre, dixoli Oria, si tu eres Maria,
De la que fabló tanto el varon Isaia,
Por seer bien certera algun signo queria,
Porque segura fuese que salvarme podria.

134. Dixol la Gloriosa: Oria, la mi lazrada,
Que de tan luengos tiempos eres emparedada,
Yo te daré un signo, sennal buena probada:
Si la sennal vidieres, estonce seras pagada.
. . . . .²

135. Esto ten tu por signo por certera senal:
Ante de pocos dias enfermaras muy mal,
Serás fuerte embargada de enfermedad mortal,
Qual nunca la oviste, terrásla bien por tal.

136. Veráste en grant quexa, de muerte serás cortada,
Serás à pocos dias desti mundo passada,
Irás do tu cobdicias à la silla honrrada,
La que tiene Voxmea para ti bien guardada.

137. En cuita yacia Oria dentro en su casiella,
Estaba un grant conviento de fuera de la ciella,
Rezando su Psalterio cada uno en su siella,
E non tenia ninguno enjuta la maxiella.

138. Yaciendo la enferma en tal tribulacion,
Maguera entre dientes facia su oracion:
Queria batir sus pechos, mas non habia sazon,
Pero queria la mano alzar en esi son.

139. Traspósose un poco, ca era quebrantada,
Fue à monte Olivete en vision levada,
Vido y tales cosas de que fue saborgada,
Si non la despertasen, cuidó seer folgada.

140. La madre en la rabia non se podia folgar,
Ca todos se cuidaban que se queria pasar:
Metiose en la casa por la cosa probar,
Comenzó de traherla, ovo de despertar.

---

2. "Aquí falta una hoja en las copias modernas, porque falta en los códices del monasterio de San Millán" [Sánchez' note].

141. Vido redor el monte una bella anchura,
     En ella de olivos una grant espesura,
     Cargados de olivas mucho sobre mesura,
     Podria vevir so ellos ome à grant folgura.

142. Vido por esa sombra muchas gentes venir,
     Todas venian gradosas à Oria rescebir,
     Todas bien aguisadas de calzar è de vestir,
     Querian si fuese tiempo al Cielo la sobir.

143. Eran estas compannas de preciosos varones,
     Todos vestidos eran de blancos ciclatones,
     Semeiaban de Angeles todas sus guaniciones:
     Otras tales vidieran en algunas sazones.

144. Vido entre los otros un ome anciano,
     Don Sancho li dixeron, varon fue Masellano,
     Nunca lo ovo visto nil tánso de la mano;
     Pero la Serraniella conosció al Serrano.

145. Con esto la enferma ovo muy gran pesar,
     En aquella sazon non querria espertar,
     Ca estaba en grant gloria en sabroso logar,
     E cuydaba que nunca alla podria tornar.

146. Aviales poco grado à los despertadores,
     Siquiera à la madre, siquiera à los serores,
     Ca estaba en grant gloria entre buenos Señores,
     Que non sentia un punto de todos los dolores.

147. Dicia entre los dientes con una voz cansada:
     Monte Olivete monte Olivete ca non dicia al nada:
     Non gelo entendia nadi de la posada,
     Ca non era la voz de tal guisa formada.

148. Otras buenas mugieres qui cerca li sedien,
     Vidian que murmuraba, mas no la entendien:
     Por una maravilla esta cosa havien,
     Estaban en gran dubda si era mal ò bien.

149. La madre de la duenna fizo à mi clamar,
     Fizome en la casa de la fija entrar,
     Yo que la afincasse si podiesse fablar,
     Ca quiera decir algo, non la podian entrar.

150. Dixeronli à ella quando yo fui entrado:
     Oria, abre los oios, è oirás buen mandado:
     Recibe à Don Munno el tu amo honrrado

Que viene despedirse del tu buen gasaiado.

151. Luego que oió este mandado Oria,
Abrió ambos los oios, entró en su memoria,
E dixo: ay mesquina! estaba en gran gloria:
Porque me despertaron so en gran querimonia.

152. Si solo un poquiello me oviesen dexada,
Grant amor me ficieran, seria terminada,
Ca entre tales omes era yo arribada
Que contra los sus bienes el mundo non es nada.

153. Ovo de estas palabras Don Muño mucho placer:
Amiga, dixo, esto fáznoslo entender:
Bien non lo entendemos, querriamoslo saber,
Esto que te rogamos tu debeslo facer.

154. Amigo, dijo ella, non te mintre en nada,
Por facer el tu ruego mucho so adebdada,
A monte Oliveti fui en vission levada,
Vidi y tales cosas por qui so muy pagada.

155. Vidi y logar bueno sobra buen arbolado,
El fruto de los arboles non seria preciado,
De campos grant anchura, de flores grant mercado.
Guarria la su olor à ome entecado.

156. Vidi y grandes gentes de personas honrradas,
Que eran bien vestidas todas, è bien calzadas,
Todas me recibieron con laudes bien cantadas,
Todas eran en una voluntat acordadas.

157. Tal era la companna, tal era el logar;
Ome que y morase nunca veria pesar:
Si oviesse mas un poco y estar,
Podria muchos bienes ende acarrear.

158. Dixoe Muño à Oria: cobdicias alla ir?
Dixol à Muño Oria: yo si, mas que vivir:
E tu non perdrias nada de conmigo venir:
Dixol Munno: quisiesselo eso Dios consentir.

159. Con sabor de la cosa quisose levantar,
Como ome que quiere en carrera entrar:
Dixoli Munno: Oria fuelga en tu logar,
Non es agora tiempo por en naves entrar.

160. En esta pleitesia no quiero detardar;
Si por bien lo tovierdes, quierovos detaiar,

A la fin de la duenna me quiero acostar,
Levarla à la siella, despues ir à folgar.

161. El mes era de Marzo la segunda semana,
Fiesta de Sant Gregorio de Leandre cormana,
Hora quando los hombres facen meridiana,
Fue quexada la duenna que siempre vistia lana.

162. La madre de la duenna, cosa de Dios amada,
[D]el duelo de la fixa estaba muy lazrada:
Non dormiera la noche, estaba apesgada,
Lo que ella comia non era fascas nada.

163. Yo Munno è Don Gomez cellerer de el logar
Oviemos à Amunna de firmes à rogar
Que fuese à su lecho un poquiello à folgar,
Ca nos la guardariamos, si quisiesse passar.

164. Quanto fue acostada fue luego adormida,
Un vision vido que fue luego complida:
Vido à su marido ome de santa vida,
Padre de la reclusa que yacia mal tanida.

165. Vido à Don Garcia que fuera su marido,
Padre era de Oria, bien ante fue transido:
Entendió bien que era por la fixa venido,
E que era sin dubda el su curso complido.

166. Preguntóli Amunna, decitme, Don Garcia,
Quál es vuestra venida? yo saberlo querria:
Si vos vala Don Christo, Madre Sante Maria,
Decitme de la fixa si verá cras el dia.

167. Sepas, dixo Garcia, fágote bien certera,
Cerca anda del cabo Oria de la carrera:
Cuenta que es finada, ca la hora espera,
Es de las sus iornadas esta la postremera.

168. Vido con Don Garcia tres personas seer
Tan blancas que nul ome non lo podria creer:
Todas de edat una et de un parescer,
Mas non fablaban nada nin querian signas fer.

169. Despierta fue Amunna, la vission pasada:
Si ante fue en cuita, despues fue mas coitada,
Ca sabia que la fixa seria luego pasada,
E que fincaria ella triste è dessarrada.

170. Non echó esti sueño la duenna en olvido
Ni lo que li dixiera Garcia su marido:

Recontógelo todo a Munno su querido:
El decorólo todo como bien entendido.

171. Bien lo decoró eso como todo lo al,
Bien gelo contó ella, non lo aprendió él mal,
Por ende de la su vida fizo libro caudal:
Yo ende lo saqué esto de esi su misal.

172. Conjuróla Amunna à su fixuela Oria:
Fixa, si Dios vos lieve à la su santa Gloria,
Si vision vidiestes ò alguna historia,
Decítmelo demientre avedes la memoria.

173. Madre, dixo la fixa, qué me afincades tanto.
Dexatme, sí vos vala Dios el buen Padre Santo:
Asaz tengo en mí lacerio è quebranto:
Mas me pesa la lengua que un pesado canto.

174. Queredes que vos fable, yo no puedo fablar:
Veedes que non puedo la palabra formar:
Madre, si me quisierdes tan mucho afincar,
Ante de la mi hora me puedo enfogar.

175. Madre, si Dios quisiesse que pudiese vevir,
Aun asaz tenia cosas que vos decir;
Mas quando no lo quiere el Criador sofrir,
Lo que à él ploguiere es todo de sofrir.

176. Fuel viniendo à Oria la hora postremera:
Fuese mas aquejando, à boca de noche era:
Alzó la mano diestra de fermosa manera:
Fizo cruz en su fruente, sanctiguó su mollera.

177. Alzó ambas las manos, juntólas en igual,
Como qui riende gracias al buen Rey espiritual:
Cerró oios è boca la reclusa leal:
Rindió à Dios la alma, nunca mas sintió mal.

178. Avia buenas compannas en essi pasamiento,
El buen Abat Don Pedro persona de buen tiento,
Monges è Hermitannos, un general conviento,
Estos facian obsequio è todo complimiento.

179. Fue esti santo cuerpo ricamente guardado,
En sus pannos de orden ricamente aguisado:
Fue muchas de vegadas el Psalterio rezado:
Non se partieron de elli fasta fue soterrado.

180. Si entender queredes toda certanidat,
Do yace esta duenna de grant santidat,

En Sant Millan de Suso, esta es la verdat:
Fáganos Dios por ella mercet è caridat.

181. Cerca de la iglesia es la su sepultura,
A pocas de pasadas en una angustura,
Dentro en una cueba so una piedra dura,
Como merescia ella non de tal apostura.

182. La fija è la madre ambas de santa vida,
Como ovieron siempre gran amor è complida,
En la muerte y todo non an cosa partida,
Cerca yace de Oria Amunna sepelida.

183. Cuerpos son derecheros que sean adorados,
Ca sufrieron por Christo lacerios muy granados:
Ellas fagan à Dios ruegos multiplicados
Que nos salve las almas, perdone los pecados.

184. Gonzalo li dixeron al versificador,
Que en su portaleyo fizo esta labor:
Ponga en el su gracia Dios el nuestro Sennor,
Que vea la su gloria en el Reyno mayor.

185. Aun no me queria, Sennores, espedir,
Aun fincan cosiellas que vos è de decir:
La obra comenzada bien la quiero complir,
Que non aya ninguno porque me escarnir.

186. Desque murió la fixa santa emparedada,
Andaba la su madre por ella fetillada:
Solo que la podiesse sonnar una vegada,
Teniase por guarida è por muy confortada.

187. Sopo Dios entender bien el su corazon,
Demostróli à Amunna una grant vission,
Que sopo de la fixa que era ò que non:
Aun esso nos finca de todo el sermon.

188. Cayó una grant fiesta un dia sennalado,
Dia de Cincuesma que es Mayo mediado,
Ensonnó esta duenna un suenno desseado,
Por qual muchas vegadas ovo à Dios rogado.

189. Cantadas las matinas, la licencia soltada,
Que fuesse quis quissiese folgar à su posada,
Acostóse un poco Amunna bien lazrada,
E luego ensonnó la su fixa amada.

190. Abrazaronse ambas como facian en vida:
Fixa, dixo la madre, avedesme guarida:

Quiero que me digades qual es vuestra venida,
O si sodes en pena ò sodes ende salida.

191. Madre, dixo la fixa, fiesta es general,
Como es Resurection, ò como la Natal:
Oy prenden los Christianos el cebo espiritual,
El cuerpo de Don Christo mi Sennor natural.

192. Pasqua es en que deben Christianos comulgar,
Recibir Corpus Domini sagrado en el altar:
Yo essi quiero, madre, rescibir è tomar,
E tener mi carrera, allá me quiero andar.

193. Madre, si bien me quieres, è pro me quieres buscar,
Manda llamar los Clerigos, venganme comulgar,
Que luego me querria de mi grado tornar,
E nin poco nin mucho non querria tardar.

194. Fixa, dixo la madre, do vos queredes ir?
Madre, dixo la fixa, à los Cielos sobir,
Sinrazon me faces, fixa, quiero voslo decir,
Que tan luego queredes de mi vos despartir.

195. Mas fixa, una cosa vos quiero demandar:
Si en el *pensamiento* [3] recibiestes pesar?
O si vos dieron luego en el cielo logar?
O vos ficieron ante à la puerta musar?

196. Madre, dixo la fixa, en la noche primera
Non entré al palacio, non sé por qual manera:
Otro dia mannana abrióme la portera,
Recibieronme, madre, todos por compannera.

197. Fixa, en esa noche que entrar non podiestes,
Quién vos fizo compaña mientre fuera estoviestes?
Madre, las santas Virgines que de suso oiestes:
Estovi en tal delicio en qual nunca oyestes.

198. La Virgo gloriosa lo que me prometió,
Ella sea laudada, bien me lo guardó:
En el mi *pensaminto* de mi non se partió:
De la su santa gracia en mi mucha metió.

199. Otra cosa vos quiero, mi fixa, preguntar,
En qual compañia sodes, facétmelo entrar?
Madre, dixo la fixa, estó en buen logar,
Qual nunca por mi merito non podria ganar.

200. Entre los Inocentes so, madre, heredada,

3. "Acaso *pasamiento*, que es el tránsito, la muerte" [Sánchez' note].

Los que puso Erodes por Christo à espada,
Yo non lo merezria de seer tan honrrada;
Mas plógo à Don Christo la su virtut sagrada.

201. Estas palabras dichas è muchas otras tales,
Oria la benedicta de fechos espiritales
Fuyóli à la madre de los oios corales,
Despertó luego ella, moyó los lagremales.

202. Vido sin estas otras muy grandes visiones,
De que formaria ome asaz buenas razones;
Mas tengo otras priesas de fer mis cabazones:
Quiero alzarme desto fasta otras sazones.

203. Qui en esto dubdare que nos versificamos,
Que non es esta cosa tal como nos contamos,
Pecara duramiente en Dios que adoramos:
Ca nos quanto decimos, escrito lo fallamos.

204. El que lo escribió non dirá falsedat,
Que ome bueno era de muy gran santidat:
Bien conosció à Oria, sopo su poridat:
En todo quanto dixo, dixo toda verdat.

205. De ello sopo de Oria, de la madre lo al,
De ambas era elli maestro muy leal:
Dios nos dé la gracia el buen Rey Spiritral
Que allá nin aqui nunca veamos mal. Amen.

Hic liber est scriptus, qui scripsit sit benedictus.

LOS VERSOS SIGUIENTES ESTAN
EN LA LAPIDA DEL SEPULCRO DE SANTA AURIA VIRGEN.

Hunc quem cernis lapidem scultum sacra tegit membra
Beata. Simul Auria Virgo cum matre Amunnia quies[c]unt
Femina. Et quia pro Xpo arctam duxerunt vitam,
Simul cum eo meruerunt coronari in gloria.

So esta piedra que vedes yace el cuerpo de Santa Oria,
E el de su madre Amunna fembra de buena memoria:
Fueron de grant abstinencia en esta vida transitoria,
Por que son con los Angeles las sus almas en gloria.

List of Works Consulted

Alanus ab Insulis, *Summa de arte praedicatoria, PL, 210,* cols. 111–98

Alonso, Amado, *Materia y forma en poesía,* Madrid, 1960.

Alonso, Dámaso, "Berceo y los *topoi*," in his *De los siglos oscuros al de oro* (Madrid, 1958), pp. 74–85.

———— and Carlos Bousoño, *Seis calas en la expresión literaria española,* Madrid, 1951.

Alphonso Maria de Liguori, St., *The Glories of Mary,* trans. R. A. Coffin, London, 1869.

Andrés, Fray Alfonso, ed., *Vida de Santo Domingo de Silos. Edición crítico-paleográfica del códice del siglo* XIII, Madrid, 1958.

Arnold, H., "Irregular Hemistichs in the *Milagros de Nuestra Señora* of Gonzalo de Berceo," *PMLA, 50* (1935), 335–51.

———— "Synalepha in Old Spanish Poetry: Berceo," *HR, 4* (1936), 141–58.

Artiles, Joaquín, *Los recursos literarios de Berceo,* Madrid, 1964.

Asensio, Eugenio, *Poética y realidad en el cancionero peninsular de la edad media,* Madrid, 1957.

Auerbach, Erich, "Figura," *Archivum Romanicum, 22* (1938), 436–89; reprinted in his *Scenes from the Drama of European Literature* (New York, 1955), pp. 11–76.

———— *Literary Language and Its Public in Late Latin Antiquity and in the Middle Ages,* trans. Ralph Manheim, New York, 1965.

———— *Mimesis. The Representation of Reality in Western Literature,* trans. Willard Trask, Princeton, 1953.

Augustine, St., *On Christian Doctrine,* trans. D. W. Robertson, Jr., New York, 1958.

Azorín, *Obras completas, 3 (Al margen de los clásicos),* Madrid, 1947.

Balbín Lucas, Rafael de, *Sistema de rítmica castellana,* Madrid, 1962.

Barrera, Carlos, "El alejandrino castellano," *BH, 20* (1918), 1–25.

Becker, Richard, *Gonzalo de Berceos Milagros und ihre Grundlagen*, Strassburg, 1910.

Bello, Andrés, *Opúsculos gramaticales, 1 (Ortología. Arte métrica)*, Madrid, 1890.

Benedict, St., *Regula*, in *San Benito: Su vida y su regla*, Madrid, 1954.

Benjamin, Walter, *Ursprung des deutschen Trauerspiels*, Frankfurt, 1963.

Berceo, Gonzalo de, *Martirio de San Lorenzo*, ed. C. Carroll Marden, in *PMLA, 45* (1930).

———— *Milagros de Nuestra Señora*, ed. Antonio García Solalinde, Madrid, 1922.

———— *Obras*, in *BAE, 57*, Madrid, 1898.

———— *El sacrificio de la misa*, ed. Antonio G. Solalinde, Madrid, 1913.

———— *Vida de Santo Domingo de Silos*, ed. John D. Fitz-Gerald, Paris, 1904.

Bonaventura, St., *Breviloquium* and *Itinerarium mentis in Deum*, in *Obras de San Buenaventura, 1*, 6 vols. Madrid, 1955.

Borges, Jorge Luis, "Tlön, Uqbar, Orbis Tertius," in his *Labyrinths* (New York, 1962), pp. 3–18.

Bourgain, L., *La chaire française au XIII*e *siècle*, Paris, 1879.

Briffault, Robert, *The Mothers, 3*, 3 vols. New York, 1927.

Bruyne, Edgar de, *Historia de la estética medieval*, trans. Fr. A. Suarez, 2 vols. Madrid, 1963.

Butler, Cuthbert, *Benedictine Monachism*, London, 1919.

Callcott, F., *The Supernatural in Early Spanish Literature*, New York, 1923.

Campo, Agustín del, "La técnica alegórica en la introducción de los *Milagros de Nuestra Señora*," *RFE, 28* (1944), 15–57.

Castro, Américo, *The Structure of Spanish History*, trans. Edmund King, Princeton, 1954.

Cirlot, J. E., *A Dictionary of Symbols*, trans. Jack Sage, London, 1962.

Cirot, Georges, "L'expression dans Gonzalo de Berceo," *RFE,* 9 (1922), 154–70.

Crosby, Ruth, "Oral Delivery in the Middle Ages," *Speculum,* 11 (1936), 88–110.

Curtius, Ernst Robert, *European Literature and the Latin Middle Ages,* trans. Willard Trask, New York, 1963.

——— "Zur Interpretation des Alexiusliedes," *ZRP,* 56 (1936), 113–37.

Daniélou, Jean, *Origène,* Paris, 1948.

Davy, M.-M., *Essai sur la symbolique romane,* Paris, 1955.

Delehaye, Hippolyte, *Les légendes hagiographiques,* Brussels, 1906; trans. V. M. Crawford, *The Legends of the Saints,* New York, 1907.

Donahue, Charles, "Patristic Exegesis: Summation," *Critical Approaches to Medieval Literature,* Selected Papers from the English Institute, 1958–59, ed. Dorothy Bethurum, New York, 1960.

Donaldson, E. Talbot, "Patristic Exegesis in the Criticism of Medieval Literature: the Opposition," *Critical Approaches to Medieval Literature,* Selected Papers from the English Institute, 1958–59, ed. Dorothy Bethurum, New York, 1960.

Dutton, Brian, review of Joaquín Artiles, *Los recursos literarios de Berceo, BHS,* 42 (1965), 184–86.

Eliade, Mircea, *Cosmos and History: The Myth of the Eternal Return,* trans. Willard Trask, New York, 1954.

——— *Images and Symbols,* trans. Philip Mairet, London, 1961.

——— *Myths, Dreams and Mysteries,* trans. Philip Mairet, London, 1960.

Faral, Edmond, *Les arts poétiques du XIIᵉ et du XIIIᵉ siècle,* Paris, 1962.

Férotin, Dom Marius, "La Légende de Sainte Potamia," *Analecta Bollandiana, 21* (1902), 40–42, 401–02.

Fitz-Gerald, John D., *Versification of the Cuaderna Via as Found in Berceo's Vida de Santo Domingo de Silos,* New York, 1905.

Fitzmaurice-Kelly, James, *Some Masters of Spanish Verse,* Oxford, 1924.

Fletcher, Angus, *Allegory: The Theory of a Symbolic Mode,* Ithaca, 1964.

Foerster, Wendelin, *Sankt Alexius,* Halle, 1915.

Frye, Northrop, *Anatomy of Criticism: Four Essays,* Princeton, 1957.

Gadamer, H. G., "Simbolo e allegoria," *Archivio di Filosofia* (Roma, 1958), pp. 29–33.

Gaiffier et al., "De B. Auria in Hispania," in the Bollandists' *Acta Sanctorum* (Paris-Rome, 1865), March, 2, 99–100.

Gallais, Pierre, "Formules de conteur et interventions d'auteur dans les manuscrits de la *Continuation-Gauvain,*" *Romania, 85* (1964), 181–229.

Gantner, J., *Romanische Plastik,* Vienna, 1948.

Gariano, Carmelo, *Análisis estilístico de los "Milagros de Nuestra Señora" de Berceo,* Madrid, 1965.

Guerrieri Crocetti, C., *Gonzalo de Berceo,* Brescia, 1947.

Guillén, Jorge, "Prosaic Language: Berceo," in his *Language and Poetry: Some Poets of Spain,* Cambridge, Mass., 1961.

Gybbon-Monypenny, G. B., "The Spanish *Mester de Clerecía* and Its Intended Public," in *Medieval Miscellany Presented to Eugène Vinaver* (New York, 1965), pp. 230–44.

Hirn, Yrjö, *The Sacred Shrine,* London, 1912.

Hugh of Saint Victor, *Didascalicon,* ed. Charles Henry Buttimer, Washington, D.C., 1939; trans. with introduction and notes by Jerome Taylor, New York, 1961.

Huppé, Bernard F., and D. W. Robertson, Jr., *Fruyt and Chaf: Studies in Chaucer's Allegories,* Princeton, 1963.

Jauss, Hans Robert, "Form und Auffassung der Allegorie in der Tradition der *Psychomachia,*" in *Festschrift für Walther Bulst* (Heidelberg, 1960), pp. 179–206.

Lage, Gaston Raynaud de, *Alain de Lille: Poète du XIIe siècle,* Montréal-Paris, 1951.

Lanchetas, Rufino, *Gramática y vocabulario de las obras de Gonzalo de Berceo,* Madrid, 1900.

Lang, Henry R., "Contributions to the Restoration of the *Poema del Cid,*" *BH, 66* (1926), 1–509.

Lehner, F. A. von, *Die Marienverehrung in den ersten Jahrhunderten,* Stuttgart, 1886.

Lewis, C. S., *The Allegory of Love: A Study in Medieval Tradition*, Oxford, 1958.

———— *The Discarded Image*, Cambridge, Eng., 1964.

Lida de Malkiel, María Rosa, "Notas para el texto de la *Vida de Santa Oria*," *RPh, 10*, (1956–57), 19–33.

Lord, Albert B., *The Singer of Tales*, Cambridge, Mass., 1960.

Lorenz, Erika, "Berceo, der 'Naive'," *RJ, 14* (1963), 255–68.

Lubac, Henri de, *Histoire et Esprit*, Paris, 1950.

———— " 'Typologie' et 'allégorisme,' " *Recherches de Science Religieuse, 34* (1947), 180–206.

Magoun, F. P., Jr., "Oral-Formulaic Character of Anglo-Saxon Poetry," *Speculum, 28* (1953), 446–67.

Manly, J. M., "Chaucer and the Rhetoricians," *Proceedings of the British Academy, 12* (1926), 95–113.

Marden, C. Carroll, ed., *Cuatro poemas de Berceo*, Madrid, 1928.

———— ed., *Libro de Apolonio*, Baltimore–Paris, 1917.

———— ed., *Poema de Fernán Gonzalez*, Baltimore, 1904.

Maritano, Giovanna, "*La Vida de Santa Oria*," introduzione e note, Varese-Milano, 1964.

Martin-Chabot, Eugène, ed., *Chanson de la croisade albigeoise*, Paris, 1960.

Menéndez Pidal, Ramón, *Manual de gramática histórica española*, 11th ed. Madrid, 1962.

Menéndez y Pelayo, Marcelino, *Antología de poetas líricos castellanos*, Madrid, 1891.

———— *Historia de la poesía castellana en la Edad Media, 1, 3* vols. Madrid, 1911–16.

Migne, *Patrologia latina*, Paris, 1844–64.

Nebrija, *Gramática castellana*, ed. Galindo Romeo and Ortiz Muñoz, Madrid, 1948.

Nichols, Stephen G., Jr., *Formulaic Diction and Thematic Composition in the "Chanson de Roland*," Chapel Hill, 1961.

Parry, Milman, "Studies in the Epic Technique of Oral Verse-Making. I: Homer and Homeric Style," *Harvard Studies in Classical Philology, 41* (1930), 73–147.

Patch, Howard, *The Other World According to Descriptions in Medieval Literature*, Cambridge, Mass., 1950.

Peña de San José, Fray Joaquín, "Glosas a la vida de Santa Oria, de Gonzalo de Berceo," *Berceo* (Logroño), *60* (1961), 371–82.

Pérez de Urbel, Justo, "Manuscritos de Berceo en el archivo de Silos," *BH, 32* (1930), 5–15.

Peter the Venerable, *De miraculis libri duo*, in *PL, 189*, cols. 851–954.

Pfandl, Ludwig, "Studien zu Prudencio de Sandoval," *ZRP, 54* (1934), 385–423; continued in 55 (1935), 88–125.

Post, Chandler Rathton, *Medieval Spanish Allegory*, Cambridge, Mass., 1915.

Robertson, D. W., Jr., *A Preface to Chaucer: Studies in Medieval Perspectives*, Princeton, 1962.

Ruiz, Juan, Arcipreste de Hita, *Libro de buen amor*, ed. Jean Ducamin, Toulouse, 1901.

Saitta, Giuseppe, *Filosofia italiana e umanesimo*, Venezia, 1928.

Salinas, Pedro, *Jorge Manrique: Tradición y originalidad*, Buenos Aires, 1947.

Sánchez, Thomás Antonio, *Colección de poesías castellanas anteriores al siglo XV, 2* and *3*, 4 vols. Madrid, 1779–90.

Sandoval, Prudencio de, *Primera parte de las fundaciones de los monesterios del . . . padre san Benito que los reyes de España fundaron y dotaron . . .* , Madrid, 1601.

Sarmiento, Martín de, *Memorias para la historia de la poesía y poetas españoles*, Madrid, 1775

Scholem, Gershom G., *Major Trends in Jewish Mysticism*, New York, 1954.

Seco Serrano, Carlos, "Vida y obra de fray Prudencio de Sandoval," in *BAE, 80* (1955), vii–xlviii.

Singleton, Charles S., *An Essay on the "Vita Nuova,"* Dante Studies, I, Cambridge, Mass., 1958.

——— *Journey to Beatrice*, Dante Studies, II, Cambridge, Mass., 1958.

Solalinde, Antonio G., review of T. C. Goode, *El sacrificio de la misa. A Study of Its Symbolism and of Its Sources*, HR, *3* (1935), 177–78.

Spicq, C., *Esquisse d'une histoire de l'exégèse latine au moyen âge*, Paris, 1944.

Unamuno, Miguel de, *Tres novelas ejemplares y un prólogo,* Madrid, 1920.

Valbuena Prat, Angel, *Historia de la literatura española, 1,* 2 vols. Barcelona, 1937.

Viereck, Peter, *The Tree Witch,* New York, 1960.

Vitae patrum, in *PL, 21,* cols. 387–462.

Webber, Ruth House, *Formulistic Diction in the Spanish Ballad,* Berkeley-Los Angeles, 1951.

Weber de Kurlat, Frida, "Notas para la cronología y composición literaria de las Vidas de Santos de Berceo," *NRFH, 15* (1961), 113–30.

Welter, J. T., *L'exemplum dans la littérature religieuse et didactique du moyen âge,* Paris, 1927.

Whallon, William, "Formulaic Poetry in the Old Testament," *CL, 15* (1963), 1–14.

Wheelwright, Philip, *The Burning Fountain: A Study in the Language of Symbolism,* Bloomington, 1954.

Willis, Raymond S., Jr., review of E. Alarcos Llorach, *Investigaciones sobre el Libro de Alexandre, HR, 19* (1951), 168–72.

Yepes, Antonio de, *Crónica general de la orden de san Benito, 3,* 4 vols. Madrid, 1960.

Index

Castro, Américo, 174, 184-85
Center, symbols of the, 101. *See also* Ladder; Tree
Chanson de la croisade albigeoise, 44 n.
Chanson de Roland, 140 n., 147 n., 155 n., 160
Chaucer, 126, 173
Christ, 75-76; compared with God the Father, 85-87. See also *Esposo*
Cirlot, J. E., 97 n., 100 n., 101 n.
Cirot, Georges, 28 n., 121, 128, 133
Columna. See Ladder
Communion, 109, 155 n.
Contemptus mundi, 51, 55-56, 183, 187. *See also* Asceticism
Crónica de la orden de San Benito. See Sandoval, Prudencio de
Crosby, Ruth, 28 n.
Cuaderna via, 43, 140, 143, 186
Curtius, Ernst R., 9 n., 22, 26 n., 33-34 n., 38 n., 98-99 n., 122 n., 136 n., 152-53 n., 172, 175

Daniélou, Jean, 89 n.
Dante, 77 n.
Davy, M.-M., 96 n., 99 n.
Day, symbolism of, 178. *See also* Light; Night
Death, 180, 187-88; in Berceo's *Vidas*, 8-13 passim; in *SOr*, 14, 16. *See also* Night
Delehaye, Hippolyte, 8-9 n., 34
Devil, 55, 60-62, 82, 109, 117, 120; symbolized, 137-38, 179, 181
Didacticism: its use of realism, 50, 53, 134; and antithesis, 161 n.; its relation to originality, 171-73
Diminutives, 117-19
Donahue, Charles, 89 n., 94 n.
Dove: symbol of the Holy Spirit, 70, 96-97, 103 n., 181; symbol of the soul, 96-97; symbol of ascent, 101; identified with the Virgin Mary, 103-04
Dutton, Brian, 7 n., 140, 143 n., 190 n.

Eliade, Mircea, 101-04, 124 n.
Encabalgamiento, 139-40, 146-47
Enjambement. See *Encabalgamiento*
Epic poetry, medieval, 2, 139. See also *Vida de Santa Oria*, epic formulas in
Epithets. *See* Binary Expressions, synonymous
Esposo (Christ), 64, 85, 87
Estoria, 20-21
Evil, defined in *SOr*, 55, 61
Exemplum: as hagiography, 48-49; general characteristics of, 49-51; distinguished from other didactic modes, 51-52; its use of realism, 53; in Berceo, 187. *See also* Visions

Faral, Edmond, 33
Fernán Gonzalez, 44-45 n., 115
Férotin, D. Marius, 4
Fitz-Gerald, John D., 141-42, 144-45, 148-49
Fitzmaurice-Kelly, James, 182
Fletcher, Angus, 89 n., 90 n., 95 n.
Folgar, 30, 40; as death, 187
Formulas: of sincerity, 31-32; in artistic composition, 139; defined as recurrence, 140-41; function of in Berceo, 190-92. See also *Abbreviatio*
Frye, Northrop, 95 n., 178 n.

Gadamer, H. G., 134 n.
Gaiffier, B. de, 4, 6
Gallais, Pierre, 22 n., 31-32, 36
Gantner, J., 187 n.
Garcia (Oria's father), 75, 79, 105
Gariano, Carmelo, 6 n., 173 n., 189 n.
Geoffroi de Vinsauf, 156
Giraldus Cambrensis, 52
God the Father: transcendence of, 76-77, 85; distinguished from Christ, 85-87; symbolic words of, 90-92. *See also* Holy Trinity
Grace, 86; counterpart of humility, 67-68; symbolized, 181
Gregory the Great, St., 49, 53, 57